THE COMPLETE
KETO
COOKBOOK
FOR BEGINNES WITH OVER

500
KETO DIET RECIPES

28 Days Weight Loss Plan

The Ultimate Beginners Keto Diet Book with 500
Healthy & Delicious Weight Loss Recipes for
Busy People on Keto Diet
incl. 28 Days Weight Loss Plan

ASIN: B08RSDPRP

Table of Contents

KETO VEGITARIAN RECIPES 134

INTRODUCTION

My goal with this book is to support and inspire people who decide to make apositive change in their lives. For that reason, this book features 500 recipes, from simple recipes for new keto-ers to festive recipes that everyone will love, so that you never run out of ideas. All of these recipes are made with common ingredients that deliver great flavor and stunning aromas. They are approved by my husband and my guests who often come over for dinner. They are designed to guide you every step of the way in order to prepare the best keto foods ever. Each recipe includes the nutritional information and has up to 7 grams of net carbs. This is the best way to track your macronutrients and customize your diet to fit your unique needs. Besides being a great source for keto recipes, the book is chock-full of cooking secrets, crafty tricks, and handy hacks. Are you ready to go keto? Go ahead! Remember, if I can do it, you can too!

What is a Keto Diet?

The ketogenic diet (also known as the keto diet) is a way of eating that encourages your body to burn the excess fat that it has already stored. In order to do that, the amount of carbohydrates that you consume per day is limited (to 20-25 g of net carbs/day), and fat and protein make up the rest of your caloric intake. When you limit the amount of carbs (i.e. sugar and starches) that you are consuming, you enter a state called "nutritional ketosis." Your body can no longer rely on carbohydrates for its energy needs and it now needs to start burning fat as its primary fuel source.

As a result, blood glucose remains much more stable throughout the day, and many people report increased energy and lower appetite, which makes it easier to control the amount of food you're eating. The ketogenic diet was primarily designed as a treatment for epilepsy and is nowadays most often used for weight loss.

It has multiple benefits that go beyond weight control, such as improving blood sugar regulation and insulin sensitivity, lowering the risks of type 2 diabetes and heart disease, and possibly even protecting against cancer.

How does the keto diet work?

You can stay on the keto diet indefinitely, do it as a weight-loss plan over a single short period or cycle in and out. Fat-rich foods are key, protein is moderate and carbs are the bad guys.

I offer some tips for getting started on keto:

Educating yourself about carbs and getting familiar with good fats is the first step.

Before jumping in, experiment with low-carb veggies in the grocery store's natural produce section, find sources of grass-fed meat and learn about hidden sources of sugar, like the coleslaw at your local eatery.

Don't assume sugar cravings will disappear right away. Instead, stock up on keto-friendly desserts like dark chocolate with nut butter.

During the first week of carb withdrawal, you might experience symptoms including muscle aches, headaches, fatigue and mental fogginess – and yes, hunger. For early cravings, try nibbling on a high-fat snack such as a bacon strip or some cucumber with avocado mayo.

As the diet moves into the second and third weeks, you'll begin to feel better. Soon, low-carb, high-fat eating will seem more natural as it becomes a habit. By week four, you can expect weight loss, especially if you've been physically active while sticking closely to the plan. Selecting the right food will be easier as you become accustomed to the keto approach. Instead of lean meats, you'll focus on skin-on poultry, fattier parts like chicken thighs, rib-eye steaks, grass-fed ground beef, fattier fish like salmon, beef brisket or pork shoulder, and bacon. Leafy greens such as spinach, kale and lettuce, along with broccoli, cauliflower and cucumbers, make healthy vegetable choices. But you'll avoid starchy root foods like carrots, potatoes, turnips and parsnips. You can work in less-familiar veggies such as kohlrabi or daikon. Oils like avocado, olive, canola, flaxseed and palm, as well as mayonnaise, will flavor salads while fattening them up. Clarified butter, or ghee, is a fat you'll use for cooking or as a spread. Start your day with a nut butter-boosted latte, coffee or tea, or have bacon and eggs as a breakfast staple. Stick with whole-fat milk, cheese and other whole dairy products. Use stevia to replace sugar and artificial sweeteners.

In "Keto in 28," details my four-week plan. In the book's menus, carbs are kept to low levels, ranging from 15 to 20 net carbs a day. Net carbs are the total amount of carbohydrates in a serving subtracted by the amount of fiber.

On the other hand, fat makes up a whopping 70% to 73% of the daily diet. Protein rounds out the meal plans, comprising a moderate one-fifth to one-quarter of breakfasts, lunches and dinners daily, along with one or two recommended snacks. (Carb/fat/protein proportions vary from diet to diet with each author.)

For maintenance over time, I suggest taking a cyclical approach and going in and out of ketosis, especially for women.

Dieters use a number of signs to know they're in ketosis, some more subjective than others. Simple DIY urine or blood test results, bad or fruity breath, reduced hunger, sharper mental focus, changes in exercise performance and weight loss can all indicate ketosis.

How it works: With keto, your body enters a state of ketosis. It's breaking down stored body fat and dietary fat into substances called ketones for energy – instead of using carbs for energy.

What is the benefit of Keto Diet?

There is a ton of hype Surrounding the ketogenic diet. Some researchers swear that it is the best diet for most people to be on, while others think it is just another fad diet.

To some degree, both sides of the spectrum are right. There isn't one perfect diet for everyone or every condition, regardless of how many people "believe In It. The ketogenic diet is no exception to this rule.

However, the ketogenic diet also has plenty of solid research backing up its benefit. It's better than most diets at helping people with:

- Epilepsy
- Parkinson's disease
- Fatty Liver Disease
- Type 2 Diabetes
- Type 1 Diabetes
- Cancer
- Chronic Inflammation
- High Blood Sugar
- Migraines
- High Blood Pressure Levels
- Ahheimer's disease
- Heart Disease

Even if you are not at risk from any of these conditions, the ketogenic diet can be helpful for you too. Some of the benefits that most people experience are:

- Better brain function
- A decrease in inflammation
- An increase in energy
- Improved body composition

What to Eat on a Keto Diet?

Keto emphasizes higher fat intake and little carb intake. This can make meal planning challenging since a large number of high carb foods are not considered keto-friendly - like grains, breads, starchy veggies, and fruits.

Additionally, carbs tend to be the bulk of most people's diets - meaning you have to find a keto alternative or change the way you think about meals in general. Some of the best staples for any keto diet should include healthy carb substitutes. Many veggies work great for this, like:

- Cauliflower rice
- Mashed cauliflower
- Portobello mushroom "buns"
- Spaghetti squash
- Zucchini or Courgette noodles
- Lettuce wraps

Help keep your nutrition in check, have the bulk of your keto diet should consist of nutrient-rich low carb veggies, quality proteins, and healthy fats to ensure you are getting the right balance and overall good nutrition to keep you going.

Keto Food List

Here is a brief overview of what you should and shouldn't eat on the keto diet:

Do Eat

Get ready for a whole lot of fat, some protein, and just about zero carbs throughout your day. Keto-approved fridges and pantries include plenty of meat, seafood, dairy, eggs, nuts, fats and oils, and some veggies that grow above ground.

Plenty of meats: Chicken, pork, steak, ground beef, lamb, bacon, turkey, ham, and sausage (in limited amounts).

Fatty seafood: Salmon, snapper, tuna, halibut, cod, trout, catfish, scallops.

Shellfish: Crab, clams, oysters, lobster, mussels.

Most fats and oils: Eggs, butter, coconut oil, olive oil, ghee, lard, avocado oil (and plenty of avocados!), mayonnaise.

High-fat dairy: Heavy cream or Double cream, soft and hard cheeses, cream cheese, and sour cream.

A selection of vegetables: Cauliflower, cabbage, broccoli, zucchini or courgette, green beans, peppers, eggplants, tomatoes, asparagus, cucumber, onion, mushroom, spinach, lettuce, and olives.

Most nuts: Almonds, peanuts, macadamia nuts, pecans, hazelnuts, walnuts, as well as their retrospective butters (look for natural varieties that aren't sweetened).

A selection of berries: Blueberries, blackberries, raspberries, all in moderation.

Some of your favorite beverages: Unsweetened coffee and black tea is OK. Dry wine, champagne, and hard liquor should be enjoyed sparingly.

All spices and some sweeteners: Enjoy stevia and sucralose every once in a while.

Do Not Eat

It's a pretty exhaustive list, and probably includes some of your favorites: Bread, rice, pasta, fruit, corn, potatoes, beans, baked goods, sweets, juice, and (most!) beer all get the axe. Basically, you have to avoid most sugars and starches.

Almost all fruits: Apples, bananas, oranges, grapes, watermelon, peaches, melon, pineapple, cherries, pears, lemons, limes, grapefruits, plums, mango, and more.

Most grains: Wheat, rice, rye, oats, corn, quinoa, barley, millet, bulgur, amaranth, buckwheat, and sprouted grains.

Starches: Bread (all of it!), bagels, cereal, pasta, rice, corn, oatmeal, crackers, pizza, popcorn, granola, muesli, flour. There are some work arounds that dieters can still enjoy, like faux tortilla wraps that are made from cheese.

Legumes: Black beans, kidney beans, pinto beans, navy beans, soybeans, peas, chickpeas, lentils.

Real sweeteners and sugar: Cane sugar, honey, maple syrup, agave nectar, Splenda, aspartame, saccharin, and corn syrup. You'll have to settle for sugar alternatives, including natural substitutes like this monkfruit sugar replacement.

Sweet treats: Candy, chocolate, cakes, buns, pastries, tarts, pies, ice cream, cookies, pudding, and custard. Dieters can shop for dessert alternatives like this keto-friendly ice cream that won't impact your blood sugar levels in a single serving.

A selection of cooking oils: Canola oil, soybean oil, grapeseed oil, peanut oil, sesame oil, and sunflower oil.

Alcohol: Beer, cider, sweet wines, and sweetened alcoholic drinks. If you're going to spring for wine, keep it as dry as possible — the bottle should have less than 10g of sugar in its entirety.

Bottled condiments: Ketchup, BBQ sauce, tomato sauce, some salad dressings and hot sauces that contain added sugar.

Low-fat dairy: Things like skim milk, skim mozzarella, fat-free yogurt, low-fat cheese and cream cheese should be swapped for higher-fat counterparts.

Healthy Fats

When following a high-fat, very-low-carb ketogenic (keto) diet, it's important to remember that not all fats are created equal.
Some sources of fat are better for you than others, and it's critical that you fill your plate with the most wholesome options to successfully reach your health goals.

Here are 14 healthy sources of fat to enjoy on the keto diet.

1. Avocados and avocado oil
2. Nuts
3. Nut and seed butters
4. Flax seeds
5. Hemp hearts
6. Chia seeds
7. Olives and cold-pressed olive oil
8. coconuts and unrefined coconut oil
9. Cacao nibs
10. Full-fat Greek yogurt
11. Whole eggs
12. Fatty fish
13. Butter
14. Cheese

Health Risk on Keto Diet

Keto could pose health risks, particularly for people with certain medical conditions. People with kidney or liver conditions should not attempt a keto diet.
Some experts caution that the diet can lead to muscle loss.
The keto diet isn't for everyone: Pregnant or nursing women, underweight people, or anyone with heart disease who hasn't first consulted a doctor should avoid the diet.
Hormonal changes aren't always beneficial, as the diet can dramatically affect insulin and reproductive hormones. The keto diet for people with diabetes is controversial, and some dietitians advise against it. A person with diabetes, especially someone taking insulin, would require careful monitoring.
Keto diets take different paths, and your nutritional mileage may vary. You could incorporate healthy fats such as avocados and nuts as much as possible and focus on whole, unprocessed foods. In that case, the diet might have disease-preventing properties. On the other hand, if you choose to max out on the least-healthy sources of animal fats and protein like nitrate-packed processed meats, the diet could become part of the problem.

How to Avoid Muscle Loss on Keto?

The most important macronutrient for preserving and building lean muscle is protein. Carbs help preserve muscle mass to some extent, but protein is — without a doubt — the most important macronutrient that you must eat enough if you don't want to lose muscle. Protein consumption is especially crucial on the ketogenic diet. Without dietary carbs to provoke an anabolic (muscle building) response, you will tend to lose muscle more rapidly without adequate protein intake on keto. With that being said, research has also found that ketones have a muscle preserving effect. Because of this, it is reasonable to suggest that you should eat just enough protein to maintain muscle mass without eating so much protein that you decrease your ketone levels.

Recipe Notes

We wanted to make it as simple as possible for you to get in the kitchen and rustle up something special, so you will find each recipe laid out in an easy to follow format.
Remember this diet is designed to rekindle your love of food not extinguish it with rules and regulations, so don't be afraid to experiment.
Use the ingredients as general guidelines and follow the instructions as best you can. You may not get everything the perfect first time, every time but that is what makes it yours!
Keep at it for a full 28 days of eating and you will no doubt establish a few firm favourites that you can turn into your speciality dishes over time.
Each recipe ends with a breakdown of key nutritional information including the number of calories and amount of fats, carbohydrates and protein.
Again, this isn't to be obsessed over. Food is something to be enjoyed, so if you are going to keep a note of your intake levels then just make it a general estimate.

Why no pic? This cookbook is full of fun and flavour and doesn't take stuff too seriously. The food is entering your mouth, not a modelling contest, and we don't like to encourage unhealthy obsession about presentation. So just cook expert: tent, and enjoy.
Once you start loving what you are eating mealtimes will become something to look forward to. Take this as encouragement, go forth and cook to your heart's content!

28-Days Keto Diet Mealplan

I created an easy-to-follow meal plan for you to kick-start your keto journeyright. This is a sample menu for four weeks on a ketogenic diet plan.
How to use this plan:
- Each day will be between 1,500-1,700 calories (designed for weight loss).
- This meal plan is designed for 1 person. If you would like to use them for multiple people, simply multiply the ingredient quantities by the total number of people.
- Be flexible! Feel free to replace any of the recipes or ingredients with your personal choices and adjust the ingredient amounts to fit your macros and situation.
- If you follow a very strict keto diet, make sure to personalize this meal plan (including the snack list suggestion at the end) to make it work for you.

28-Days Keto Diet Weight Loss Challenge

First Week Meal Plan

Monday	B: 2. Keto Blueberry Smoothie L: 102. Spicy Chicken Satay D: 241. Omelet Wrap with Salmon
Tuesday	B: 5. Keto Coffee Recipe L: 142. Egg & Bacon Sandwich D: 380. Keto fried chicken
Wednesday	B: 57. Breakfast Pizza Eggs L: 213. Blueberry Smoothie D: 285. Hot chicken with sausages
Thursday	B: 66. Keto Golden Eggs L: 123. Peanut butter chicken D: 333. Keto Cream Cheese
Friday	B: 36. Keto Easy Breakfast L: 225. Tuna Lunch Bowl D: 247. Delicious Keto Salad
Saturday	B: 33. Avocado Breakfast Boats L: 142. Egg & Bacon Sandwich D: 380. Keto fried chicken
Sunday	B: 2. Keto Blueberry Smoothie L: 190. Brekkie bakes for lunch D: 285. Hot chicken with sausages

Third Week Meal Plan

Monday	B: 5. Keto Coffee Recipe L: 123. Peanut butter chicken D: 241. Omelet Wrap with Salmon
Tuesday	B: 66. Keto Golden Eggs L: 190. Brekkie bakes for lunch D: 285. Hot chicken with sausages
Wednesday	B: 33. Avocado Breakfast Boats L: 225. Tuna Lunch Bowl D: 333. Keto Cream Cheese
Thursday	B: 2. Keto Blueberry Smoothie L: 142. Egg & Bacon Sandwich D: 380. Keto fried chicken
Friday	B: 57. Breakfast Pizza Eggs L: 102. Spicy Chicken Satay D: 247. Delicious Keto Salad
Saturday	B: 66. Keto Golden Eggs L: 213. Blueberry Smoothie D: 280. Cashew Chicken
Sunday	B: 33. Avocado Breakfast Boats L: 123. Peanut butter chicken D: 333. Keto Cream Cheese

Second Week Meal Plan

Monday	B: 5. Keto Coffee Recipe L: 225. Tuna Lunch Bowl D: 247. Delicious Keto Salad
Tuesday	B: 57. Breakfast Pizza Eggs L: 123. Peanut butter chicken D: 333. Keto Cream Cheese
Wednesday	B: 66. Keto Golden Eggs L: 142. Egg & Bacon Sandwich D: 285. Hot chicken with sausages
Thursday	B: 5. Keto Coffee Recipe L: 102. Spicy Chicken Satay D: 241. Omelet Wrap with Salmon
Friday	B: 36. Keto Easy Breakfast L: 213. Blueberry Smoothie D: 380. Keto fried chicken
Saturday	B: 2. Keto Blueberry Smoothie L: 225. Tuna Lunch Bowl D: 280. Cashew Chicken
Sunday	B: 33. Avocado Breakfast Boats L: 213. Blueberry Smoothie D: 285. Hot chicken with sausages

Furth Week Meal Plan

Monday	B: 57. Breakfast Pizza Eggs L: 102. Spicy Chicken Satay D: 380. Keto fried chicken
Tuesday	B: 1. Keto Blueberry Smoothie L: 142. Egg & Bacon Sandwich D: 241. Omelet Wrap with Salmon
Wednesday	B: 5. Keto Coffee Recipe L: 123. Peanut butter chicken D: 333. Keto Cream Cheese
Thursday	B: 66. Keto Golden Eggs L: 190. Brekkie bakes for lunch D: 241. Omelet Wrap with Salmon
Friday	B: 57. Breakfast Pizza Eggs L: 213. Blueberry Smoothie D: 285. Hot chicken with sausages
Saturday	B: 36. Keto Easy Breakfast L: 102. Spicy Chicken Satay D: 333. Keto Cream Cheese
Sunday	B: 33. Avocado Breakfast Boats L: 225. Tuna Lunch Bowl D: 380. Keto fried chicken

Keto Breakfast Recipes

1. Bulletproof Coffee

Made for: Breakfast | **Prep Time:** 5 minutes | **Servings:** 01
Per Serving: Kcal: 320, Protein: 0g, Fat: 36g, Net Carb: 0g

INGREDIENTS
- 1 tbsp MCT Oil
- 2 tbsp Butter
- 12 oz Coffee

INSTRUCTIONS
1. Brew a cup of coffee using any brewing method you'd like.
2. Add butter, MCT oil, and coffee to a blender. Blend on high for 30 seconds. Enjoy.

2. Keto Blueberry Smoothie

Prep Time: 5 minutes | **Servings:** 01
Per Serving: Kcal: 251, Protein: 23g, Fat: 10g, Net Carb: 5g

INGREDIENTS
- 1 cup (240 ml) Coconut Milk or almond milk
- 1/4 cup (150 g) Blueberries
- 1 tsp Vanilla Extract
- 1 tsp MCT Oil or coconut oil
- 30 g Protein Powder optional

INSTRUCTIONS
3. Put all the ingredients into a blender, and blend until smooth.

3. Avocado Smoothie

Made for: Breakfast | **Prep Time:** 15 minutes | **Servings:** 02
Per Serving: Kcal: 517, Protein: 23g, Fat: 47g, Net Carb: 1g

INGREDIENTS
- 1 large ripe avocado
- 1 cup (150 g) ice
- 1 cup (240 ml) almond milk or other milk
- 3 tbsp any sugar free syrup

INSTRUCTIONS
1. Bring a large saucepan of salted water to the boil. Carefully drop the eggs into the water and boil for 5 mins for runny yolks.
2. Meanwhile, heat the oil in a non-stick pan and wrap each avocado slice in pancetta. Fry for 2-3 mins over a high heat until cooked and crisp.
3. Serve the eggs in egg cups with the pancetta avocado soldiers on the side for dipping.

4. Keto Butter Coffee

Made for: Breakfast | **Prep Time:** 5 minutes | **Servings:** 01
Per Serving: Kcal: 230, Protein: 0g, Fat: 25g, Net Carb: 0g

INGREDIENTS
- 1 cup of water
- 2 tbsp coffee
- 1 tbsp grass-fed butter
- 1 tbsp coconut oil

INSTRUCTIONS
1. Make a cup of coffee in your favourite way. We like to use Turkish Coffee Pot. We simply simmer ground coffee in water for about 5 minutes and then strain it into our cup. You can also use a Moka Pot, a French press, or a coffee machine!
2. Pour your brewed coffee into your blender (like a Nutribullet) and butter and coconut oil. Blend for about 10 seconds. You'll see it instantly become light and creamy!
3. Pour the butter coffee into a mug and enjoy! Add in any other ingredients you'd like in this step like cinnamon or whipped cream!

5. Keto Coffee Recipe

Prep Time: 7 minutes | **Servings:** 01
Per Serving: Kcal: 200, Protein: 1g, Fat: 22g, Net Carb: 0g

INGREDIENTS
- 12 oz freshly brewed coffee
- 1-2 tbsp Butter
- 1/4 tsp liquid stevia

INSTRUCTIONS
1. Add all ingredients to a blender jar and blend for 10 seconds.
2. Carefully remove the lid and pour into a coffee mug.

6. Scrambled eggs

Made for: Breakfast | **Prep Time:** 10 minutes | **Servings:** 2
Per Serving: Kcal: 298, Protein: 20g, Fat: 21g, Net Carb: 2g

INGREDIENTS
- 1 tbsp rapeseed oil, plus 1 tsp

- 3 tomatoes, halved
- 4 large eggs
- 4 tbsp natural bio yogurt
- ⅓ small pack basil, chopped
- 175g (4 cup) baby spinach, dried well (if it needs washing)

INSTRUCTIONS

1. Heat 1 tsp oil in a large non-stick frying pan, add the tomatoes and cook, cut-side down, over a medium heat. While they are cooking, beat the eggs in a jug with the yogurt, 2 tbsp water, plenty of black pepper and the basil.
2. Transfer the tomatoes to serving plates. Add the spinach to the pan and wilt, stirring a few times while you cook the eggs.
3. Heat the rest of the oil in a non-stick pan over a medium heat, pour in the egg mixture and stir every now and then until scrambled and just set. Spoon the spinach onto the plates and top with the scrambled eggs.

7. Keto Boosted Coffee

Made for: Breakfast | **Prep Time:** 3 minutes | **Servings:** 1
Per Serving: Kcal: 280, Protein: 1g, Fat: 31g, Net Carb: 1g

INGREDIENTS

- 2 cup freshly brewed hot coffee
- Two tablespoons grass-fed butter
- One scoop Perfect Keto MCT Powder
- One teaspoon Ceylon cinnamon

INSTRUCTIONS

1. Combine all of the ingredients in a blender.
2. Using an immersion blender or frother, blend on low bringing the speed up to high for 30 seconds or until frothy.
3. Serve, sip, and enjoy.

8. Herb omelette with fried tomatoes

Made for: Breakfast | **Prep Time:** 10 minutes | **Servings:** 02
Per Serving: Kcal: 204, Protein: 17g, Fat: 14g, Net Carb: 4g

INGREDIENTS

- 1 tsp rapeseed oil
- 3 tomatoes, halved
- 4 large eggs
- 1 tbsp chopped parsley
- 1 tbsp chopped basil

INSTRUCTIONS

1. Heat the oil in a small non-stick frying pan, then cook the tomatoes cut-side down until starting to soften and colour. Meanwhile, beat the eggs with the herbs and plenty of freshly ground black pepper in a small bowl.
2. Scoop the tomatoes from the pan and put them on two serving plates. Pour the egg mixture into the pan and stir gently with a wooden spoon so the egg that sets on the base of the pan moves to enable uncooked egg to flow into the space. Stop stirring when it's nearly cooked to allow it to set into an omelette. Cut into four and serve with the tomatoes.

9. Bacon and Avocado with eggs

Made for: Breakfast | **Prep Time:** 25 minutes | **Servings:** 02
Per Serving: Kcal: 410, Protein: 13g, Fat: 36g, Net Carb: 7g

INGREDIENTS

- 2 eggs
- 2 tbsp heavy cream (optional)
- to taste salt
- to taste pepper
- 2 tsp butter
- 2 tbsp mayonnaise
- 1 cup (47g) romaine lettuce (chopped)
- 1 roma tomato (sliced)
- 4 cooked bacon strips
- 1/2 avocado (sliced)

INSTRUCTIONS

1. Whisk the eggs well with the heavy cream, salt and pepper.
2. Heat up a non-stick pan to a medium heat.
3. Melt half the butter in the pan, and pour in half the egg mixture. Immediately tilt the pan back and forth to ensure the egg covers the entire base.
4. Cover the pan and let the cook for about a minute.
5. When you are able to move the entire crepe when shaking the pan back and forth, carefully flip it over with a spatula.
6. When it's fully cooked, transfer to a paper towel to remove excess oiliness.
7. Repeat with the other half of the egg mix.
8. Spread the mayonaisse on the crepe.
9. Add the lettuce, tomato, bacon and avocado.
10. Season with salt and pepper.
11. Roll and enjoy!

10. Tomato & Ham Omelette

Made for: Breakfast | **Prep Time:** 15 minutes | **Servings:** 2
Per Serving: Kcal: 206, Protein: 21g, Fat: 14g, Net Carb: 5g

INGREDIENTS
- 2 whole eggs and 3 egg whites
- 1 tsp olive oil
- 1 red pepper, deseeded and finely chopped
- 2 spring onions, white and green parts kept separate and finely chopped
- few slices wafer-thin extra-lean ham, shredded
- 25g (1/6 cup) reduced-fat mature cheddar

INSTRUCTIONS
1. Mix the eggs and egg whites with some seasoning and set aside. Heat the oil in a medium non-stick frying pan and cook the pepper for 3-4 mins. Throw in the white parts of the spring onions and cook for 1 min more. Pour in the eggs and cook over a medium heat until almost completely set.
2. Sprinkle on the ham and cheese and continue cooking until just set in the centre, or flash it under a hot grill if you like it more well done.
Serve straight from the pan with the green part of the spring onion sprinkled on top, the chopped tomato and some wholemeal toast.

11. Mushroom omelette

Made for: Breakfast | **Prep Time:** 20 minutes | **Servings:** 2
Per Serving: Kcal: 197, Protein: 15g, Fat: 14g, Net Carb: 4g

INGREDIENTS
- 2 tomatoes, halved
- 3 medium eggs
- 1 tbsp snipped chive
- 300g (3 cup) chestnut mushroom, sliced
- 1 tsp unsalted butter
- 2 tbsp low-fat cream cheese
- 1 tbsp finely chopped basil leaves

INSTRUCTIONS
1. Heat the grill to its highest setting and place the tomatoes on a square of foil underneath, turning occasionally to prevent burning. When the tomatoes are slightly scorched, remove from the grill, squashing them slightly to release the juices.
2. Break the eggs into a bowl and mix with a fork. Add a small splash of water and mix. Add the chives and some black pepper, and beat some more. Set aside while you prepare the mushrooms.
3. In a non-stick frying pan, heat the butter over a medium heat until foaming. Add the mushrooms and cook for 5-8 mins until tender, stirring every few mins. Remove and set aside.
4. Briskly stir the egg mixture, then add to the hot pan (tilting it so that the mixture covers the entire base) and leave for 10 secs or so until it begins to set. With a fork, gently stir the egg here and there so that any unset mixture gets cooked.
5. While the egg mixture is still slightly loose, spoon the mushroom mix onto one side of the omelette, and top with the cream cheese and basil leaves. Flip the other side of the omelette over to cover, if you like. Leave to cook for 1 min more, then cut in half and slide each half onto a plate. Serve immediately with the tomatoes on the side.

12. Eggs with Bacon & Asparagus

Made for: Breakfast | **Prep Time:** 35 minutes | **Servings:** 02
Per Serving: Kcal: 307, Protein: 20g, Fat: 19g, Net Carb: 7g

INGREDIENTS
- 4 asparagus spears (about 150g), woody ends discarded
- 2 long thin slices rustic bread (preferably sourdough)
- 4 rashers smoked streaky bacon or pancetta
- 2 duck eggs

INSTRUCTIONS
1. Heat your grill to high. Snap off the woody ends of the asparagus spears and discard. Cut the bread into 12 soldiers, a little shorter than the asparagus.
2. Place a spear onto each soldier and wrap tightly with a rasher of bacon. Place on a baking tray, season and grill for 15 mins or until the bacon is crisp.
3. Bring a pan of salted water to the boil and simmer the duck eggs for about 7 mins, to get a runny yolk and a cooked white. Serve immediately with the warm soldiers for dipping.

13. Mushroom hash with poached eggs

Made for: Breakfast | **Prep Time:** 35 minutes | **Servings:** 02
Per Serving: Kcal: 285, Protein: 15 g, Fat: 17g, Net Carbs: 3 g

INGREDIENTS
- 1 tbsp rapeseed oil
- 1 large onions, halved and sliced
- 250g (2 cup) closed cup mushrooms, quartered
- 1/2 tbsp fresh thyme leaves, plus extra for sprinkling
- 250g (3/2 cup) fresh tomatoes, chopped
- 1/2 tsp smoked paprika
- 2 tsp omega seed mix (see tip)
- 2 large eggs

INSTRUCTIONS
1. Heat the oil in a large non-stick frying pan and fry the onions for a few mins. Cover the pan and leave the onions to cook in their own steam for 5 mins more.
2. Tip in the mushrooms with the thyme and cook, stirring frequently, for 5 mins until softened. Add the tomatoes and paprika, cover the pan and cook for 5 mins until pulpy. Stir through the seed mix.
3. If you're making this recipe as part of our two-person Summer Healthy Diet Plan, poach two of the eggs in lightly simmering water to your liking. Serve on top of half the hash with a sprinkling of fresh thyme and some black pepper. Chill the remaining hash to warm in a pan and eat with freshly poached eggs on another day. If you're serving four people, poach all four eggs, divide the hash between four plates, sprinkle with thyme and black pepper and serve with the eggs on top.

14. Bacon Egg and Cheese

Made for: Breakfast | **Prep Time:** 10 minutes | **Servings:** 01
Per Serving: Kcal: 589, Protein: 28g, Fat: 89g, Net Carb: 3g

INGREDIENTS
- 2 slices homemade keto white bread
- 1 slice cheddar cheese
- 2 slices bacon cooked until crispy
- 1 egg fried

INSTRUCTIONS
1. Place the cheese on top of the slice of bread, and broil until the cheese is melted (stay with it, this happens fast!).

2. Top with the bacon, egg, and microgreens (if using).
3. Serve.

15. Kale smoothie

Made for: Breakfast | **Prep Time:** 5 minutes | **Servings:** 02
Per Serving: Kcal: 153, Protein: 4g, Fat: 11g, Net Carb: 3g

INGREDIENTS
- 2 handfuls kale
- ½ avocado
- ½ lime, juice only
- large handful frozen pineapple chunks
- medium-sized chunk ginger
- 1 tbsp cashew nuts
- 1 banana, optional

INSTRUCTIONS
1. Put all of the ingredients into a bullet or smoothie maker, add a large splash of water and blitz. Add more water until you have the desired consistency.

16. Low Carb Pancakes

Prep Time: 15 minutes | **Servings:** 2
Per Serving: Kcal: 391, Protein: 14g, Fat: 31g, Net Carb: 1.8g

INGREDIENTS
- 2 large eggs
- 1 tablespoon water
- 2 oz cream cheese, cubed
- 2/3 cup (75g) almond flour
- 1 teaspoon baking powder
- 2 teaspoons vanilla extract
- 1/2 teaspoon cinnamon
- 1/2 teaspoon Sweetleaf - stevia sweetener (or 2 tablespoons regular sugar)
- butter and syrup (sugar free syrup for low carb option)

INSTRUCTIONS
1. Add all ingredients to blender. Start with eggs and water and cream cheese so you don't have anything get stuck at bottom.
2. Blend until smooth, scraping down the sides if needed. Let batter sit for 2 minutes.
3. Heat a non-stick skillet to medium heat. For each pancake, pour 3 to 4 tablespoons of batter onto skillet.
4. Once you start to see little bubbles form, flip and continue to cook until pancake is browned on each side. Continue until you have used all pancake batter.

5. Serve pancakes topped with butter and syrup!

17. Chaffle Breakfast Sandwich

Prep Time: 15 minutes | **Servings:** 1
Per Serving: Kcal: 6581, Protein: 43g, Fat: 51g, Net Carb: 4g

INGREDIENTS
For the chaffles
- 1 egg
- 1/2 cup Cheddar cheese, shredded

For the sandwich
- 2 strips bacon
- 1 egg
- 1 slice Cheddar.

INSTRUCTIONS
1. Preheat the waffle maker according to manufacturer instructions.
2. In a small mixing bowl, mix together egg and shredded cheese. Stir until well combined.
3. Pour one half of the waffle batter into the waffle maker. Cook for 3-4 minutes or until golden brown. Repeat with the second half of the batter.
4. In a large pan over medium heat, cook the bacon until crispy, turning as needed. Remove to drain on paper towels.
5. In the same skillet, in 1 tbsp of reserved bacon drippings, fry the egg over medium heat. Cook until desired doneness.
6. Assemble the sandwich, and enjoy!

18. Boiled Egg Breakfast Bites

Prep Time: 7 minutes | **Servings:** 02
Per Serving: Kcal: 134, Protein: 9g, Fat: 10g, Net Carb: 1g

INGREDIENTS
- 2 slice - 6" long Bacon
- 2 cracker-size slice Cheddar Cheese
- 2 large Hard-Boiled Egg
- ¼ teaspoon Salt
- ¼ teaspoon Black Pepper, Ground

INSTRUCTIONS
1. Prep your ingredients by cooking and cutting your bacon into 8 pieces (2 pieces per egg), arrange 4 slices of cheddar (1 per egg), and slice 4 hard-boiled eggs in half.
2. Sandwich 2 pieces of chopped bacon and

3. 1 piece of cheese between 2 egg halves, and secure the bites together with a toothpick. Sprinkle a small pinch each of salt and pepper over the top of each egg bite. Enjoy!

19. Breakfast Fat Bombs

Made for: Breakfast | **Prep Time:** 30 minutes | **Servings:** 08
Per Serving: Kcal: 365, Protein: 12g, Fat: 34g, Net Carb: 0g

INGREDIENTS
- 4 hardboiled eggs chopped
- 8 ounces cream cheese
- 2 tablespoons minced green onion
- 1 lb bacon cooked and crumbled

INSTRUCTIONS
1. In a medium bowl mix together the egg, cream cheese, and green onion. Roll into 8 balls. Place the balls in the freezer for 10 minutes to set just a bit.
2. Place the crumbled bacon on a plate and roll the balls in the bacon pressing the bacon slightly into the ball. Store in an airtight container in the refrigerator for up to 4 days.

20. Scrambled Egg with Bacon and Avocado

Made for: Breakfast | **Prep Time:** 15 minutes | **Servings:** 01
Per Serving: Kcal: 329, Protein: 12g, Fat: 30g, Net Carb: 2g

INGREDIENTS
- 3 small Raw Egg
- 2 slice - 6" long Bacon
- 2oz cheddar cheese
- 1-½ tablespoon Olive Oil
- 1 each Avocado
- ¼ teaspoon Salt, Sea Salt
- ⅛ teaspoon Black Pepper

INSTRUCTIONS
1. Heat half a tablespoon of oil in a skillet over a medium heat. Roughly dice the bacon and add to the skillet, cooking through until crisp and golden. Set aside.
2. Add the eggs to a small bowl and season to taste. Beat together.
3. Heat the remaining olive oil in a saucepan over a medium heat. Add the beaten egg and allow to settle and cook for a moment before scrambling.
4. Dice the avocado into half inch cubes. Once the egg has just cooked to preference, add the bacon and avocado

to the pan and stir through.

21. Keto Breakfast Sandwich

Made for: Breakfast | Prep Time: 15 minutes | Servings: 01
Per Serving: Kcal: 604, Protein: 22g, Fat: 55g, Net Carb: 4g

INGREDIENTS
- 2 sausage patties
- 1 egg
- 1 tbsp cream cheese
- 2 tbsp sharp cheddar
- 1/4 medium avocado, sliced
- 1/4–1/2 tsp sriracha (to taste)
- Salt, pepper to taste

INSTRUCTIONS
1. In skillet over medium heat, cook sausages per package instructions and set aside
2. In small bowl place cream cheese and sharp cheddar. Microwave for 20-30 seconds until melted
3. Mix cheese with sriracha, set aside
4. Mix egg with seasoning and make small omelette
5. Fill omelette with cheese sriracha mixture and assemble sandwich

22. Keto Chia Pudding

Made for: Breakfast | **Prep Time:** 35 minutes | **Servings:** 2
Per Serving: Kcal: 336, Protein: 8g, Fat: 27g, Net Carb: 5g

INGREDIENTS
- 2 tbsp low carb sugar (Sukrin:1, Swerve, Lakanto, Truvia, or Besti)
- 1 tbsp Cocoa Powder (sift before measuring)
- 1 tsp Vanilla Extract
- 1 cup/240 ml Coconut Milk (from a can) (or Almond Milk for less calories)
- 1/4 cup/170g Chia Seeds

INSTRUCTIONS
1. Add the cocoa powder and sweetener to a mason jar. Close the lid and shake well to remove any lumps.
2. Add the coconut milk and vanilla extract to the mason jar. Close the lid and shake to combine.
3. Add the chia seeds to the jar and shake again. Once the mixture is well combined, transfer the jar to the fridge.
4. Chill for at least 30 minutes.
5. Serve the chocolate chia pudding in your favourite jars, with coconut yogurt and seasonal fruit. Enjoy!

23. Parfait Recipe

Made for: Breakfast | **Prep Time:** 10 minutes | **Servings:** 2
Per Serving: Kcal: 335, Protein: 11g, Fat: 15g, Net Carb: 0g

INGREDIENTS
- ½ cup (140g) Greek Yogurt full fat
- ¼ cup (58g) Heavy Cream/ Double Cream
- 1 teaspoon Vanilla Essence
- ½ cup (75g) Keto Chocolate Almond Clusters
- 2 Strawberries diced
- 8 Blueberries

INSTRUCTIONS
1. In a mixing bowl, add together the yogurt, cream and vanilla. Whisk together until thick and smooth.
2. Spoon half the yogurt between two glasses, then sprinkle over half the granola.
3. Add the remaining yogurt, followed by the remaining granola.
4. Top with the berries and enjoy!

24. Keto Avocado Toast

Made for: Breakfast | **Prep Time:** 5 minutes | **Servings:** 2
Per Serving: Kcal: 225, Protein: 7g, Fat: 18g, Net Carb: 3g

INGREDIENTS
- 1 large avocados
- ¼ large lemon squeezed
- ½ teaspoon salt
- ¼ teaspoon pepper
- 2 slices keto bread

INSTRUCTIONS
1. In a mixing bowl, add your avocado and mash very well, until mostly smooth. Add in the lemon juice and spices and mix until combined.
2. Toast your slices of keto bread. Distribute the avocado mixture amongst the toast and serve immediately.

25. Crispy Bacon

Prep Time: 30 minutes | **Servings:** 2 slices bacon
Per Serving: Kcal: 366, Protein: 11g, Fat: 35g, Net Carb: 1g

INGREDIENTS
- 8 bacon slices

INSTRUCTIONS

1. Preheat your oven to 400 degrees fahrenheit.
   Line a baking tray with parchment paper, then place the bacon side-by-side on the tray.
2. Cook the bacon for 18-20 minutes or until it's reached your desired level of crispiness. Remove the tray from the oven and transfer the bacon with tongs to a paper towel-lined plate.
3. If you're rendering the bacon fat, line a fine mesh sieve with a paper towel. Then place the sieve over a glass storage container and pour the bacon fat from the sheet tray into the sieve. Cover the glass storage container and place it in the refrigerator for future cooking needs.
   Tips:
1. If you don't have a heavy-duty baking sheet, I recommend purchasing some. They never warp or bend in the oven!
2. Please note that all ovens cook slightly differently. It's best to keep an eye on the bacon past the 10 minute mark so you can ensure it's cooked to your personal preference.

26. Bacon Fat Bombs

Made for: Breakfast | **Prep Time:** 50 minutes | **Servings:** 2
Per Serving: Kcal: 184, Protein: 5g, Fat: 10g, Net Carb: 1g

INGREDIENTS
- 1/2 Hardboiled Egg
- 1/4 Avocado
- 2 Tbsp Unsalted or Clarified Butter
- 1/2 Tbsp Mayonnaise
- 1/2 Serrano Pepper seeded and diced
- 1/2 Tbsp Cilantro chopped
- Kosher Salt to taste
- Cracked Pepper to taste
- Juice of ¼ Lime
- 1 Tbsp Bacon Grease
- 3 Cooked Bacon Slices

INSTRUCTIONS
1. In a large bowl, combine the hardboiled egg, avocado, butter, mayonnaise, serrano pepper, and cilantro. Mash into a smooth paste with a fork or potato smasher. Season with salt and pepper, then add the lime juice and stir.
2. Prepare bacon in your favorite fashion until crispy, reserving 2 tablespoons of bacon grease. Add the bacon grease to

the fat bomb mixture and stir gently. Cover and place in the fridge for 30 minutes, or until the mixture has cooled and can form solid balls. Crumble the bacon into small bits in a small bowl.
3. Using a spoon, scoop out 6 even-sized amounts of the fat bomb mixture and form into balls. Add the balls to the bacon bits and roll around until completely covered. Serve immediately.

27. Dollar Pancakes

Made for: Breakfast | **Prep Time:** 15 minutes | **Servings:** 02
Per Serving: Kcal: 257, Protein: 18g, Fat: 19g, Net Carb: 4g

INGREDIENTS
- 3 (3) Eggs
- 1/2 cup (105 g) cottage cheese
- 1/3 cup (37.33 g) Superfine Almond Flour
- 1/4 cup (62.5 g) Unsweetened Almond Milk
- 2 tablespoons (2 tablespoons) Truvia
- Vanilla extract
- 1 teaspoon (1 teaspoon) Baking Powder
- Cooking Oil Spray

INSTRUCTIONS
1. Place ingredients in a blender jar in the order listed. Blend until you have a smooth, liquid batter.
2. Heat a nonstick saucepan on medium-high heat. Spray with oil or butter.
3. Place 2 tablespoons of batter at a time to make small, dollar pancakes. This is a very liquid, delicate batter so do not try to make big pancakes with this one as they will not flip over as easily.
4. Cook each pancake until the top of the pancake has made small bubbles and the bubbles have disappeared, about 1-2 minutes.
5. Using a spatula, gently loosen the pancake, and then flip over.
6. Make the rest of the pancakes in this manner and serve hot.

28. Keto Breakfast Cake

Made for: Breakfast | **Prep Time:** 20 minutes | **Servings:** 02
Per Serving: Kcal: 432, Protein: 12g, Fat: 40g, Net Carb: 3g

INGREDIENTS
- 2 tablespoons butter
- 4 eggs
- 4 oz. softened cream cheese
- 1/4 cup (50.75g) granular erythritol

- 1/4 cup (58g) heavy cream/double cream
- 1/4 cup (28g) coconut flour
- 1 teaspoon almond extract

INSTRUCTIONS
1. Heat your oven to 425°F.
2. Place the butter in a cast iron skillet (or other oven-proof skillet) and transfer to the oven.
3. Meanwhile, mix the remaining ingredients together in a mixing bowl to make the batter.
4. Carefully with oven mitts or a pot holder, remove the skillet from the oven when the butter is melted and pour batter into skillet. Make sure the batter covers the bottom of the skillet completely.
5. Bake for 15-18 minutes or until it gets bubbly and golden brown.
6. Top with confectioner erythritol, slivered almonds, and sugar-free syrup before serving.

29. Keto egg muffins

Made for: Breakfast | **Prep Time:** 25 minutes | **Servings:** 06
Per Serving: Kcal: 337, Protein: 24g, Fat: 26g, Net Carb: 2g

INGREDIENTS
- Two scallions, finely chopped
- 5 oz. chopped air-dried chorizo
- 12 eggs
- 2 tbsp red pesto or green pesto (optional)
- salt and Pepper
- 6 oz. shredded cheese

INSTRUCTIONS
1. Preheat the oven to 350°F (175°C).
2. Line a muffin tin with nonstick, insertable baking cups or grease a silicone muffin tin with butter.
3. Add scallions and chorizo to the bottom of the tin.
4. Whisk eggs together with pesto, salt, and pepper. Add the cheese and stir.
5. Pour the batter on top of the scallions and chorizo.
6. Bake for 15–20 minutes, depending on the size of the muffin tin.

30. Keto breakfast burrito

Made for: Breakfast | **Prep Time:** 10 minutes | **Servings:** 01
Per Serving: Kcal: 332, Protein: 12g, Fat: 32g, Net Carb: 1.4g

INGREDIENTS

- 1 tablespoon butter
- 2 eggs - medium medium
- 2 tablespoon cream full fat
- choice of herbs or spices
- salt/pepper to taste

INSTRUCTIONS
1. In a small bowl, whisk the eggs, cream, and chosen herbs and spices.
2. Melt the butter in the frying pan then pour in the burrito egg mixture.
3. Swirl the frying pan until the burrito mixture is evenly spread and thin as shown in the cooking video.
4. Place a lid over the burrito and leave to cook for 2 minutes.
5. Gently lift the burrito from the frying pan with a clean spatula onto a plate.
6. Add your favourite fillings then roll up and enjoy.

31. Fried Tomatoes

Made for: Breakfast | **Prep Time:** 5 minutes | **Servings:** 01
Per Serving: Kcal: 320, Protein: 0g, Fat: 36g, Net Carb: 0g

INGREDIENTS
- 1 tsp rapeseed oil
- Three tomatoes halved
- Four large eggs
- 1 tbsp chopped parsley
- 1 tbsp chopped basil

INSTRUCTIONS
1. Heat the oil in a small nonstick frying pan, then cook the tomatoes cut-side down until starting to soften and colour. Meanwhile, beat the eggs with the herbs and plenty of freshly ground black pepper in a small bowl.
2. Scoop the tomatoes from the pan and put them on two serving plates. Pour the egg mixture into the pan and stir gently with a wooden spoon, so the egg that sets on the base of the pan moves to enable the uncooked egg to flow into space. Stop stirring when it's nearly cooked to allow it to put into an omelette. Cut into four and serve with the tomatoes.

32. Breakfast Casserole

Made for: Breakfast | **Prep Time:** 45 minutes | **Servings:** 02
Per Serving: Kcal: 322, Protein: 22g, Fat: 27g, Net Carb: 4g

INGREDIENTS

- 1 cup shredded swiss cheese or gruyere
- 2 tablespoon unsalted butter plus more for greasing the dish
- 1/2 cup (120g/4.3 oz) whole milk
- 1 tablespoon dry white wine
- 5 eggs
- 1/4 teaspoon salt
- 1/8 teaspoon black pepper
- 1/8 teaspoon ground mustard
- fresh chives for garnish

INSTRUCTIONS

1. Preheat the oven to 325 F degrees. A grease casserole dish with extra butter. Spread the cheese in the bottom of the casserole dish. Cut the butter into small chunks and dot over the cheese.
2. Combine the milk and wine. Pour half the mixture over the cheese.
3. Pour the remaining milk/wine mixture over eggs.
4. Bake until the eggs are slightly puffed and just set, approximately 35 to 40 minutes. Beginning checking at 30 minutes, then every few minutes until the center is just slightly jiggly. Rest for 5 minutes before cutting into squares, garnish with chives.

33. Avocado Breakfast Boats

Made for: Breakfast | Prep Time: 12 minutes | Servings: 01
Per Serving: Kcal: 442, Protein: 12g, Fat: 40.5g, Net Carb: 3g

INGREDIENTS

- 2 avocados
- 2 large egg
- 2-⅛ tablespoon cream
- 2 medium slices bacon
- 1 tbsp butter without salt
- ⅛ teaspoon salt
- 1-⅛ tsp black pepper

INSTRUCTIONS

1. Prepare the avocados by halving them and removing the stones and outer skin. Reserve to one side.
2. Add the diced bacon to a large dry frying pan over a medium heat and cook for 3 minutes until crispy. Reserve to one side.
3. While the bacon cooks, add the eggs to a mixing bowl with the cream and season generously with salt and pepper. Whisk until smooth.
4. Heat the butter in a pan over a low/medium heat. Pour in the egg

mixture and allow it to settle for a minute before stirring. Cook the eggs through until soft and fluffy, stirring regularly.
5. Divide the scrambled egg mixture evenly between the four avocado halves and sprinkle with the crispy bacon.
6. Season with salt and pepper and scatter with fresh chives to serve

34. Blueberry Smoothie

Made for: Breakfast | Prep Time: 5 minutes | Servings: 02
Per Serving: Kcal: 257, Protein: 10g, Fat: 20.5g, Net Carb: 5g

INGREDIENTS

- 1 large avocado
- 1/2 cup (82g) frozen blueberries
- 4 tsp flax seeds
- 2 tbsp collagen powder
- 1 1/2 cups (375ml) of almond milk

INSTRUCTIONS

1. Put all the ingredients into a blender, and blend until smooth.

35. Almond Cream Cheese

Made for: Breakfast | Prep Time: 12 minutes | Servings: 02
Per Serving: Kcal: 203, Protein: 15g, Fat: 15g, Net Carb: 0.1g

INGREDIENTS

- ½ cup plus 1 tbsp almond flour (60g)
- ½ cup full fat cream cheese (125g)
- 4 eggs
- 1 tsp granulated sweetener
- ½ tsp cinnamon (optional)
- butter for frying

INSTRUCTIONS

1. Mix all ingredients in a blender.
2. Fry pancakes in melted butter in a non-stick pan over a medium heat. Turn over once the centre begins to bubble. The pancakes should be smallish, ca 10-12 cm in diameter. About the right size to fit them in the toaster the next day should you be so lucky to have any leftovers.

36. Keto Easy Breakfast

Made for: Breakfast | Prep Time: 15 minutes | Servings: 01
Per Serving: Kcal: 497, Protein: 17g, Fat: 44g, Net Carb: 4.8g

INGREDIENTS

- 1 large egg

- 4 to 5 thin-cut or 2 regular slices bacon (60 g/2.1 oz)
- 4 to 5 brown mushrooms or 1 large Portobello mushroom (84 g/3 oz)
- 1/2 large avocado (100 g/3.5 oz)
- 1 tbsp ghee or duck fat
- salt and pepper, to taste

INSTRUCTIONS
1. Heat a skillet greased with ghee over a medium-high heat. Cook the mushrooms, top side down, for about 5 minutes. Flip and cook for about 2 more minutes. Transfer to a plate.
2. Fry the bacon until crispy. Finally, fry the egg until the white is cooked through and opaque, and the yolk is still runny.
3. Serve with sliced avocado. Season to taste and serve immediately.

37. Keto Breakfast Biscuits

Made for: Breakfast | **Prep Time:** 15 minutes | **Servings:** 02
Per Serving: Kcal: 320, Protein: 12g, Fat: 41g, Net Carb: 2g

INGREDIENTS
- 1 ounce's cream cheese
- 1 cup mozzarella, shredded
- 1 egg, beaten
- 1 cup (125g) almond flour
- pinch salt & pepper
- 1 ounces colby jack cheese, thin cubes (or your choice of cheese)
- 2 breakfast sausage patties

INSTRUCTIONS
1. Preheat oven to 400.
2. In a microwave safe bowl, add cream cheese and mozzarella.
3. Microwave for 30 seconds at a time until cream cheese is very soft and mozzarella starts to melt.
4. Mix well! And by mix well I mean, stir stir stir! You want this really combined.
5. In a small separate bowl, combine beaten egg and almond flour. Add cheese mixture and mix well, again, REALLY well.
6. Dough may be sticky, this is ok. Dust it with additional almond flour and form into a ball. Place on plastic wrap and refrigerate until firm.
7. Cut into sections to form 6 3" balls, depending on the size of the sausage.
8. Flatten dough balls, place sausage on the dough, then cheese and wrap dough around.

9. Put the stuffed dough into a greased muffin tin.
10. Bake for 12-15 minutes or until golden and set. Top with more mozzarella if desired.

38. Egg Medley Muffins

Made for: Breakfast | **Prep Time:** 15 minutes | **Servings:** 02
Per Serving: Kcal: 320, Protein: 22g, Fat: 36g, Net Carb: 2g

INGREDIENTS
- 6 large eggs.
- 1 onion (finely chopped).
- 3 oz cheddar cheese (grated).
- 2 oz bacon (cooked and diced).
- Pinch salt and pepper.

INSTRUCTIONS
1. Preheat the oven at 175 degrees and grease a 12-hole muffin tray.
2. Equally, place onion and bacon to the bottom of each muffin tray hole.
3. In a large bowl, whisk the eggs, cheese, salt and pepper.
4. Pour the egg mixture into each hole; on top of the onions and bacon.
5. Bake for 20-25 minutes, until browned and firm to the touch.

39. Keto Breakfast Salads

Made for: Breakfast | **Prep Time:** 20 minutes | **Servings:** 01
Per Serving: Kcal: 260, Protein: 12g, Fat: 8g, Net Carb: 3g

INGREDIENTS
- 2 cups greens arugula, kale, spinach, power greens
- 1/2 cup (50g) vegetables mushrooms, cherry tomatoes, asparagus, zucchini
- 1/4 cup (50g) berries raspberries, strawberries, blackberries
- 2 tablespoons nuts or seeds pecans, walnuts, almonds, sunflower seeds, pumpkin seeds, etc.
- 1-2 eggs prepared any way
- 2 slices bacon or use sausage or leftover meats

INSTRUCTIONS
1. Add all ingredients for dressing to a jar and shake well. Use about 1 tablespoon per salad.
2. Start building a breakfast salad by choosing any type of greens.
3. Add veggies to the salad. Veggies can be sauteed or added raw.

4. Add optional berries to the salad.
5. Choose healthy fats, such as avocado, nuts or seeds.
6. If choosing to add bacon or sausage, cook to package directions.
7. Top salads with an egg prepared any way.

40. Egg & Celeriac Nests

Made for: Breakfast | **Prep Time:** 20 minutes | **Servings:** 02
Per Serving: Kcal: 126, Protein: 9g, Fat: 9g, Net Carb: 2g

INGREDIENTS
- 4 large eggs
- 2 cups grated celeriac or turnip (180 g/6.3 oz)
- freshly ground black pepper or cayenne pepper
- sea salt to taste
- fresh parsley for garnish
- 4 thinly-cut bacon slices (100 g/3.5 oz)

INSTRUCTIONS
1. Peel and grate the celeriac. Low-Carb Egg & Celeriac Nests
2. Distribute the grated celeriac equally into silicone muffin molds. Crack an egg into each mold. Low-Carb Egg & Celeriac Nests
3. Reduce the oven temperature to 175 °C/ 350 °F. Season the eggs with salt and pepper and place in the oven for about 20-25 minutes. Low-Carb Egg & Celeriac Nests
4. Remove from the oven and let the cups cool down before you remove them from the molds. Garnish with fresh parsley and serve with crisped up bacon rashers. The egg cups and bacon can be stored in the fridge for up to 4 days.

41. Green Smoothie

Made for: Breakfast | **Prep Time:** 5 minutes | **Servings:** 01
Per Serving: Kcal: 380, Protein: 12g, Fat: 36g, Net Carb: 5g

INGREDIENTS
- 2 cups (60 g) spinach
- 1/3 cup (46 g) raw almonds
- 2 Brazil nuts
- 1 cup (240 ml) coconut milk
- 1 Tablespoon (10 g) psyllium seeds (or psyllium husks) or chia seeds

INSTRUCTIONS
1. Place the spinach, almonds, Brazil nuts,

and coconut milk into the blender first.
2. Blend until pureed.
3. Add in the rest of the ingredients (greens powder, psyllium seeds) and blend well.

42. Low Carb Breakfast Balls

Made for: Breakfast | **Prep Time:** 50 minutes | **Servings:** 01
Per Serving: Kcal: 401, Protein: 31g, Fat: 261g, Net Carb: 0.3g

INGREDIENTS
- 1/3 lb (150g) Poultry sausage
- 1/4 lb (113g) ground beef
- 1 egg
- 1/3 tablespoon dried onion flakes
- 1/8 teaspoon black pepper
- 1/8 lb sharp cheddar cheese, shredded

INSTRUCTIONS
1. Mix all the ingredients together until thoroughly blended (it is best to use your hands or an electric mixer).
2. Form into about 4 dozen 1 to 1 1/2-inch balls and place on a cookie sheet or broiler pan.
3. Bake at 375°F for about 25 minutes.
4. Once they are cool, they can be sorted into individual zip bags and frozen for a grab-and-go breakfast.

43. Breakfast Porridge

Made for: Breakfast | **Prep Time:** 5 minutes | **Servings:** 02
Per Serving: Kcal: 430, Protein: 8g, Fat: 40g, Net Carb: 6g

INGREDIENTS
- 1/2 cup (60 g) almonds, ground using a food processor or blender
- 3/4 cup (180 ml) coconut milk
- 1 teaspoon (2 g) cinnamon powder
- Dash of nutmeg
- Dash of cloves

INSTRUCTIONS
1. Heat the coconut milk in a small saucepan on medium heat until it forms a liquid.
2. Add in the ground almonds and sweetener and stir to mix in.
3. Keep stirring for approximately 5 minutes (it'll start to thicken a bit more).
4. Add in the spices (have a taste to check whether you want more sweetener or spices) and serve hot.

44. Avocado Sandwich

Made for: Breakfast | Prep Time: 15 minutes | Servings: 01
Per Serving: Kcal: 544, Protein: 23g, Fat: 46g, Net Carb: 11g

INGREDIENTS
- 6 slices bacon.
- 2 avocados.
- 2 small onions (diced).
- 2 tbsp lime juice.
- 2 tbsp garlic powder.
- Cooking spray.

INSTRUCTIONS
1. Preheat the oven at 180 degrees.
2. Spray a baking tray with cooking spray, cook the bacon 20-25 minutes until crispy.
3. Remove seeds from avocados; in a large bowl mash avocado flesh with a fork.
4. Add onions, garlic and lime juice; mash until well combined.
5. Allow the crispy bacon to cool and place one slice on a plate; top with 2 tbsp of avocado guacamole. Place another bacon slice on top and add another 2 tbsp of guacamole and top with bacon. Repeat to make another sandwich.

45. Avocado Coconut Milk

Made for: Breakfast | Prep Time: 5 minutes | Servings: 01
Per Serving: Kcal: 437, Protein: 5g, Fat: 43g, Net Carb: 10g

INGREDIENTS
- ½ avocado
- ½ cups (120ml) Unsweetened Coconut Milk
- 5 drops stevia
- 5 Ice Cubes

INSTRUCTIONS
1. Add all the ingredients to the blender. Blend until smooth.

46. Coconut oil Coffee

Made for: Breakfast | Prep Time: 5 minutes | Servings: 01
Per Serving: Kcal: 61, Protein: 0g, Fat: 6g, Net Carb: 0.1g

INGREDIENTS
- 1 cup coffee
- 1 1/2 tsp coconut oil
- 1/2 cup (120ml) warm coconut milk optional
- 1/8 tsp cinnamon optional
- 1/8 tsp cayenne pepper optional

- Whole cloves for garnish
- Coconut cream for garnish
- Star anise for garnish

INSTRUCTIONS
1. Make a cup of coffee as you normally would and pour it into a blender.
2. Add the coconut oil to the blender and blend for 1-2 minutes until the mixture lightens in colour and becomes frothy.
3. Add any extras you'd like, including warm coconut milk, cinnamon, and or cayenne pepper, and give it a quick blend for 10-20 seconds.
4. Pour into a mug, top with coconut cream, and grind fresh cloves over the cream, if desired.
5. Garnish with star anise, and enjoy warm.

47. Keto Breakfast Bowl

Made for: Breakfast | Prep Time: 15 minutes | Servings: 01
Per Serving: Kcal: 916, Protein: 40g, Fat: 35g, Net Carb: 04g

INGREDIENTS
- 2 eggs (size of your choice)
- 2 Tbsp butter
- 1/2 avocado, sliced
- 3 strips of bacon, cooked and crumbled
- 1/2 cup (115g) cheddar cheese, shredded
- sour cream (optional)

INSTRUCTIONS
1. In a medium sized skillet, melt the two Tbsp of butter on medium heat.
2. In a separate bowl, scramble the two eggs.
3. Place the eggs into the skillet and cook to your preferred texture.
4. Once cooked, place the eggs at the bottom of a soup bowl.
5. Top the eggs with the shredded cheese.
6. Top the shredded cheese with bacon.
7. Slice your avocado and then place the slices on top of the bacon.
8. Top with salsa and sour cream and enjoy!

48. Fried Avocados

Made for: Breakfast | Prep Time: 5 minutes | Servings: 02
Per Serving: Kcal: 200, Protein: 2g, Fat: 10g, Net Carb: 2g

INGREDIENTS
- 1 ripe avocado (not too soft), cut into slices
- 1 Tablespoon (15 ml) coconut oil
- 1 Tablespoon (15 ml) lemon juice

- Salt to taste

INSTRUCTIONS
1. Add coconut oil to a frying pan. Place the avocado slices into the oil gently.
2. Fry the avocado slices (turning gently) so that all sides are slightly browned.
3. Sprinkle the lemon juice and salt over the slices and serve warm

49. Smoked Salmon Frittata

Made for: Breakfast | Prep Time: 40 minutes | Servings: 2
Per Serving: Kcal: 326, Protein: 23g, Fat: 22g, Net Carb: 1.8g

INGREDIENTS
- 1/2 leek, cleaned with white and light green parts diced
- 1/2 shallot, diced
- 1 scallion, thinly sliced
- 1 tbsp olive oil, divided
- 4 large eggs
- 1/2 cup yogurt, or dairy-free yogurt
- 1/2 bunch fresh parsley, roughly chopped
- 1/2 bunch fresh dill, roughly chopped
- 3 oz smoked salmon, torn into small pieces
- 2 oz goat cheese
- salt and pepper, to taste

INSTRUCTIONS
1. Heat one tablespoon of olive oil in a 10-inch cast iron skillet over medium heat. Add the leek, shallot and scallions and saute for 1-2 minutes, or until slightly translucent. Then, remove the vegetables to a plate and set aside.
2. In a large mixing bowl, add the eggs and yogurt and whisk together. Stir in the herbs, smoked salmon, goat cheese, sauteed leek, shallot and scallions, salt and pepper.
3. Once your skillet has cooled, clean it (or use a paper towel to quickly wipe it clean). Over low heat, add two tablespoons of olive oil to the skillet and ensure that the bottom is full coated.
4. Pour the frittata egg mixture into the skillet and cook for 8-10 minutes, or until the sides are just starting to set.
5. Transfer the frittata to the oven (on a middle shelf) and turn the top broiler on. Continue cooking for another 8-10 minutes, checking on it every few
6. minutes to ensure the top isn't browning too much. If the top cooks faster than

the inside of the frittata, turn the broiler off and let it continue cooking in the oven.
7. Serve the frittata with extra herbs.

50. Berry Crumble Pots

Made for: Breakfast | Prep Time: 40 minutes | Servings: 02
Per Serving: Kcal: 160, Protein: 01g, Fat: 12g, Net Carb: 2g

INGREDIENTS
- 1 cup (164g) fresh or frozen unsweetened mixed berries defrosted
- 1/3 cup (42g) Swerve sweetener divided in half
- 1/2 teaspoon xanthan gum thickener
- 1/3 cup (37g) almond flour
- 1/8 cup unsweetened finely shredded coconut
- 1/2 teaspoon ground cinnamon
- 1/8 teaspoon sea salt
- 2 tablespoon butters melted or coconut oil

INSTRUCTIONS
1. Preheat oven to 350 F and spray six 4-ounce ramekins with coconut oil non-stick spray. Set aside.
2. In a large mixing bowl add: mixed berries, ⅓ cup Swerve, and xanthan gum. Using a large spoon, gently toss berries to coat with the sweetener and xanthan gum. Set aside.
3. In a large bowl combine: almond flour, ⅓ cup Swerve sweetener, shredded coconut, cinnamon, sea salt and melted butter or coconut oil. Stir and press with a fork until a pasty crumble forms. Set aside.
4. Fill prepared ramekins halfway full with the berry mixture. Top each ramekin with equal amounts of the cinnamon crumble mixture.
5. Place ramekins on a large baking sheet and bake for 35 to 40 minutes or until crumble starts browning.
6. Remove and cool for 10 minutes. Serve with sugar-free whipped cream or whipped coconut cream.

51. Cabbage Hash Browns

Made for: Breakfast | Prep Time: 25 minutes | Servings: 02
Per Serving: Kcal: 320, Protein: 28g, Fat: 60g, Net Carb: 4g

INGREDIENTS
- 2 large eggs

- 1/2 tsp. garlic powder
- 1/2 tsp. kosher salt
- Freshly ground black pepper
- 2 cup (140g) shredded cabbage
- 1/4 small yellow onion, thinly sliced
- 1 tbsp. vegetable oil

INSTRUCTIONS
1. In a large bowl, whisk together eggs, garlic powder, and salt. Season with black pepper. Add cabbage and onion to egg mixture and toss to combine.
2. In a large skillet over medium-high heat, heat oil. Divide mixture into 4 patties in the pan and press with spatula to flatten. Cook until golden and tender, about 3 minutes per side.

52. Baked Eggs

Made for: Breakfast | Prep Time: 25 minutes | Servings: 2
Per Serving: Kcal: 338, Protein: 21g, Fat: 24g, Net Carb: 5g

INGREDIENTS
- 4 Eggs
- 4 Slices Bacon
- Salt and pepper to taste 1 Oz Cheddar
- 1 Small Onion (80g)

INSTRUCTIONS
1. Fry four slices of Bacon
2. Cut a small onion in half and fry
3. In a ramekin or equivalent ovenproof bowl, place onion and Bacon
4. Crack two eggs into each container, making sure to not break the yolk
5. Add salt and pepper
6. Add cheddar cheese
7. Bake at 350 degrees for 20 minutes or until eggs have set

53. Almond Butter Fat Bombs

Made for: Breakfast | Prep Time: 5 minutes | Servings: 01
Per Serving: Kcal: 190, Protein: 4g, Fat: 20g, Net Carb: 1.4g

INGREDIENTS
- 1/4 Cup (63.75g) Almond Butter
- 1/4 Cup (62ml) Unrefined Coconut Oil
- 2 Tbsp Cacao Powder
- 1/4 Cup (50g) Erythritol

INSTRUCTIONS
1. Mix together almond butter and coconut oil in a medium bowl
2. Microwave for 30-45 seconds
3. Stir until smooth

4. Stir in erythritol and cacao powder
5. Pour into silicone molds
6. Refrigerate until firm

54. Tuna & Spinach Mix

Made for: Breakfast | Prep Time: 15 minutes | Servings: 02
Per Serving: Kcal: 952, Protein: 53g, Fat: 80g, Net Carb: 3g

INGREDIENTS
- 4 large eggs.
- 10 oz tinned tuna (in olive oil).
- ½ cup (120g) mayonnaise.
- 1 avocado (sliced).
- 1 onion (finely diced).
- Salt and pepper (to season).

INSTRUCTIONS
1. Bring a large pan of water to the boil and lower in the eggs. Cook for 8 minutes.
2. In a bowl, mix together tuna, mayonnaise, onion, salt and pepper.
3. Chop the hard boiled eggs into halves and place on a plate with avocado slices and spinach.
4. Place the tuna mixture on top of spinach.

55. Keto cheese omelet

Made for: Breakfast | Prep Time: 15 minutes | Servings: 02
Per Serving: Kcal: 897, Protein: 40g, Fat: 80g, Net Carb: 4g

INGREDIENTS
- 3 oz. butter
- 6 eggs
- 7 oz. shredded cheddar cheese
- salt and pepper to taste

INSTRUCTIONS
1. Whisk the eggs until smooth and slightly frothy. Blend in half of the shredded cheddar. Salt and pepper to taste.
2. Melt the butter in a hot frying pan. Pour in the egg mixture and let it set for a few minutes.
3. Lower the heat and continue to cook until the egg mixture is almost cooked through. Add the remaining shredded cheese. Fold and serve immediately.

56. Cheat's Eggs Benedict

Made for: Breakfast | Prep Time: 10 minutes | Servings: 01
Per Serving: Kcal: 240, Protein: 15g, Fat: 19g, Net Carb: 3g

INGREDIENTS
- 1 large egg
- 2 tsp white vinegar
- ½ tsp salt
- 1½ oz ham steak
- 2 tbs Hollandaise sauce from a jar
- black pepper

INSTRUCTIONS
1. Use an Egg Cooker or poach the egg as follows: Crack the egg into a ramekin and set aside.
2. Add an inch of water to a small saucepan, add the vinegar, and season generously with salt. Bring the water to a fast simmer, and use a spoon handle to swirl the water round in one direction.
3. When the water is swirling, drop the egg into the center of the swirl. Turn off the heat, cover, and leave undisturbed for 5 minutes.
4. While the egg is cooking, warm through the ham steak on a grill pan - about 2 minutes on each side.
5. Transfer the ham to a plate, then use a slotted spoon to remove the cooked egg from the water. Pour over some of the Hollandaise sauce, season with black pepper, and enjoy!

57. Breakfast Pizza Eggs

Made for: Breakfast | **Prep Time:** 10 minutes | **Servings:** 01
Per Serving: Kcal: 602, Protein: 30g, Fat: 51g, Net Carb: 5g

INGREDIENTS
- 1/4 cup homemade Marinara Sauce or any sugar-free pizza sauce (60 ml/2 fl oz)
- 1 tbsp extra virgin olive oil (15 ml)
- 3 large eggs
- 1/4 cup (28g) shredded mozzarella cheese
- 6 slices of pepperoni or cured chorizo (18 g/0.6 oz)
- fresh basil to serve

INSTRUCTIONS
1. If you need to make some marinara sauce, follow this recipe. It will only take 5 minutes to prepare. You can also use any sugar-free pizza sauce. Heat a medium pan greased with olive oil over a medium-high heat. Add the marinara sauce and spread evenly over the pan. Crack in the eggs. Use a spatula to gently break the egg whites. This will help them cook faster and combine with

the marinara sauce. Tip: if you don't like runny yolks, use the spatula to break the yolks and swirl through the whites and marinara.
2. When the egg whites are almost set, sprinkle with the shredded cheese and top with the pepperoni (or cured chorizo) slices. Cook for another 2-3 minutes until the cheese is melted and the egg yolks are still runny. Keto Breakfast Pizza Eggs
3. Sprinkle with fresh basil and serve while still warm.

58. Cream Cheese Pancakes

Made for: Breakfast | **Prep Time:** 15 minutes | **Servings:** 01
Per Serving: Kcal: 346, Protein: 16g, Fat: 30g, Net Carb: 3g

INGREDIENTS
- 2 large eggs
- 2 oz cream cheese.
- 1 tsp granulated sugar substitute.
- ½ tsp ground cinnamon.

INSTRUCTIONS
1. Blend all ingredients until smooth. Allow to rest for 2 minutes.
2. Grease a large frying pan and pour in ¼ of the mixture.
3. Cook for 2 minutes until golden, flip and cook for an additional minute.
4. Repeat process until all mixture has gone.

59. Keto Breakfast Tacos

Made for: Breakfast | **Prep Time:** 20 minutes | **Servings:** 01
Per Serving: Kcal: 652, Protein: 33g, Fat: 53g, Net Carb: 2g

INGREDIENTS
- 2 keto friendly wraps (I love these ones that I get at Sprouts)
- breakfast meat of choice (bacon, sausage, chorizo, taco meat, carnitas, verde chicken, barbacoa, etc)
- 2 eggs, scrambled in ghee
- shredded cheese
- sliced avocado
- salsa

INSTRUCTIONS
1. On your keto friendly wraps, place the breakfast meat, eggs, shredded cheese, avocado and salsa. Serve warm and enjoy!

60. Keto Breakfast Pizza

Made for: Breakfast | **Prep Time:** 45 minutes | **Servings:** 02
Per Serving: Kcal: 364, Protein: 19g, Fat: 31g, Net Carb: 3g

INGREDIENTS
- Pizza crust
- 1/2 oz cream cheese
- 1/2 cups (113g) mozzarella cheese
- 1/4 cup (30g) almond flour
- 1/2 tsp seasonings optional

Pizza toppings
- 1/2 lbs cooked breakfast sausage
- 1.5 slices cooked crumbled bacon
- 1/2 mini peppers
- 1/2 TB onion chopped
- 1/2 eggs beaten
- 1/4 cup (20g) grated cheese any kind

INSTRUCTIONS
1. Grease a 9-inch cast iron skillet, or similar size baking dish. Prepare your pizza crust. Melt cream cheese and mozzarella by increments in your microwave. When melted, incorporate your almond flour.
2. Add seasonings if desired. Add egg, kneading to form your dough. Dock with a fork to prevent air bubbles.
3. Bake at 400° For 10 minutes. Remove. Add beaten eggs first, followed by meats and veggies.
4. Top with cheese. Return to oven. Bake 15 minutes. Broil if desired.
5. Remove from oven, let rest 15 minutes. Slice and serve.

61. Keto Chaffle Sandwich

Made for: Breakfast | **Prep Time:** 15 minutes | **Servings:** 01
Per Serving: Kcal: 658, Protein: 43g, Fat: 26g, Net Carb: 3g

INGREDIENTS
For the chaffles
- 1 egg
- 1/2 cup (60g) Cheddar cheese, shredded

For the sandwich
- 2 strips bacon
- 1 egg
- 1 slice Cheddar or American cheese.

INSTRUCTIONS
1. Preheat the waffle maker according to manufacturer instructions.
2. In a small mixing bowl, mix together egg and shredded cheese. Stir until well combined.
3. Pour one half of the waffle batter into the waffle maker. Cook for 3-4 minutes or until golden brown. Repeat with the second half of the batter.
4. In a large pan over medium heat, cook the bacon until crispy, turning as needed. Remove to drain on paper towels.
5. In the same skillet, in 1 tbsp of reserved bacon drippings, fry the egg over medium heat. Cook until desired doneness.
6. Assemble the sandwich, and enjoy!

62. Breakfast Burrito Bowl

Made for: Breakfast | **Prep Time:** 15 minutes | **Servings:** 02
Per Serving: Kcal: 287, Protein: 17g, Fat: 22g, Net Carb: 3g

INGREDIENTS
- 3 cooked scrambled eggs
- 1/2 cup (100g) keto taco meat
- 1/2 avocado, diced
- 3 tablespoons sugar free salsa
- 2 tablespoons full fat sour cream
- 1 tablespoon cotija cheese
- lime wedges (optional)

INSTRUCTIONS
1. Split all ingredients evenly between two bowls, adding cooked scrambled eggs, warm keto taco meat and diced avocado first.
2. Add a dollop of sour cream to each bowl and sprinkle with the cotija cheese. Enjoy!

63. Bacon and Egg Breakfast

Made for: Breakfast | **Prep Time:** 20 minutes | **Servings:** 2
Per Serving: Kcal: 450, Protein: 34g, Fat: 35g, Net Carb: 4g

INGREDIENTS
- ¾ Cup (84.75g) Mozzarella Cheese
- ¾ Cup (90g) Cheddar Cheese
- 4 Slices Bacon
- 3 Eggs
- ⅛ Cup (18.75g) Diced Tomato
- 1 Tbsp Green Onion

INSTRUCTIONS
1. Preheat oven to 400 F. Cover a pizza pan with Parchment Paper (NOT wax paper).
2. Mix the Cheeses together, then evenly spread them over the parchment paper

(in a circle shape). Bake the cheese shell for 5 minutes. Pour off any extra oil as soon as it comes out of the oven.

64. Low Carb Sandwich

Prep Time: 10 minutes | **Servings:** 02 sandwiches
Per Serving: Kcal: 272, Protein: 22g, Fat: 14g, Net Carb: 4g

INGREDIENTS
- 4 slices Carbonaut Seeded Bread
- 1 8 ounces firm tofu
- 1 teaspoon olive oil
- 1/2 teaspoon turmeric
- 1/2 teaspoon garlic powder
- 1/2 teaspoon chili powder
- 1 tablespoon nutritional yeast
- 1 cups sprout
- Himalayan Sea Salt and Pepper to Taste

INSTRUCTIONS
1. In a frying pan, mash the tofu with a fork and begin to saute over low heat.
2. Add the olive oil, turmeric, chili powder, garlic powder, and nutritional yeast. Saute on low heat for about 5 minutes, stirring well to combine. Taste, and add salt and pepper if desired.
3. Toast the Carbonaut seeded bread. For each sandwich, add half of the tofu and top with sprouts. Mangia!

65. Sandwich with Pancakes

Made for: Breakfast | **Prep Time:** 30 minutes | **Servings:** 02
Per Serving: Kcal: 591, Protein: 34g, Fat: 43g, Net Carb: 4g

INGREDIENTS
- ½ lb ground breakfast sausage
  Pancakes
- 2 tbsp Coconut flour or ¼ cup almond flour
- 2 large eggs
- 1 tsp baking powder
- 1 ½ tbsp oil
- 1 tbsp Erythritol
- pinch of salt
- cooking spray
  eggs
- 4 large eggs
- 1 tbsp butter
- kosher salt to taste
  garnish
- sugar free syrup
- butter

INSTRUCTIONS
1. Patty up the breakfast sausage into 2 patties and place in a cast iron skillet over medium high heat. Cook on each side until a crust forms and an internal temperature reads 145F
2. Heat a large non-stick skillet over medium heat. Mix all of the ingredients for the pancakes into a small bowl. Spray the skillet with cooking spray and spoon the batter into 4 round pancakes in the skillet. Let the pancakes cook until bubbles start to form in the batter around the side. Flip and continue to cook on the other side until the center on the pancake springs back when lightly touched.
3. For the eggs, beat the 4 eggs in a medium sized bowl until whites and yolks are combined. Heat a medium skillet (I used the same skillet as the pancakes) over medium-low heat. Add the butter and then the beaten eggs. Let the eggs cook until the edges begin to set. push the eggs with a rubber spatula scraping the bottom of the pan. scrape occasionally to get large folds of soft scrambled eggs. When the eggs are just set and still a little runny, remove from the heat.
4. To assemble the sandwiches: place a sausage patty on one pancake, followed by half of the eggs, followed by another pancake. Garnish with butter and sugar free syrup.

66. Keto Golden Eggs

Made for: Breakfast | **Prep Time:** 10 minutes | **Servings:** 01
Per Serving: Kcal: 470, Protein: 20g, Fat: 41g, Net Carb: 3g

INGREDIENTS
- 1/8 cup extra virgin olive oil or ghee (30 ml/1 fl oz)
- 1/2 packed cup chopped kale (33 g/1.2oz)
- 3 large eggs
- 1/2 tsp ground turmeric
- 1/4 tsp ground cumin
- salt and black pepper, to taste

INSTRUCTIONS
1. Crack the eggs into a bowl. Chop the kale and remove the hard stems (weight excludes the stems). Easy Keto Golden Eggs
2. Crack the eggs into a bowl, and add the turmeric, cumin, salt and pepper. Whisk

with a fork. Easy Keto Golden Eggs
3. Heat the olive oil (or ghee) in a sauce pan on a medium heat.
4. Add the chopped kale and stir until well coated. Cover with a lid and cook the kale for about 5 minutes over a medium heat. Easy Keto Golden Eggs
5. Pour the eggs to the pan with the kale and cook for about 1 minute, stirring the eggs with a spatula to prevent sticking. Remove from the heat and allow to firm up.
Place on a plate and serve immediately.

67. Keto Breakfast Bake

Made for: Breakfast | **Prep Time:** 30 minutes | **Servings:** 02
Per Serving: Kcal: 616, Protein: 31g, Fat: 50g, Net Carb: 2g

INGREDIENTS
- 4 bacon rashers
- 1 bunch asparagus
- 2 tablespoons olive oil
- 100 grams (1/2 cup) cherry tomatoes
- 6 eggs
- 50 grams (1/3 cup) feta
- salt and pepper to taste

INSTRUCTIONS
1. Preheat the oven to 200C / 392F and grease a small baking dish. Chop the asparagus into 3cm long pieces, halve the cherry tomatoes and cut the feta into cubes
2. Lay the bacon and asparagus in the baking dish and toss with olive oil.
3. Bake for 5 - 7 minutes until starting to crispy up.
4. Scatter the dish with the cherry tomatoes and feta, then crack the eggs over the top. Season with salt and pepper.
5. Bake for a further 15 - 20 minutes until the eggs are done to your liking.

68. Buttered Cabbage

Made for: Breakfast | **Prep Time:** 5 minutes | **Servings:** 02
Per Serving: Kcal: 380, Protein: 4g, Fat: 43g, Net Carb: 3g

INGREDIENTS
- 10 oz cabbage (cut in long strips).
- 4 oz butter.
- 4 bacon slices.

INSTRUCTIONS
1. In a large frying pan, melt half of the

butter and fry the bacon until crispy.
2. Add the remaining butter and stir in the cabbage; cook until cabbage begins to change colour.

69. Perfect Keto Breakfast

Made for: Breakfast | **Prep Time:** 10 minutes | **Servings:** 01
Per Serving: Kcal: 174, Protein: 12g, Fat: 11g, Net Carb: 2g

INGREDIENTS
- 2 Slices Hearty Thick Sliced Bacon
- 1 Large Egg
- 1/2 oz Avocado
- 1/4 oz Roma Tomatoes
- 1 Tbsp, Shredded Mozzarella Cheese
- 2 Medium Strawberries

INSTRUCTIONS
1. Pan fry bacon slices
2. Cook egg in bacon grease as desired, I prefer over easy
3. Top with sliced tomatoes, avocado, and cheese

70. Egg Foo Young

Prep Time: 35 minutes | **Servings:** 10 patties
Per Serving: Kcal: 124, Protein: 7g, Fat: 9g, Net Carb: 1g

INGREDIENTS
- 6 large eggs
- ¼ cup (28g) coconut flour or ½ cup cassava flour
- 1 teaspoon Red Boat fish sauce or kosher salt, to taste
- ½ teaspoon apple cider vinegar
- 1 cup diced ham or cooked meat of choice
- 10 ounces frozen spinach thawed and squeezed dry
- 2 scallions sliced
- 1 tablespoon minced fresh cilantro
- ½ teaspoon baking soda
- Freshly ground black pepper
- ghee or avocado oil

INSTRUCTIONS
1. In a large bowl, whisk together the eggs, coconut flour (or cassava flour), fish sauce, and apple cider vinegar until smooth.
2. Mix in the ham, spinach, scallions, cilantro, and baking soda, and some freshly ground black pepper.
3. Melt a tablespoon of ghee in a cast iron skillet over medium heat. Use a large

disher (3-tablespoon size) to plop the batter in the pan, and flatten the pancake to ½-inch thick with the back of a spoon. I can comfortably fit 3 pancakes in my 12-inch skillet at a time – don't overcrowd them!

4. Fry without disturbing the patties for 2 minutes before flipping the pancakes over and cooking it on the other side for about 1-2 minutes more. The pancakes are cooked through when the centers bounce back when you press down on them with your finger.
5. Repeat until you're out of batter. As each pancake finishes cooking, transfer it to a wire rack to cool. Then, plate 'em up and serve!

71. 2 Ingredient Chaffles

Prep Time: 10 minutes | Servings: 04 chaffles
Per Serving: Kcal: 230, Protein: 18g, Fat: 16g, Net Carb: 3g

INGREDIENTS
- 2 large eggs
- 1 cup (113g) finely mozzarella or cheddar

INSTRUCTIONS
1. Pre-heat dash waffle iron.
2. Whisk egg and cheese in a medium bowl.
3. Spray waffle iron with cooking spray or butter.
4. Pour about 1/4th of the mixture into the waffle iron and cook for 2-3 minutes or until golden. Remove and repeat for remaining batter.
5. Serve as waffles with pancake syrup or use as bread for sandwiches!

72. Keto Crepes Recipe

Made for: Breakfast | Prep Time: 15 minutes | Servings: 04
Per Serving: Kcal: 690, Protein: 14g, Fat: 70g, Net Carb: 4g

INGREDIENTS
- 8 large eggs.
- 2 cups (460g) thick whipping cream.
- ½ cup (125ml) water (room temperature).
- 3 oz butter.
- 2 tbsp psyllium husk (powder).

INSTRUCTIONS
1. In a large bowl, whisk together eggs, cream and water. Gradually mix in the psyllium husk until a smooth batter is formed. Allow to rest for 20 minutes.
2. Use a little butter and ½ cup of batter

mixture for one pancake.
3. When the top of the pancake is lightly browned and almost dry, flip and cook the other side.
4. Repeat until all batter has gone.

73. English Keto Breakfast

Made for: Breakfast | Prep Time: 15 minutes | Servings: 01
Per Serving: Kcal: 658, Protein: 30g, Fat: 55g, Net Carb: 6g

INGREDIENTS
- 1 tbsp ghee, lard or duck fat (15 ml)
- 4 to 5 brown mushrooms or 1 large Portobello mushroom (85 g/3 oz)
- 5-6 thin-cut or 2-3 regular slices bacon (75 g/2.7 oz)
- 2 large eggs
- 1/2 cup frozen and thawed spinach (78 g/2.8 oz), excess juices drained
- 4-5 cherry tomatoes on the vine (40 g/1.4 oz)
- 1/2 medium avocado, sliced (75 g/2.7 oz)
- salt, pepper and/or chili pepper flakes to taste

INSTRUCTIONS
1. Heat a skillet greased with ghee over a medium-high heat. Cook the mushrooms seasoned with salt and pepper, top side down, for about 5 minutes. Flip and cook for about 2 more minutes until they are tender. Transfer to a plate.
2. Fry the bacon until crispy. Fry the eggs until the white is cooked through and opaque, and the yolk is still runny. Tilt the skillet and pour the hot oil over the egg white to help it cook faster.
3. Place the cherry tomatoes in the pan where you cooked the bacon and egg and fry on high for just about a minute. Frying is optional and you can serve the tomatoes fresh if you prefer that.
4. Drain the spinach (once you squeeze out the water, you'll get about 40% of the original weight, about 30 g/ 1 oz drained spinach). Optionally, throw in the pan where you cooked the egg to heat through.
5. Serve everything with sliced avocado. Season to taste and enjoy immediately.

74. Crustless Quiche Recipe

Made for: Breakfast | Prep Time: 25 minutes | Servings: 02
Per Serving: Kcal: 216, Protein: 11g, Fat: 7g, Net Carb: 1g

INGREDIENTS

- 1/4 cup (28g) bacon chopped
- 1/4 cup (38g) broccoli chopped
- 1/4 cup (37.5g) cherry tomatoes chopped
- 1/4 cup (240g) milk
- 1/4 cup (250ml) half
- 2/3 cup shredded mozzarella cheese
- 2 eggs
- 1/4 tsp salt adjust to taste
- 1/8 tsp ground black pepper adjust to taste

INSTRUCTIONS

1. Preheat the oven to 325F.
2. Spray a 9-inch baking dish with cooking spray. Spread broccoli, tomatoes and bacon pieces evenly on the baking dish.
3. In a separate bowl, combine together eggs, milk, half-and-half, salt and pepper. Whisk until you get a smooth, even mixture.
4. Pour egg mixture over the veggies. Sprinkle with cheese.
5. Bake for about 25 minutes, or until the quiche is fully cooked through.
6. Let the quiche rest for a few minutes before serving. Enjoy!

75. Almond Flour Crepes

Made for: Breakfast | **Prep Time:** 35 minutes | **Servings:** 02
Per Serving: Kcal: 158, Protein: 7g, Fat: 13g, Net Carb: 2g

INGREDIENTS

- 1 ounce's cream cheese softened
- 1 large eggs
- 1/4 cup (28g) almond flour
- 1/2 tablespoon granulated Swerve Sweetener
- 1/16 cup (15 ml) unsweetened almond milk
- Pinch salt
- Oil or butter for the pan

INSTRUCTIONS

1. Line a large baking sheet with parchment paper.
2. In a blender, combine cream cheese, eggs, almond flour, sweetener, almond milk and salt. Puree until smooth and well combined. Let rest 5 minutes.
3. Set a 10-inch skillet over medium-low heat. Add just enough oil or butter to the pan to lightly coat it. Once hot, add a few tablespoons of batter to the pan and swirl or spread into a thin layer that reaches almost to the edges (8 to 9

inches in diameter).
4. Cook until edges are cooked and can be loosened with a spatula. Loosen all the way around and then lift one edge gently and work spatula underneath (I found it easiest to grab the loosened edge with my fingers while working the spatula under the crepe so I could flip it).
5. Flip and cook on the other side until lightly browned. Remove and lay on prepared baking sheet, then continue with remaining batter. You can layer another piece of parchment on top of the first set of crepes as more come off the pan.
6. Fill with whatever your little heart desires. We love them with sugar-free Nutella!

76. Bacon Wrapped Egg

Made for: Breakfast | **Prep Time:** 25 minutes | **Servings:** 2
Per Serving: Kcal: 115, Protein: 9g, Fat: 9g, Net Carb: 0g

INGREDIENTS

- 3 strips of bacon
- 3 large eggs
- pepper, to taste

INSTRUCTIONS

1. Preheat oven to 400°F and spray a nonstick muffin tin with coconut oil cooking spray. Set aside.
2. Next, use one piece of bacon per muffin to create a basket of sorts for the egg. Place the bacon on the inside of each muffin so that it covers the sides completely. Then, use a pair scissors to cut the remaining bacon. Use this excess piece of bacon for the bottom of your basket. Repeat with all pieces of bacon.
3. Place bacon in the oven at 400°F for around 7 minutes. Remove before they start to get crispy.
4. Crack 1 egg inside of each bacon basket. Make sure that you use large eggs as anything bigger will be too much egg to hold in the muffins.
5. Bake for an additional 10-15 minutes depending on how runny you like your eggs.
6. Finally, season with pepper and enjoy!

77. Cinnamon Almond Butter

Made for: Breakfast | **Prep Time:** 5 minutes | **Servings:** 1
Per Serving: Kcal: 326, Protein: 19g, Fat: 27g, Net Carb: 6g

INGREDIENTS

- 1 1/2 cups (360 ml) unsweetened nut milk
- 1 scoop collagen peptides
- 2 Tbsp almond butter
- 2 Tbsp golden flax meal
- ½ tsp cinnamon
- 15 drops liquid stevia
- 1/8 tsp almond extract
- 1/8 tsp salt
- 6–8 ice cubes

INSTRUCTIONS

1. Add all the ingredients to a blender and combine for 30 seconds or until you get a smooth consistency.

78. Keto Chocolate Crepes

Made for: Breakfast | Prep Time: 5 minutes | Servings: 04
Per Serving: Kcal: 186, Protein: 11g, Fat: 14g, Net Carb: 2g

INGREDIENTS

- 4 oz = 115 g full-fat cream cheese
- 4 eggs
- 1/4 cup = 60 ml powdered erythritol
- 3 tablespoons coconut flour
- 2 tablespoons dark, unsweetened cocoa powder
- (Optional: 1 teaspoon vanilla extract)

INSTRUCTIONS

1. Combine all ingredients in a medium bowl.
2. Beat with an electric mixer until well combined and fluffy, about 1-2 minutes. Start with a low speed to prevent the powdered erythritol and the cocoa powder from spreading all over your kitchen. Increase the speed after the ingredients have combined.
3. Heat a skillet or a griddle over medium-low heat. Add butter if you are not using a non-stick pan.
4. Add 1/4 of the batter to the skillet or griddle. Tilt to make the batter spread evenly.
   Cover with a lid and cook, until the top is set, a few minutes. Flip, and cook a half a minute without the lid.
5. Remove the crepe from the skillet or griddle and repeat the cooking with the rest of the batter so that you get 4 crepes altogether. Mix the batter properly before pouring it into the skillet or the griddle.
6. Serve with berries and whipped cream, or fill with keto chocolate frosting. You can also melt some dark chocolate as a sauce, or prepare Keto Hot Fudge Sauce.

79. Pumpkin Chaffles

Made for: Breakfast | Prep Time: 15 minutes | Servings: 02
Per Serving: Kcal: 116, Protein: 5g, Fat: 10g, Net Carb: 2g

INGREDIENTS

- 1 oz cream cheese softened
- 1 large egg
- 1 tbsp pumpkin puree
- 1/2 tsp pumpkin spice
- 1 tbsp superfine almond flour
- 1/4 tsp baking powder optional
- 1/2 tsp erythritol granular optional

INSTRUCTIONS

1. Add cream cheese to a medium bowl and whisk cream cheese until it becomes a whipped consistency. If your cream cheese is too hard to whisk, heat in the microwave for a few seconds (no more than 5 seconds at a time) to soften the cream cheese. Be careful not to heat the cream cheese too long or it will overheat and make a mess in your microwave.
2. Whisk in egg and pumpkin puree until batter is smooth. Add in pumpkin spice and almond flour and whisk until evenly combined.
   If using baking powder and sweetener, whisk in until evenly combined.
3. Preheat waffle iron. When it is ready, grease waffle iron with a cooking oil spray.
4. Pour half of the batter into the mini waffle maker. Your batter should cover all the holes. Close waffle iron. Let it cook for about 4-5 minutes, or until waffle is a dark brown and crispy on the outside. Repeat with remaining batter. You should have enough batter for two chaffles using the Dash mini waffle maker.

80. Bacon Omelet Recipe

Made for: Breakfast | Prep Time: 30 minutes | Servings: 02
Per Serving: Kcal: 470, Protein: 17g, Fat: 20g, Net Carb: 3g

INGREDIENTS

- 4 eggs
- 1 leek, sliced
- 2 bacon slices, cooked and chopped

- 1 tbsp. ghee
- Fresh chives, minced
- Microgreens of your choice
- Sea salt and freshly ground black pepper

INSTRUCTIONS
1. Lightly beat the eggs in a bowl and season to taste with salt and pepper.
2. In a skillet, melt the ghee over medium heat.
3. Add the leek and cook until soft, 5 to 6 minutes, stirring frequently.
4. Pour in egg mixture and add the cooked bacon pieces.
5. As eggs set around the edge of skillet, gently push cooked portions toward the center of skillet. Tilt and rotate skillet to allow uncooked egg to flow into empty spaces.
6. Carefully flip the omelet over and cook another 2 to 3 minutes are until eggs are fully cooked.
7. Let rest 4 to 5 minutes and serve topped with fresh microgreens and chives.

81. Keto Waffles

Made for: Breakfast | Prep Time: 15 minutes | Servings: 02
Per Serving: Kcal: 294, Protein: 10g, Fat: 27g, Net Carb: 2g

INGREDIENTS
- 2 large eggs
- 2 oz cream cheese ½ block
- 1/4 cup (28g) almond flour
- 1 tablespoon melted butter or coconut oil
- 1/2 teaspoon vanilla extract
- 1/2 teaspoon baking powder

INSTRUCTIONS
1. Add all the ingredients into a blender. Blend until mixed through and smooth, about 1 minute.
2. Grease pre-heat waffle iron with cooking spray or butter. Pour batter into waffle iron depending on the iron size.
3. Cook until golden and crispy. Repeat until all the batter is finished. Enjoy!

82. Bacon & Brie Frittata

Made for: Breakfast | Prep Time: 35 minutes | Servings: 2
Per Serving: Kcal: 389, Protein: 18g, Fat: 28g, Net Carb: 1.7g

INGREDIENTS
- 4 slices bacon chopped
- 4 large eggs

- 1/2 cup (120ml) heavy whipping cream/double cream
- 1 cloves garlic minced
- 1/4 teaspoon salt
- 1/4 teaspoon pepper
  2 ounces brie sliced thin

INSTRUCTIONS
1. Cook the chopped bacon in a 10-inch oven-proof skillet over medium heat until crisp. Remove the bacon with a slotted spoon and let drain on a paper towel lined plate. Leave at least 2 tablespoon of bacon grease in the skillet (if you are using cast iron, you may want to leave more) and remove from heat. Let the skillet cool before proceeding.
2. In a large bowl, whisk the eggs with the cream, garlic, salt and pepper and about two thirds of the cooked bacon. Set the skillet over medium low heat and swirl remaining bacon grease to coat bottom and sides.
3. Pour the egg mixture into skillet and cook undisturbed until edges are set up center is still somewhat loose, 7 to 10. Layer the sliced brie overtop. Sprinkle with the remaining bacon.
4. Preheat the broiler to high and set an oven rack on the second highest setting in the oven. Broil until puffed and golden brown,2 to 5 minutes, watching carefully to make sure it doesn't burn.
5. Remove and let cool a few minutes before serving.

83. Almond Keto Smoothie

Made for: Breakfast | Prep Time: 05 minutes | Servings: 1
Per Serving: Kcal: 560, Protein: 34g, Fat: 40g, Net Carb: 6g

INGREDIENTS
- 1 cup (240 ml) unsweetened almond milk
- 1/4 cup (60 ml) unsweetened all-natural almond butter
- 1 scoop vanilla-flavored stevia-sweetened whey protein OR rice protein
- 2 tablespoons raw cacao powder

INSTRUCTIONS
1. Place all ingredients into a high-speed blender. Close the lid tightly and blend until smooth.
2. Enjoy! Decorate the smoothie with grated dark chocolate, if you like.

84. Kimchi Fried Cauliflower

Made for: Breakfast | **Prep Time:** 20 minutes | **Servings:** 2
Per Serving: Kcal: 260, Protein: 9g, Fat: 21g, Net Carb: 7g

INGREDIENTS
- 2 tablespoon unsalted butter
- 2 tablespoon diced onion
- 1 clove garlic minced
- ½ cup (65g) Kimchi
- 10 ounces frozen cauliflower rice
- 1 tablespoon tamari
- 2 teaspoon sesame oil
- 2 eggs
  Toppings
- 1 tablespoon nori flakes
- 1 teaspoon sesame seeds
- 1 green onion, thinly sliced
- 1 serrano pepper, thinly sliced
- 2 tablespoon minced cilantro

INSTRUCTIONS
1. Place the butter in a large skillet over medium high heat. Once bubbling add in the onion and garlic, saute for about 3 minutes until just starting to soften.
2. Add in the kimchi, cauliflower rice, and tamari. Continue to cook for about 5 minutes until the cauliflower is starting to crisp. Taste for salt and add if necessary. Remove from heat and set aside.
3. Place the sesame oil in a small ceramic non-stick skillet over medium heat. Crack in the eggs and cook until the whites are set, flip and continue to cook about 30 seconds. The yolk should still be runny.
4. Divide the cauliflower rice between two bowls and top each with an egg and half of the toppings.

85. Sheet Pan Breakfast

Made for: Breakfast | **Prep Time:** 5 minutes | **Servings:** 01
Per Serving: Kcal: 320, Protein: 0g, Fat: 36g, Net Carb: 0g

INGREDIENTS
- 1 tbsp MCT Oil
- 2 tbsp Butter
- 12 oz Coffee

INSTRUCTIONS
1. Brew a cup of coffee using any brewing method you'd like.
2. Add butter, MCT oil, and coffee to a blender. Blend on high for 30 seconds.

Enjoy.

86. Turkey Wrap

Made for: Breakfast | **Prep Time:** 25 minutes | **Servings:** 01
Per Serving: Kcal: 360, Protein: 20g, Fat: 30g, Net Carb: 3g

INGREDIENTS
- 2 slices of turkey breast (use more if the slices break easily)
- 2 romaine lettuce leaves (or 2 slices of avocado)
- 2 slices of bacon
- 2 eggs
- 1 Tablespoon (15 ml) coconut oil to cook in

INSTRUCTIONS
1. Cook the 2 slices of bacon to the crispness you like.
2. Scramble the 2 eggs in the coconut oil (or bacon fat).
3. Make 2 wraps by placing half the scrambled eggs, 1 slice of bacon, and 1 romaine lettuce leaf on each slice of turkey breast.

87. Green eggs

Made for: Breakfast | **Prep Time:** 15 minutes | **Servings:** 012
Per Serving: Kcal: 298, Protein: 18g, Fat: 21g, Net Carb: 2g

INGREDIENTS
- 1½ tbsp rapeseed oil, plus a splash extra
- 2 trimmed leeks, sliced
- 2 garlic cloves, sliced
- ½ tsp coriander seeds
- ½ tsp fennel seeds
- pinch of chilli flakes, plus extra to serve
- 200g spinach
- 2 large eggs
- 2 tbsp Greek yogurt
- squeeze of lemon

INSTRUCTIONS
1. Heat the oil in a large frying pan. Add the leeks and a pinch of salt, then cook until soft.
   Add the garlic, coriander, fennel and chilli flakes. Once the seeds begin to crackle, tip in the spinach and turn down the heat. Stir everything together until the spinach has wilted and reduced, then scrape it over to one side of the pan. Pour a little oil into the pan, then crack in the eggs and fry until cooked to your liking.

2. Stir the yogurt through the spinach mix and season. Pile onto two plates, top with the fried egg, squeeze over a little lemon and season with black pepper and chilli flakes to serve.

88. Mexican egg roll

Made for: Breakfast | **Prep Time:** 10 minutes | **Servings:** 02
Per Serving: Kcal: 133, Protein: 9g, Fat: 11g, Net Carb: 2g

INGREDIENTS
- 1 large egg
- a little rapeseed oil for frying
- 2 tbsp tomato salsa
- about 1 tbsp fresh coriander

INSTRUCTIONS
1. Beat the egg with 1 tbsp water. Heat the oil in a medium non-stick pan. Add the egg and swirl round the base of the pan, as though you are making a pancake, and cook until set. There is no need to turn it.
2. Carefully tip the pancake onto a board, spread with the salsa, sprinkle with the coriander, then roll it up. It can be eaten warm or cold – you can keep it for 2 days in the fridge.

89. Buffalo Deviled Eggs

Made for: Breakfast | **Prep Time:** 20 minutes | **Servings:** 06
Per Serving: Kcal: 167, Protein: 8g, Fat: 14g, Net Carb: 1g

INGREDIENTS
- 6 large eggs
- 3 tbsp paleo mayonnaise (45 g/1.6 oz) - you can make your own
- 2 tbsp buffalo sauce + more for topping (30 ml) - you can use our homemade Fermented Sriracha
- 1/3 cup crumbled blue cheese (57 g /2 oz)
- 1 celery stalk (40 g/1.4 oz)
- 1 tbsp chopped chives ned, peeled and cubed
- juice 1 lemon

INSTRUCTIONS
1. Place the eggs in a large pot and cover with cold water by 2 1/2 cm/ 1 inch. Bring to a boil over medium-high heat.
2. Once boiling cover and remove from the heat, set aside 8 to 10 minutes. Rinse the eggs with cool water then peel and cut in half.

3. Scoop the yolks into a small bowl with the buffalo sauce and mayonnaise.
4. Keto Buffalo Deviled Eggs
5. Place the egg whites on a serving platter and fill each with the yolk mixture.
6. Keto Buffalo Deviled Eggs
7. Top with a dash of hot sauce, blue cheese, celery, and chives.
8. Keto Buffalo Deviled Eggs
9. Store in an airtight container in the refrigerator for up to 4 days.

90. Chorizo Egg Muffins

Made for: Breakfast | **Prep Time:** 30 minutes | **Servings:** 02
Per Serving: Kcal: 198, Protein: 13g, Fat: 14g, Net Carb: 4g

INGREDIENTS
- 100 g Spanish chorizo or pepperoni, diced (3.5 oz)
- 100 g chopped parboiled kale or fresh kale (3.5 oz)
- 6 large eggs
- 1 cup unsweetened pumpkin purée (200 g/ 7.1 oz)
- Salt and pepper, to taste
- Optional: 1/2 cup grated Manchego, Cheddar or crumbled feta (60 g/ 2.1 oz)
- Optional: Sriracha sauce, greens, sliced avocado

INSTRUCTIONS
1. Preheat the oven to 180 °C/ 355 °F (fan assisted), or 200 °C/ 400 °F (conventional). Dice the chorizo and place on a hot dry pan. Cook for 1 to 2 minutes to release the juices and crisp it up.
2. Add the parboiled kale and cook for another minute. (If using fresh kale: Cover with a lid and cook for 5 to 7 minutes over a medium-low heat.) Remove from the heat and set aside.
3. Crack the eggs into a bowl and mix with the pumpkin purée. Add the chorizo (or use pepperoni) and kale. Season with salt and pepper, and mix until combined. Add the grated cheese (if using).
4. You can optionally add some grated cheese such as Manchego or even crumbled feta cheese.
5. Spoon the mixture into a muffin tray (a silicone tray works best). Use a ladle to distribute the mixture evenly among 10 muffin cups. (Or, bake in a skillet to make a frittata.)
6. Bake for 20 to 25 minutes, and set aside to cool slightly before serving.

7. Serve with Sriracha sauce, greens, or sliced avocado, if you like. Store in the fridge in an airtight container for up to 5 days.

91. Bacon & avocado frittata

Made for: Breakfast | Prep Time: 25 minutes | Servings: 04
Per Serving: Kcal: 468, Protein: 22g, Fat: 38g, Net Carb: 5g

INGREDIENTS

- 8 rashers smoked streaky bacon
- 3 tbsp olive oil
- 6 eggs, beaten
- 1 large avocado, halved, stoned, peeled and cut into chunky slices
- 1 small red chilli, finely chopped
- 1 heaped tsp Dijon mustard
- 2 tsp red wine vinegar
- 200g (4.5 cup) bag mixed salad leaves (we used watercress, rocket & spinach)
- 12 baby plum tomatoes, halved

INSTRUCTIONS

1. Heat a 24cm non-stick ovenproof pan and fry the bacon rashers in batches on a high heat until cooked through and crisp. Chop 4 roughly and break the other 4 into large pieces. Set aside on kitchen paper and clean the pan.
2. Heat the grill to high. Warm 1 tbsp oil in the pan. Season the eggs, add the chopped bacon and pour into the pan. Cook on a low heat for around 8 mins or until almost set. Arrange the avocado slices and bacon shards on top. Grill briefly for about 4 mins until set.
3. Mix the remaining oil, the chilli, mustard, vinegar and seasoning in a large bowl. Toss in the salad leaves and tomatoes. Serve alongside the frittata, cut into wedges.

92. Tomato baked eggs

Made for: Breakfast | Prep Time: 55 minutes | Servings: 02
Per Serving: Kcal: 204, Protein: 9g, Fat: 17g, Net Carb: 3g

INGREDIENTS

- 450g (3 cup) ripe vine tomatoes
- 2 garlic cloves
- 2 tbsp olive oil
- 4 large free-range eggs
- 1 tbsp chopped parsley and/or chives

INSTRUCTIONS

1. Preheat the oven to fan 180C/ conventional 200C/gas 6. Cut the tomatoes into quarters or thick wedges, depending on their size, then spread them over a fairly shallow 1.5 litre ovenproof dish. Peel the garlic, slice thinly and sprinkle over the tomatoes. Drizzle with the olive oil, season well with salt and pepper and stir everything together until the tomatoes are glistening.
2. Slide the dish into the oven and bake for 40 minutes until the tomatoes have softened and are tinged with brown.
3. Make four gaps among the tomatoes, break an egg into each gap and cover the dish with a sheet of foil. Return it to the oven for 5-10 minutes until the eggs are set to your liking. Scatter over the herbs and serve piping hot with thick slices of toast or warm ciabatta and a green salad on the side.

93. Mushroom baked eggs

Made for: Breakfast | Prep Time: 30 minutes | Servings: 02
Per Serving: Kcal: 148, Protein: 12g, Fat: 9g, Net Carb: 3g

INGREDIENTS

- 2 large flat mushrooms (about 85g each), stalks removed and chopped
- rapeseed oil, for brushing
- ½ garlic clove, grated (optional)
- a few thymes leave
- 2 tomatoes, halved
- 2 large eggs
- 2 handfuls rocket

INSTRUCTIONS

1. Heat oven to 200C/180C fan/gas 6. Brush the mushrooms with a little oil and the garlic (if using). Place the mushrooms in two very lightly greased gratin dishes, bottom-side up, and season lightly with pepper. Top with the chopped stalks and thyme, cover with foil and bake for 20 mins.
2. Remove the foil, add the tomatoes to the dishes and break an egg carefully onto each of the mushrooms. Season and add a little more thyme, if you like. Return to the oven for 10-12 mins or until the eggs are set but the yolks are still runny. Top with the rocket and eat straight from the dishes.

94. Baked eggs brunch

Made for: Breakfast | **Prep Time:** 35 minutes | **Servings:** 04
Per Serving: Kcal: 211, Protein: 12g, Fat: 14g, Net Carb: 4g

INGREDIENTS

- 2 tbsp olive oil
- 2 leeks, thinly sliced
- 2 onions, thinly sliced
- 2 x 100g bags baby spinach leaves
- handful fresh wholemeal breadcrumbs
- 25g (1/3 cup) parmesan (or vegetarian alternative), finely grated
- 4 sundried tomatoes, chopped
- 4 medium eggs

INSTRUCTIONS

1. Heat oven to 200C/180C fan/gas 6. Heat the oil in a pan and add the leeks, onions and seasoning. Cook for 15-20 mins until soft and beginning to caramelise.
2. Meanwhile, put the spinach in a colander and pour over a kettle of boiling water. When cool enough to handle, squeeze out as much liquid as possible. Mix the breadcrumbs and cheese together.
3. Arrange the leek and onion mixture between 4 ovenproof dishes, then scatter with the spinach and pieces of sundried tomato. Make a well in the middle of each dish and crack an egg in it. Season and sprinkle with cheese crumbs. Put the dishes on a baking tray and cook for 12-15 mins, until the whites are set and yolks are cooked to your liking.

95. Veggie breakfast bakes

Made for: Breakfast | **Prep Time:** 30 minutes | **Servings:** 2
Per Serving: Kcal: 127, Protein: 9g, Fat: 8g, Net Carb: 4g

INGREDIENTS

- 2 large field mushrooms
- 4 tomatoes, halved
- 1 garlic clove, thinly sliced
- 2 tsp olive oil
- 100g bag spinach
- 2 eggs

INSTRUCTIONS

1. Heat oven to 200C/180C fan/gas 6. Put the mushrooms and tomatoes into 4 ovenproof dishes. Divide garlic between the dishes, drizzle over the oil and some seasoning, then bake for 10 mins.
2. Meanwhile, put the spinach into a large colander, then pour over a kettle of

boiling water to wilt it. Squeeze out any excess water, then add the spinach to the dishes. Make a little gap between the vegetables and crack an egg into each dish. Return to the oven and cook for a further 8-10 mins or until the egg is cooked to your liking.

96. Herby Persian frittata

Made for: Breakfast | **Prep Time:** 20 minutes | **Servings:** 2
Per Serving: Kcal: 198, Protein: 14g, Fat: 11g, Net Carb: 1g

INGREDIENTS

- 3 eggs
- ½ tsp baking powder
- ¼ tsp turmeric
- 1 small pack of coriander and parsley, roughly chopped
- ½ small pack dill, roughly chopped
- 4 spring onions, thinly sliced
- 1 tbsp currants or barberries, if you can find them
- 1 tbsp toasted walnuts (optional), roughly chopped
- 1 tbsp cold pressed rapeseed oil
- 30g (1/4 cup) feta, crumbled

INSTRUCTIONS

1. Heat grill to high. Whisk the eggs together in a large bowl, add the baking powder and turmeric, then season with salt and pepper. Stir in most of the herbs, then add the spring onions, currants and walnuts.
2. Drizzle the oil into a small ovenproof, non-stick frying pan over a medium heat. Pour in the herby egg mixture and cook for 8-10 mins until the egg is nearly set, then put the frittata under the grill for a final minute until cooked through. Sprinkle over the remaining herbs and the crumbled feta to serve.

97. Mushroom & basil omelette

Made for: Breakfast | **Prep Time:** 20 minutes | **Servings:** 04
Per Serving: Kcal: 196, Protein: 14g, Fat: 14g, Net Carb: 4g

INGREDIENTS

- 2 tomatoes, halved
- 3 medium eggs
- 1 tbsp snipped chive
- 300g (3.8 cup) chestnut mushroom, sliced
- 1 tsp unsalted butter
- 2 tbsp low-fat cream cheese

- 1 tbsp finely chopped basil leaves

INSTRUCTIONS

1. Heat the grill to its highest setting and place the tomatoes on a square of foil underneath, turning occasionally to prevent burning. When the tomatoes are slightly scorched, remove from the grill, squashing them slightly to release the juices.
2. Break the eggs into a bowl and mix with a fork. Add a small splash of water and mix. Add the chives and some black pepper, and beat some more. Set aside while you prepare the mushrooms.
3. In a non-stick frying pan, heat the butter over a medium heat until foaming. Add the mushrooms and cook for 5-8 mins until tender, stirring every few mins. Remove and set aside.
4. Briskly stir the egg mixture, then add to the hot pan (tilting it so that the mixture covers the entire base) and leave for 10 secs or so until it begins to set. With a fork, gently stir the egg here and there so that any unset mixture gets cooked.
5. While the egg mixture is still slightly loose, spoon the mushroom mix onto one side of the omelette, and top with the cream cheese and basil leaves. Flip the other side of the omelette over to cover, if you like. Leave to cook for 1 min more, then cut in half and slide each half onto a plate. Serve immediately with the tomatoes on the side.

98. Coconut Porridge

Made for: Breakfast | Prep Time: 15 minutes | Servings: 01
Per Serving: Kcal: 444, Protein: 10g, Fat: 36g, Net Carb: 6g

INGREDIENTS

- ½ cup (120g) almond milk.
- ¼ cup (35g) of mixed berries.
- ⅓ cup (76g) of coconut milk.
- 2 tbsp flaxseed.
- 1 tbsp desiccated coconut.
- 1 tbsp almond meal.
- 1 tsp pumpkin seeds.
- ½ tsp cinnamon.
- ½ tsp vanilla extract.

INSTRUCTIONS

1. To a large saucepan, add coconut milk, almond milk, flaxseed, almond meal, coconut, cinnamon, and vanilla; stir continuously until mixture thickens.

2. Pour into a bowl and top with pumpkin seeds and mixed fruit.

99. Breakfast Roll Ups

Made for: Breakfast | Prep Time: 15 minutes | Servings: 02
Per Serving: Kcal: 350, Protein: 15g, Fat: 17g, Net Carb: 3g

INGREDIENTS

- 2 eggs
- 1/8 lb (56.5g) gourjd sausage
- 2 slicesmozzarella cheese
- salt & pepper taste

INSTRUCTIONS

1. Preheat oven to 400 degrees.
2. Cook sausage through and add eggs.
3. Stir until cooked and set aside.
4. Place parchment paper on the cookie sheet and top with mozzarella cheese slices.
5. Bake cheese for 5-6minutes or until edges starts to brown. Remove cheese from the oven and allow to cool down.
6. Divide sausage and eggs evenly among the slices of cheese and roll.
   Optional
1. Lightly grease your pan with butter and cook until crunchy.

100. Vegan Keto Breakfast

Made for: Breakfast | Prep Time: 15 minutes | Servings: 01
Per Serving: Kcal: 152, Protein: 5g, Fat: 10g, Net Carb: 1.5g

INGREDIENTS

- 50g (1/3 cup) frozen berries (strawberry, raspberry, blueberry, blackberry – or a mix of them)
- 200g (4/3 cup) Alpro soy yogurt with coconut (or plain)
- 1/2 tsp cinnamon
- optional 1/4 tsp stevia (if you like it extra sweet – I used Natvia)
- 30g (1/5 cup) Pip & Nut almond & coconut butter
- 1 tsp cacao nibs

INSTRUCTIONS

1. Add the frozen berries, cinnamon and stevia to a large container and add the yogurt on top.
2. Using a stick blender combine all ingredients. I figured a stick blender works best for me as it is quite a small amount for a regular blender size.
3. Add to a bowl, top with the almond &

coconut butter and cacao and voila: breakfast is served!

Keto Lunch Recipes

101. Crispy Fried KFC Chicken

Made for: Lunch | **Prep Time:** 25 minutes | **goujons:** 08
Per Goujon: Kcal: 230, Protein: 20g, Fat: 16g, Net Carb: 0.9g

INGREDIENTS
- 1 1/2 tsp paprika
- 1/2 tsp dried thyme
- 1 tsp garlic powder
- 1/4 tsp cayenne pepper
- 1/2 tsp dried oregano
- 3/4 tsp sea salt
- 1/4 tsp cracked black pepper
- 3/4 cup unflavoured whey protein powder or egg white protein powder (75 g/2.7 oz)
- 1 large egg
- 1 tbsp heavy whipping cream or coconut milk or almond milk (15 ml)
- 1 tsp Sriracha hot sauce, or to taste
- 1/2 tsp Dijon mustard
- 400 g chicken fillets, equivalent to 4 breasts or 6 skinless and boneless chicken thighs (14.1 oz)
- enough oil for deep frying (avocado oil, ghee or coconut oil)

INSTRUCTIONS
1. Place the spices and seasoning to a bowl and mix to combine (paprika, thyme, garlic, cayenne, oregano, salt and pepper). Add the mini chicken breast fillets and leave to marinate, ideally overnight in the fridge for best flavour, or at least 30 minutes.
2. Once the chicken is marinated, prepare the coating. To another bowl, add the egg, cream, Sriracha and Dijon mustard. Mix to combine.
3. Add protein powder (whey or egg white protein isolate) to a third bowl. Dip the seasoned chicken in the egg wash (shaking off any excess) and then in the whey protein to fully coat.
4. Note: The amount of protein powder in this recipe will be enough for one coating. If you want to do double coating, you will need to use more protein powder and possibly more egg. Also keep in mind that some of the whey will clump up and be wasted so you may

need to use a few tablespoons more to fully coat the chicken.
5. For deep frying, add your chosen oil to a deep pan, enough for the chicken pieces to be fully submerged when fried. The pan should ideally be about 20-23 cm/ 8-9" in diameter so you can get about 3 or 4 pieces in at once. (Note: you will need 1 1/2 to 2 cups (360 to 480 ml) of oil although only about 1/2 cup oil will contribute to the nutrition facts, the remaining oil is discarded.)
6. Once the oil is hot, fry the chicken tenders on a medium-low heat for about 5 minutes or until golden and cooked through.
7. The chicken should be cooked once the internal temperature reaches at least 75 °C/ 165 °F but cut one open to test.
8. If you want to keep the skin crispy skin, serve fresh. They can be reheated in the oven, after storing in the fridge for 1 day, but the crumb may be a little softer.

102. Spicy Chicken Satay

Made for: Lunch | **Prep Time:** 20 minutes | **Servings:** 01
Per Serving: Kcal: 545, Protein: 45g, Fat: 36g, Net Carb: 9g

INGREDIENTS
- 150 g chicken breasts, sliced into tenders (5.3 oz)
- sea salt and pepper to taste
- 1/2 tbsp ghee, duck fat or avocado oil (8 ml)
- 1/6 cup almond butter or peanut butter (40 g/2 oz)
- 1 tsp coconut aminos
- 1 tsp Sriracha hot sauce, or to taste
- 1-2 tbsp water, to thin the sauce
- 100 g broccolini or broccoli florets (4 oz)

INSTRUCTIONS
1. Slice the chicken breasts into smaller tenders. Season with salt and pepper. Put a pot of water on to boil.
2. Heat a griddle pan greased with ghee or a non-stick frying pan. Lay the chicken tenders on the pan and cook for about five minutes on either side.
3. While they cook, mix the almond butter, coconut aminos and Sriracha together in a small bowl or jug and then add water, a little at a time, until you get a nice smooth consistency.
4. Meanwhile, cook the broccolini. Place the broccolini in a steamer basket over the boiling water and cook until just

tender.

5. Drizzle about a third of the sauce over the chicken tenders and toss to coat. Retain the rest of the sauce to serve, heating it gently if desired.
6. Serve the chicken with more sauce and the steamed broccolini on the side.
7. Serve warm. To store, refrigerate for up to 4 days.

103. Keto Monterey Chicken

Made for: Lunch | **Prep Time:** 40 minutes | **Servings:** 02
Per Serving: Kcal: 430, Protein: 40g, Fat: 29g, Net Carb: 1g

INGREDIENTS
- 3 slices bacon cooked
- 2 tablespoons butter
- 1 tablespoon olive oil
- 1/2 lb of thin cut boneless skinless chicken breasts
- 5 tablespoons sugar-free bbq sauce
- 2/3 cup (150g) Cheddar Cheese shredded
- 1/4 cup (29.5g) Monterey Jack Cheese shredded
- 1/2 teaspoon garlic powder
- 1 teaspoon parsley
- 1/4 teaspoon salt and pepper

INSTRUCTIONS
1. In a hot oven-safe skillet, add olive oil and butter. (I use a cast-iron skillet)
2. Season chicken generously with salt, pepper, and garlic powder.
3. Sear chicken on each side for about 4 minutes on medium/high, then cover with a lid and reduce heat to low.
4. Simmer until chicken is cooked all the way through.
5. Spoon sugar-free BBQ sauce on top of each chicken breast.
6. Divide the cooked bacon evenly and place it on top of each chicken breast.
7. Sprinkle cheddar cheese on top of the bacon.
8. Finish off the chicken with Monterey Jack Cheese and sprinkle parsley on top.
9. Turn oven to broil and place skillet in the oven on top rack.
10. Broil for 2-3 minutes or until cheese is melted and bubbly. (Make sure skillet is oven safe)

104. Spicy Shrimp

Made for: Lunch | **Prep Time:** 25 minutes | **Servings:** 02
Per Serving: Kcal: 122, Protein: 16g, Fat: 6g, Net Carb: 3g

INGREDIENTS:
- 1 pound peeled and deveined shrimp
- 1 tablespoon paprika
- 2 teaspoons garlic powder
- ½ teaspoon cayenne pepper
- 1 tablespoon extra-virgin olive oil
- Salt and freshly ground Black Pepper

INSTRUCTIONS:
1. Place the shrimp in a large zip-top plastic bag. In a small bowl, stir the paprika with the garlic powder and cayenne to combine. Pour the mixture into the container with the shrimp and toss well until they are coated with the spices. Refrigerate while you make the grits.

105. Baked Feta Chicken

Made for: Lunch | **Prep Time:** 30 minutes | **Servings:** 02
Per Serving: Kcal: 650, Protein: 52g, Fat: 43g, Net Carb: 7g

INGREDIENTS
- 2 skinless and boneless chicken breasts (340 g/ 12 oz)
- pinch of sea salt and pepper
- 300 g (10.6 oz) cherry tomatoes
- 1/2 block feta cheese (100 g/ 3.5 oz)
- 1/4 cup (60 ml/2 fl oz) extra virgin olive oil
- 2 cloves garlic, minced
- 300 g (10.6 oz) frozen spinach, drained
- fresh basil or parsley, to serve

INSTRUCTIONS
1. Preheat the oven to 200 °C/ 400 °F (fan assisted), or 220 °C/ 425 °F (conventional). Season the chicken breasts with salt and pepper. Mince the garlic.
2. Wash the cherry tomatoes and remove the green parts. Once defrosted, squeeze out any liquids from the spinach.
3. Place the chicken breasts in a hot pan greased with about a tablespoon of the olive oil. Cook for 1 to 2 minutes per side, until lightly browned.
4. To the hot skillet, add the cherry tomatoes and feta. Drizzle the remaining olive oil all over. Place in the oven and bake for about 20 minutes.
5. Remove from the oven. Transfer the cooked chicken breasts on a plate and set aside. Add the drained spinach to the hot skillet and stir through the

ingredients. If needed, place back in the oven for a minute or two to heat up.

6. Serve with the cooked chicken breasts and fresh herbs (parsley or basil work best).
7. To store, place in a sealed container and refrigerate for up to 3 days.

106. Keto Chicken Parmesan

Made for: Lunch | **Prep Time**: 30 minutes | **Servings**: 02
Per Serving: Kcal: 443, Protein: 46g, Fat: 26g, Net Carb: 4g

INGREDIENTS
- 1 (8 ounce) skinless, boneless chicken breast
- 1 egg
- 1 tablespoon heavy whipping cream
- 1-ounce grated Parmesan cheese
- ½ teaspoon salt
- ½ teaspoon garlic powder
- ½ teaspoon ground black pepper
- ½ teaspoon Italian seasoning
- ½ cup (122.5g) jarred tomato sauce
- ¼ cup (56.25g) shredded mozzarella cheese
- 1 tablespoon ghee (clarified butter)

INSTRUCTIONS
1. Set oven rack about 6 inches from the heat source and preheat the oven's broiler.
2. Slice chicken breast through the middle horizontally from one side to within 1/2 inch of the other side. Open the two sides and spread them out like an open book. Pound chicken flat until about 1/2-inch thick.
3. Beat egg and cream together in a bowl.
4. Combine Parmesan cheese, salt, garlic powder, red pepper flakes, ground black pepper, and Italian seasoning in bowl; transfer breading to a plate.
5. Dip chicken into egg mixture; coat completely. Press chicken into breading; thickly coat both sides.
6. Heat a skillet over medium-high heat; add ghee. Place chicken in the pan; cook until no longer pink in the center and the juices run clear, about 3 minutes per side. An instant-read thermometer inserted into the center should read at least 165 degrees F (74 degrees C). Be careful to keep breading in place.
7. Transfer chicken to a baking sheet. Cover with tomato sauce; top with mozzarella cheese.

8. Broil until cheese is bubbling and barely browned, about 2 minutes

107. Bacon Wrapped Chicken

Made for: Lunch | **Prep Time**: 60 minutes | **Servings**: 04
Per Serving: Kcal: 492, Protein: 56g, Fat: 30g, Net Carb: 2g

INGREDIENTS
- 4 medium chicken breasts (800 kg/1.76 lb)
- 200 g (7.1 oz) cream cheese
- 1/2 cup (45 g) grated Parmesan cheese or hard cheese of choice
- 2 tbsp chopped parsley or herbs of choice
- sea salt and pepper, to taste
- 8 thin-cut slices of bacon or 4 regular slices halved widthwise (120g)

INSTRUCTIONS
1. Start by preparing the cheese stuffing.
2. Place the cream cheese, parmesan and parsley together in a bowl and beat well to combine. Divide into four and, using cling wrap, roll into logs the length of your chicken. Place in the freezer until frozen, approx. half an hour.
3. Preheat oven to 200 °C/400 °F (fan assisted), or 220 °C/425 °F (conventional).
   Line a baking tray. Place the chicken on the tray and cut a pocket into the top of each one. Don't cut all of the way through, just pocket for your cheese. Place the frozen cream cheese mixture into each one.
4. Wrap each breast in two slices of thin bacon, securing with a toothpick if necessary. Bake for 30 minutes.
5. Keto Bacon Wrapped Chicken Parcels
6. Broil for an additional 2 minutes if the bacon needs crisping up. Store, wrapped in cling wrap, in the fridge for up to 4 days.

108. Keto Sandwich Bowl

Made for: Lunch | **Prep Time**: 10 minutes | **Servings**: 01
Per Serving: Kcal: 1038, Protein: 62g, Fat: 80g, Net Carb: 2g

INGREDIENTS
- 5 slices smoked deli ham
- 1 cup (45g) romaine hearts, chopped
- 3 slices provolone cheese
- 3 pickles
- 4 banana peppers

- ½ cucumber
- ⅓ orange bell pepper
- 3 cherry tomatoes

Dressing
- 2 tbsp olive oil
- 4 tsp red wine vinegar
- ¼ tsp Italian seasoning

INSTRUCTIONS
1. Chop ham, cheese, and veggies then put them in a bowl.
2. Add olive oil, red wine vinegar, and Italian seasoning, and mix together.
3. Dress the keto sandwich bowl.
4. Enjoy! (This keto sandwich bowl tastes best after sitting for a few minutes so the oil/vinegar mixture can infuse all the other ingredients.

109. Cucumber Avocado Salad

Made for: Lunch | **Prep Time:** 30 minutes | **Servings:** 04
Per Serving: Kcal: 75, Protein: 2g, Fat: 7g, Net Carb: 3g

INGREDIENTS
- 1 large English Cucumber cubed
- 3 ripe Avocados cubed
- 6 Small Cherry Tomatoes cut in quarters
- ¼ cup Pine Nuts or sliced almonds or sunflower seeds
- ¼ cup Italian Flat Parsley finely chopped

INSTRUCTIONS
1. Trim the English cucumber ends. Keep their skin on or peel off if you prefer. Cut cucumber halfway lengthwise, then cut into small cubes. Set aside in a large bowl.
2. Cut the cherry tomatoes in quarters. Set aside in the bowl with diced cucumbers.
3. Cut avocados in half until you hit the stone. Then, with your hands, rotate both avocado parts to open. Next, remove the stone and, using a sharp knife, cut the flesh into cubes - see my picture above in this post for tips and tricks.
4. Slide a spoon under the skin of your avocado to release the cut avocado cubes. Set aside in the mixing bowl.
5. Just before serving, fry the pine nuts over medium heat in a non-stick frying pan. You don't need to add oil, but you can add 1 teaspoon of olive oil if desired. Stir fry for 1 minute until the nuts are hot, roasted, and fragrant.

6. Serve the salad immediately with hot pine nuts or freshly chopped herbs

STORE
Store the salad for up to 24 hours in the fridge in an airtight container. Store the dressing in a separate sealed container.

110. Avocado Chicken Salad

Made for: Lunch | **Prep Time:** 30 minutes | **Servings:** 02
Per Serving: Kcal: 268, Protein: 19g, Fat: 20g, Net Carb: 3g

INGREDIENTS
- 2 cups poached chicken finally diced (10 oz)
- 1 medium Hass Avocado, mashed
- 1/3 cup celery, finely diced (1 large rib)
- 2 tbsp red onion or scallion, minced
- 2 tbsp cilantro, finely chopped
- 2 tbsp avocado oil (or your favorite)
- 1 tbsp fresh lemon juice (or lime juice)
- salt and pepper to taste

INSTRUCTIONS
1. Prepare the celery, onion, and cilantro, placing in a medium bowl. Dice the chicken and add it to the bowl with the vegetables.
2. Cut into the avocado with a chef's knife until the blade hits the pit. Slide the knife around the pit, cutting the avocado in half. Twist the halves to separate. Remove the pit by tapping the knife into the pit until it sticks, make sure the avocado half is held steadily on a cutting board before attempting. Scoop out the avocado flesh with a spoon and place into a small bowl. Mash with a fork until smooth and creamy. Stir in the lemon juice and oil.
3. Add the mashed avocado to the to the chicken and vegetables and stir to mix. Serve over lettuce or enjoy on a low carb bagel.

111. English Parsley Sauce

Made for: Lunch | **Prep Time:** 20 minutes | **Servings:** 04
Per Serving: Kcal: 104, Protein: 3g, Fat: 7g, Net Carb: 6g

INGREDIENTS
- 2 tablespoons/25 grams butter
- 2 tablespoons/20 grams all-purpose flour
- 1 1/2 teaspoons English mustard, optional

- 1 cup/250 milliliters milk, more as needed
- 1 handful fresh flat-leaf parsley, chopped
- Sea salt, to taste
- Freshly ground pepper, to taste

INSTRUCTIONS

1. Gather the ingredients.
2. In a medium-sized saucepan, melt the butter over medium heat.
3. Stir in the flour and mustard (if using).
4. Stir thoroughly to form a thick paste.
5. Cook gently for 2 to 3 minutes more, watching the heat to ensure the paste does not burn. This will cook off the taste of raw flour in the finished sauce.
6. Gradually whisk in the milk.
7. Bring to a boil, lower the heat, and simmer for 5 minutes, frequently whisking to make sure there are no lumps. The sauce should be quite thick but still pouring consistency. If too thick, add a little more milk.
8. Add the fresh parsley and stir well.
9. Season with a good pinch of sea salt and a few black pepper grinds. Taste and add more as needed.
10. Keep the sauce warm, on low heat, until needed. If keeping sauce warm for more than 15 minutes, laying a piece of buttered parchment paper on the surface will prevent a skin from forming. If a slight skin does form, whisk thoroughly over heat, and it should disappear.
11. Serve and enjoy.

112. Buffalo Chicken Casserole

Made for: Lunch | **Prep Time:** 40 minutes | **Servings:** 02
Per Serving: Kcal: 390, Protein: 32g, Fat: 25g, Net Carb: 3g

INGREDIENTS

- 1 cup chopped cauliflower
- 2 oz cream cheese
- 1 cup cooked chicken
- 1 cloves garlic, crushed
- 1/2 cup hot sauce (like Franks or Red Hot)
- 2 tablespoons heavy cream
- 2 oz cheddar cheese, grated

INSTRUCTIONS

1. Preheat the oven to 400°F. Then microwave the cauliflower for 5 minutes.
2. In the mean time add the cream cheese, hot sauce and garlic to a skillet.

Whisk and when the cream cheese has melted, add in the chicken and cauliflower. Mix well and take off stove.
3. Spray a baking dish and spoon the mixture in and smooth out. The pour the heavy cream over the top and next sprinkle the cheddar cheese.
4. Pop in the oven and bake for about 30 minutes until it's nice and browned on top.
5. Let cool a bit before eating.

113. Bacon Wrapped Chicken

Made for: Lunch | **Prep Time:** 40 minutes | **Servings:** 02
Per Serving: Kcal: 998, Protein: 66g, Fat: 77g, Net Carb: 4g

INGREDIENTS

- 1 package (12 ounces) North Country Smokehouse Bacon
- 2 skinless boneless chicken breasts
- 1 tablespoon olive oil
- 1 teaspoon smoked paprika
- 1 teaspoon salt, divided
- 1/4 teaspoon garlic powder
- 1/4 teaspoon onion powder
- 1 1/4 cup (195g) chopped broccoli
- 4 ounces cream cheese, softened
- 1/4 cup (22.5g) grated Parmesan Cheese
- 2 Tablespoons mayonnaise
- 1 clove garlic, minced

INSTRUCTIONS:

1. Preheat oven to 375 degrees Fahrenheit.
2. Place chicken on cutting board.
3. Using a sharp knife, cut a pocket on the side of each chicken breast.
4. Drizzle olive oil over each piece of chicken.
5. In a small bowl add spices plus 1/2 teaspoon of salt. Mix with a spoon.
6. Sprinkle spices over the chicken, front and back.
7. In another bowl mix cream cheese, Parmesan, Mayo, minced garlic, remaining 1/2 tsp salt, mix well, stir in broccoli.
8. Spoon broccoli cheese mixture evenly into each chicken breast. Close chicken breasts with toothpicks.
9. Wrap bacon around each chicken breast until covered.
10. Place chicken on a foil covered baking sheet.
11. Bake for 30-40 minutes, or until chicken is cooked through.

12. Place pan under broiler to make the bacon crispier if desired. Keep a close eye to make sure it doesn't burn.
13. Remove toothpicks.
14. Serve while hot.
15. To reheat, cover with foil.

114. Zucchini Pizza Boats

Made for: Lunch | **Prep Time:** 35 minutes | **Servings:** 04
Per Serving: Kcal: 242, Protein: 14g, Fat: 15g, Net Carb: 1g

INGREDIENTS
- 4 medium Zucchini
- 1 tbsp Olive oil
- 1/4 tsp Sea salt
- 1/4 tsp Black pepper
- 16 tbsp Marinara sauce
- 1/3 cup (46g) Mini pepperoni slices
- 1 1/3 cup (150.5g) Mozzarella cheese

INSTRUCTIONS
1. Preheat the oven to 400 degrees F (204 degrees C). Line a baking sheet with parchment paper.
2. Slice the zucchini lengthwise. Use a spoon or melon baller to scoop out some of the centers of the zucchini to make wells.
3. Place the zucchini onto the baking sheet, cut side up. Drizzle with olive oil and sprinkle with sea salt and black pepper.
4. Roast the zucchini in the oven for about 15-20 minutes, until soft.
5. When the zucchini are done roasting, use paper towels to pat any moisture from the wells.
6. Spread 2 tablespoons (29.5 milliliters) of marinara inside each zucchini boat. Then top with mozzarella cheese and mini pepperoni slices
7. Bake for 5 minutes. Then, broil for about 3-5 minutes, until the cheese is melted and browned.

115. Keto chicken enchilada

Made for: Lunch | **Prep Time:** 25 minutes | **Servings:** 04
Per Serving: Kcal: 282, Protein: 15g, Fat: 21g, Net Carb: 1g

INGREDIENTS
- 1 cup (260g) of Keto Enchilada Sauce
- 1/3 cup (80g) of Sour Cream
- 2 teaspoons of Garlic Powder
- 2 teaspoons of Onion Powder
- 1 teaspoon of Salt
- 1/2 teaspoon of Pepper
- 1 pound of Chicken, cooked and shredded
- 1/2 Red Pepper, seeded and diced
- 3 cups (320g) of Raw Cauliflower Rice
- 1 cup (112g) of Cheddar Cheese, shredded
- 1/4 cup (32g) of Black Olives, sliced
- 1 tablespoon of Cilantro, chopped

INSTRUCTIONS
1. Preheat your oven to 175C/350F.
2. In a large mixing bowl, add the enchilada sauce, sour cream, garlic powder, onion powder, salt, and pepper.
   Whisk together.
3. Add the shredded chicken and peppers, reserving 1 tablespoon for garnish, and mix well.
4. Add the cauliflower rice to the base of your casserole dish and spread evenly.
5. Spoon over the chicken mixture and smooth out.
6. Sprinkle over the cheddar cheese.
7. Bake for 25-30 minutes, until the cheese is golden brown.
8. Serve sprinkled with the reserved peppers, olives, and cilantro. Enjoy!

116. Creamy Lemon Chicken

Made for: Lunch | **Prep Time:** 25 minutes | **Servings:** 04
Per Serving: Kcal: 328, Protein: 35g, Fat: 20g, Net Carb: 2g

INGREDIENTS
- 1-pound thin sliced chicken breasts
- 1/2 teaspoon salt
- 1/2 teaspoon pepper
- 1 tablespoon olive oil
- 1 cup (96g) chicken broth
- 1 tablespoon lemon juice
- 3 cloves garlic, minced
- 2 tablespoons butter
- 1/4 cup (60g) heavy cream/double cream
- 1 tablespoon dill

INSTRUCTIONS
1. Season the chicken on both sides with salt and pepper.
2. Heat a large, heavy-bottomed skillet over medium heat. Add the oil and heat until shimmering.
3. Add the chicken to the skillet and cook until browned on each side and cooked through, about 8 minutes total. Remove chicken to a plate and set aside.
4. Add the chicken broth, to the pan and whisk to deglaze the pan. Add the lemon juice and garlic to the pan and bring to a boil over medium heat.

5. Allow chicken stock to reduce by half, about 10 minutes.
6. Whisk the butter and cream into the chicken stock until butter has melted and mixture is smooth and creamy.
7. Return chicken to the skillet and sprinkle with fresh dill. Cook for 1 minute to rewarm the chicken.
8. Serve immediately.

117. Creamy Garlic Shrimp

Made for: Lunch | **Prep Time:** 20 minutes | **Servings:** 04
Per Serving: Kcal: 488, Protein: 31g, Fat: 45g, Net Carb: 4g

INGREDIENTS
- 1 tablespoon olive oil
- 1 pound (500 grams) shrimp, tails on or off
- Salt and pepper, to taste
- 2 tablespoons unsalted butter
- 6 cloves garlic minced
- 1/2 cup dry white wine or chicken broth
- 1 1/2 cups reduced fat cream
- 1/2 cup fresh grated Parmesan cheese
- 2 tablespoons fresh chopped parsley

INSTRUCTIONS
1. Heat oil a large skillet over medium-high heat. Season shrimp with salt and pepper and fry for 1-2 minutes on each side, until just cooked through and pink. Transfer to a bowl; set aside.
2. Melt the butter in the same skillet. Sauté garlic until fragrant (about 30 seconds). Pour in the white wine or broth; allow to reduce to half while scraping any bits off of the bottom of the pan.
3. Reduce heat to low-medium heat, add the cream and bring to a gentle simmer, while stirring occasionally. Season with salt and pepper to your taste.
4. Add the parmesan cheese and allow sauce to gently simmer for a further minute or so until the cheese melts and sauce thickens.
5. Add the shrimp back into the pan, sprinkle with parsley. Taste test sauce and adjust salt and pepper, if needed
6. Serve over pasta, rice or steamed veg.

118. Keto Chili Kicker

Made for: Lunch | **Prep Time:** 20 minutes | **Servings:** 02
Per Serving: Kcal: 330, Protein: 35g, Fat: 15g, Net Carb: 4g

INGREDIENTS
- 16 oz minced beef.
- Two avocados (chopped).
- One tomato (finely chopped).
- One garlic clove (crushed).
- 3 tbsp lime juice (fresh).
- 2 tbsp red onion (finely chopped).
- 1 tbsp coriander (ground).
- 1 tbsp cumin (ground).
- ½ tsp cayenne pepper.
- ½ tsp garlic powder.
- ¼ tsp black pepper.

INSTRUCTIONS
1. In a large frying pan, add minced beef, coriander, cumin, cayenne pepper, and garlic powder. Fry for 6-8 minutes or until meat is thoroughly cooked.
2. In a bowl, mix avocados, tomatoes, crushed garlic, onion, lime juice, and black pepper; mix until well combined.
3. Put chilli into a bowl and serve avocado salsa on top.

119. Lemon Garlic Salmon

Made for: Lunch | **Prep Time:** 25 minutes | **Servings:** 04
Per Serving: Kcal: 521, Protein: 29g, Fat: 41g, Net Carb: 6g

INGREDIENTS
- 4 4 Ounce Salmon filets (skin on or skinless)
- kosher salt and pepper
- 2 Tablespoons avocado oil (Click here for my favorite brand on Amazon)
- 1 ¼ Cup (290g) Heavy cream
- 2 Tablespoons Lemon juice
- 3 Cloves garlic, minced
- 2 Tablespoons freshly chopped parsley

INSTRUCTIONS
1. Heat the oil in a cast iron skillet over medium high heat.
2. Add in the salmon filets skin side up. Cook until the salmon is browned and the fish easily releases from the pan. Try not to flip early or the salmon will stick.
3. Flip to the other side (skin side if your salmon has skin) and cook until the salmon skin is crispy and releases from the pan.
4. Remove the salmon from the pan and set aside.
5. Turn the heat of the skillet down to medium and whisk together the heavy cream, garlic, parsley and lemon juice. Let simmer for a few minutes to thicken.

6. Season with salt and pepper to taste.
7. Serve the salmon with cream sauce.

120. Keto Chicken Recipe

Made for: Lunch | **Prep Time:** 15 minutes | **Servings:** 04
Per Serving: Kcal: 192, Protein: 24g, Fat: 10g, Net Carb: 1g

INGREDIENTS:
- 4 small skinless chicken breast fillets or chicken thighs
- 2 small limes juiced
- 1 clove garlic minced
- 1 tsp oregano dried
- 1/2 tsp salt
- 1/2 tsp pepper
- 2 tbsp olive oil

INSTRUCTIONS:
1. In a ziplock bag, add the four pieces of chicken and set aside.
2. In a mixing bowl, whisk together the marinade ingredients until combined. Pour over the chicken and using your hands, rub it into the meat until coated. Refrigerate the chicken for at least an hour, to marinate.
3. After the chicken has marinated, remove it from the refrigerator bake or grill the chicken.

Grilled chicken
1. Preheat the grill on medium/high heat and lightly grease the grill grates. Once hot, add the chicken and grill for 20 minutes, flipping halfway through. Ensure the chicken is cooked by checking the internal temperature and ensuring it has an internal temperature of 165F.

Baked chicken
1. Preheat the oven to 230C/450F. Place marinated chicken in a lined baking dish and bake uncovered for 24 minutes, flipping halfway through. Chicken is cooked once the internal temperature reaches 165F and is no longer pink in the middle.

121. Mushroom soup

Made for: Lunch | **Prep Time:** 30 minutes | **Servings:** 04
Per Serving: Kcal: 309, Protein: 11g, Fat: 23g, Net Carb: 7g

INGREDIENTS:
- 90g (1/3 cup) butter

- 2 medium onions, roughly chopped
- 1 garlic clove, crushed
- 500g (6.5 cup) mushrooms, finely chopped (chestnut or button mushrooms work well)
- 2 tbsp plain flour
- 1l hot chicken stock
- 1 bay leaf
- 4 tbsp single cream
- small handful flat-leaf parsley, roughly chopped, to serve (optional)

INSTRUCTIONS:
1. Heat the butter in a large saucepan and cook the onions and garlic until soft but not browned, about 8-10 mins.
2. Add the mushrooms and cook over a high heat for another 3 mins until softened. Sprinkle over the flour and stir to combine. Pour in the chicken stock, bring the mixture to the boil, then add the bay leaf and simmer for another 10 mins.
3. Remove and discard the bay leaf, then remove the mushroom mixture from the heat and blitz using a hand blender until smooth.
Gently reheat the soup and stir through the cream (or, you could freeze the soup at this stage – simply stir through the cream when heating). Scatter over the parsley, if you like, and serve.

122. Coconut Chicken Curry

Made for: Lunch | **Prep Time:** 25 minutes | **Servings:** 04
Per Serving: Kcal: 1190, Protein: 32g, Fat: 112g, Net Carb: 5g

INGREDIENTS:
- 27 oz coconut milk.
- 16 oz chicken thighs (boneless and skinless, cubed).
- 8 oz broccoli (cut into small florets).
- 3 oz green beans (cut in half).
- One onion (finely chopped).
- One chilli pepper (finely chopped).
- 3 tbsp coconut oil.
- 1 tbsp fresh ginger (grated).
- 1 tbsp curry paste.
- Salt and Pepper.

Cauliflower rice:
- 24 oz cauliflower head (grated).
- 3 oz coconut oil.
- ½ tsp salt.

INSTRUCTIONS:
1. Heat coconut oil in a frying pan. Add onion, chilli, and ginger and fry until softened.
2. Add chicken and curry paste; fry until chicken is cooked and lightly browned.
3. Add broccoli and green beans.
4. Add the substantial part of coconut milk, salt, and Pepper. Allow simmering for 15-20 minutes.
5. In another large frying pan, add 3 oz coconut oil. When hot, add the grated cauliflower.
6. Add salt and cook for 5-10 minutes until rice has softened.
7. Place rice on a serving plate and top with chicken curry.

123. Peanut butter chicken

Made for: Lunch | **Prep Time:** 40 minutes | **Servings:** 01
Per Serving: Kcal: 572, Protein: 33g, Fat: 43g, Net Carb: 1g

INGREDIENTS:
- 2 tbsp vegetable oil
- 1 skinless boneless chicken thighs, cut into chunks
- 1 onion, finely chopped
- 1 garlic clove, crushed
- 1 red chillies, finely sliced (deseeded if you don't like it too hot)
- ½ tsp fresh ginger, grated
- ½ tbsp garam masala
- 25g (1/4 cup) smooth peanut butter
- 100ml (1/2 cup) coconut milk
- 100g (1/2 cup) can chopped tomatoes
- coriander, ½ roughly chopped, ½ leaves picked
- roasted peanuts, to serve
- cooked basmati rice, to serve

INSTRUCTIONS:
1. Heat 1 tbsp of the oil in a deep-frying pan over a medium heat. Brown the chicken in batches, setting aside once golden. Fry the onion for 8 minutes until softened. Then add the garlic, chilli and ginger and fry in the other 1 tbsp oil for 1 min. Add the garam masala and fry for 1 min more.
2. Stir in the peanut butter, coconut milk and tomatoes, and bring to a simmer. Return the chicken to the pan and add the chopped coriander. Cook for 30 mins until the sauce thickens and the chicken is cooked through.
3. Serve with the remaining coriander,

roasted peanuts and rice, if you like.

124. Baked salmon

Made for: Lunch | **Prep Time:** 20 minutes | **Servings:** 04
Per Serving: Kcal: 354, Protein: 35g, Fat: 23g, Net Carb: 0.4g

INGREDIENTS:
- 4 skinless salmon fillets
- 1 tbsp olive oil or melted butter
- chopped herbs, lemon slices and steamed long-stem broccoli, to serve (optional)

INSTRUCTIONS:
1. Heat the oven to 180C/160C fan/gas 4. Brush each salmon fillet with the oil or butter and season well.
2. Put the salmon fillets in an ovenproof dish. Cover if you prefer your salmon to be tender, or leave uncovered if you want the flesh to roast slightly.
3. Roast for 10-15 mins (or about 4 mins per 1cm thickness) until just opaque and easily flaked with a fork. Serve with a sprinkling of chopped herbs, lemon slices and steamed long-stem broccoli, if you like.

125. Masala omelette muffins

Made for: Lunch | **Prep Time:** 35 minutes | **Servings:** 04
Per Serving: Kcal: 180, Protein: 15g, Fat: 10g, Net Carb: 3g

INGREDIENTS:
- rapeseed oil, for greasing
- 2 medium courgettes, coarsely grated
- 6 large eggs
- 2 large or 4 small garlic cloves, finely grated
- 1 red chilli, deseeded and finely chopped
- 1 tsp chilli powder
- 1 tsp ground cumin
- 1 tsp ground coriander
- handful fresh coriander, chopped
- 125g (1 cup) frozen peas
- 40g (1/3 cup) feta

INSTRUCTIONS:
1. Heat oven to 220C/200C fan/ gas 7 and lightly oil four 200ml ramekins. Grate the courgettes and squeeze really well, removing as much liquid as possible. Put all the ingredients except the feta in a large jug and mix really well.
2. Pour into the ramekins, scatter with the

feta and bake on a baking sheet for 20-25 mins until risen and set. You can serve the muffins hot or cold with salad, slaw or cooked vegetables.

126. Chicken & pistachio salad

Made for: Lunch | **Prep Time:** 15 minutes | **Servings:** 02
Per Serving: Kcal: 521, Protein: 37g, Fat: 30g, Net Carb: 3g

INGREDIENTS:
- 2 large eggs
- 2 tbsp extra virgin olive oil
- 1 large lemon, zested and juiced
- 2 tbsp natural yogurt
- 1 large skinless cooked chicken breast fillet
- 40g (1/8 cup) mixed olives, halved
- 40g (1/3 cup) sundried tomatoes
- small bunch basil, chopped
- 3 Little Gem lettuces, leaves separated
- 30g (1/4 cup) pistachios, roughly chopped and toasted

INSTRUCTIONS:
1. Bring a large pan of water to a simmer. Add the eggs and cook gently for 7 mins. Remove with a slotted spoon and transfer to a bowl of cold water. Once cooled, carefully peel off the shell and slice each egg in half.
2. Meanwhile, whisk the oil with the lemon zest, juice and yogurt, and season well. Shred the chicken and toss with the olives, sundried tomatoes, basil and lettuce. Pour in the dressing, season and toss together.
3. Divide the salad between two bowls and top with the egg halves and pistachios.

127. Cheesy Chicken Chunks

Made for: Lunch | **Prep Time:** 20 minutes | **Servings:** 02
Per Serving: Kcal: 399, Protein: 41g, Fat: 24g, Net Carb: 2g

INGREDIENTS:
- 2 large chicken breasts (cut into strips).
- One large egg.
- ¾ cup (90g) parmesan cheese (grated).
- ¾ cup (84g) almond flour.

INSTRUCTIONS:
1. Preheat oven at 400 degrees.
2. Mix the parmesan and flour.
3. In a separate bowl, whisk the egg.

4. Dip each strip of chicken nto the egg mixture and then into the flour mixture. Place on a wire rack.
5. Spray chicken with cooking spray and bake for 18-20 minutes or until browned and thoroughly cooked.

128. Meatballs without breadcrumbs

Made for: Lunch | **Prep Time:** 35 minutes | **Servings:** 04
Per Serving: Kcal: 287, Protein: 23g, Fat: 18g, Net Carb: 2g

INGREDIENTS:
Meatballs:
- 1 lb. 85% lean ground beef
- 1 teaspoon Diamond Crystal kosher salt
- ¼ teaspoon black pepper
- 1 teaspoon onion powder
- 1 teaspoon garlic powder
- ¼ cup grated Parmesan cheese (not shredded cheese)

Sauce:
- 2 tablespoons unsweetened ketchup
- 1 tablespoon erythritol
- 1 tablespoon reduced sodium soy sauce (or use a gluten-free alternative and add salt as needed)
- 1 teaspoon garlic powder
- ⅛ teaspoon cayenne pepper

INSTRUCTIONS:
1. Preheat your oven to 400 degrees F. Line a large rimmed baking sheet with parchment paper.
2. In a medium bowl, use your hands to mix together the meatball ingredients.
3. Form the mixture into 20 meatballs. I find it easiest to shape the mixture into a log, slice it into five slices, then divide each slice into four.
4. Place the shaped meatballs on the prepared baking sheet, not touching each other. Bake 15 minutes.
5. Meanwhile, in a medium saucepan, whisk together the sauce ingredients. 5 minutes before meatballs should be done, heat the sauce gently over medium-low heat. If the sauce seems too thick, add a tablespoon or two of water.
6. When meatballs are done, use tongs to transfer them to the sauce. Gently toss to coat. Serve immediately.

129. Cheeseburger Casserole

Made for: Lunch | **Prep Time:** 30 minutes | **Servings:** 04
Per Serving: Kcal: 680, Protein: 57g, Fat: 46g, Net Carb: 3g

INGREDIENTS:
- Olive oil spray for the baking dish
- 2 tablespoons olive oil
- 2 lb. extra lean ground beef
- 1 medium onion finely chopped (6 oz)
- 2 teaspoons Diamond Crystal kosher salt or 1 teaspoon fine salt
- ¼ teaspoon black pepper
- 1 tablespoon minced fresh garlic
- ¼ cup (60g) avocado oil mayonnaise
- ¼ cup (68g) unsweetened ketchup
- 1 tablespoon mustard
- 1 ½ cup shredded sharp cheddar divided (6 oz)

INSTRUCTIONS:
1. Preheat your oven to 400 degrees F. Spray a 2-quart baking dish with olive oil.
2. Heat the olive oil in a large skillet over medium-high heat, about 2 minutes. Add the beef and the onions. Cook, stirring to break up the beef, until the meat is browned and the onion is soft, about 5 minutes.
3. If there are liquids at the bottom of the skillet, carefuly drain the mixture and return it to the skillet.
4. Stir in the kosher salt, black pepper, and garlic. Cook, stirring, 1 more minute.
5. Turn the heat off. Stir in the mayonnaise, unsweetened ketchup, mustard, and 1 cup cheddar.
6. Transfer the mixture to the prepared baking dish. Sprinkle with the remaining cheese.
7. Bake until the cheese is melted and the casserole is heated through, about 15 minutes. Or, if your baking dish is broiler-safe, broil the casserole 6 inches below the heating element (not directly below) until the cheese is melted, 1-2 minutes.

130. Keto Kheema

Made for: Lunch | **Prep Time:** 35 minutes | **Servings:** 04
Per Serving: Kcal: 589, Protein: 36g, Fat: 47g, Net Carb: 3g

INGREDIENTS
- 500 grams (3.37 cup) Mutton or Lamb Minced (Ground)
- 100 grams (1/2 cup) Tomato

- 80 grams (1/2 cup) Onion
- 10 grams Ginger Garlic Paste I recommend this
- 100 grams (1/2 cup) Heavy Whipping Cream Try this one
- 50 grams (1/2 cup) Cheddar Cheese
- 1 Tsp Cumin Try this one
- 3 Tbsp Ghee Try this one
- 1/2 Tsp Tumeric I recommend this one
- 1/2 Tsp Kashmiri Red Chilly Powder I use this one
- 1/2 Tsp Coriander Powder I recommend this one
- 1/2 Tsp Garam Masala Powder I recommend this one
- Salt to Taste
- Fresh Coriander Also known as Cilantro

INSTRUCTIONS:
1. Heat the ghee in a sauceman and chop and add the onions. Once they turn translucent add the cumin seeds.
2. When the onions start browning add in the minced meat and stir well. Keep stirring and breaking the pieces of meat so they do not lump up together. Keep the pan on a high heat.
3. Once the meat is separated and the moisture is released add in the tomato, ginger garlic paste, salt, tumeric, chilly powder, coriander powder, garam masala and mix well. Then add some water and cover and cook for 15-20 minutes
4. Keep stirring the meat every 2-3 mintues and once it's reduced to your liking add in cheese and mix well.
5. Once the cheese is fully melted add in the cream and cook for a further 2-3 minutes after which turn off the gas and finish with the coriander.
6. Serve with Keto bread or Keto naan.

131. Keto Taco Salad

Made for: Lunch | **Prep Time:** 20 minutes | **Servings:** 04
Per Serving: Kcal: 487, Protein: 34g, Fat: 35g, Net Carb: 3g

INGREDIENTS:
- 1 lb (450g) ground beef
- 3 tbsp homemade taco seasoning (see notes)
- 6 cups chopped romaine lettuce
- 1 cup fresh tomato salsa (pico de gallo)
- 1/2 cup (120g) sour cream
- 1 cup (112g) shredded cheese (cheddar or Mexican blend)
- 1 avocado, sliced

- 1 lime (optional)

INSTRUCTIONS:

1. In a large pan over medium-high heat, brown the ground beef. Cook, breaking it up with a wood spoon, until no longer pink and cooked through. Drain excess grease.
2. Season the beef with the homemade taco seasoning. Let cool slightly.
3. Prepare the vegetables: Wash and chop the lettuce. Slice the avocados.
4. Assemble the salads: Place the lettuce in a large bowl and top with the seasoned beef, salsa, sour cream, cheese, and avocado. Serve with a lime wedge (optional)

132. Cauliflower steaks

Made for: Lunch | Prep Time: 20 minutes | Servings: 02
Per Serving: Kcal: 277, Protein: 9g, Fat: 21g, Net Carb: 1g

INGREDIENTS:

- 1 cauliflower
- ½ tsp smoked paprika
- 2 tbsp olive oil
- 1 roasted red pepper
- 4 black olives, pitted
- small handful parsley
- 1 tsp capers
- ½ tbsp red wine vinegar
- 2 tbsp toasted flaked almonds

INSTRUCTIONS:

1. Heat oven to 220C/200C fan/gas 7 and line a baking tray with baking parchment. Slice the cauliflower into two 1-inch steaks – use the middle part as it's larger, and save the rest for another time. Rub the paprika and ½ tbsp oil over the steaks and season. Put on the tray and roast for 15-20 mins until cooked through.
2. Meanwhile, make the salsa. Chop the pepper, olives, parsley and capers, and put into a bowl and mix with the remaining oil and vinegar. Season to taste. When the steaks are cooked, spoon over the salsa and top with flaked almonds to serve.

133. Pepperoni Pizza

Made for: Lunch | Prep Time: 25 minutes | Servings: 02
Per Serving: Kcal: 1043, Protein: 52g, Fat: 90g, Net Carb: 5g

INGREDIENTS:

- 4 large eggs.
- 6 oz mozzarella (grated)

Topping:

- 3 tbsp tomato puree.
- 5 oz mozzarella (grated).
- 1 ½ oz pepperoni (sliced).
- ½ tsp dried mixed herbs.

INSTRUCTIONS:

1. Preheat oven at 400 degrees.
2. Mix the eggs with 6oz grated mozzarella, until well combined.
3. Line a baking tray with greaseproof paper. I was using a spatula, spread mixture into one large rectangular pizza.
4. Bake for 15-20 minutes until lightly browned. Remove from the oven.
5. Adjust oven temperature to 450 degrees.
6. Spread tomato puree on to the pizza and sprinkle on the herbs. Load with the remaining cheese and place pepperoni on top.
7. Bake for an additional 10 minutes or until golden brown and cheese has melted.

134. Bacon, Egg & Brussels Sprout

Made for: Lunch | Prep Time: 20 minutes | Servings: 02
Per Serving: Kcal: 520, Protein: 26g, Fat: 41g, Net Carb: 8g

INGREDIENTS:

- 1/2 small red onion, sliced (30 g/1.1 oz)
- 1 clove garlic, minced
- 4 slices bacon, chopped (120 g/4.2 oz)
- 250 g Brussels sprouts, slices (8.8 oz)
- 2 tbsp ghee or duck fat (30 ml)
- 1 tsp Dijon mustard
- 1/4 cup (60ml) chicken stock, bone broth or water
- 4 large eggs
- sea salt and pepper, to taste

INSTRUCTIONS:

1. Slice the onion and mince the garlic. Bacon, Egg & Brussels Sprout Hash
2. Trim and slice the Brussels sprouts. Bacon, Egg & Brussels Sprout Hash
3. Grease a skillet with ghee or duck fat. Add sliced bacon and cook on medium-high for about 5 minutes, until lightly browned and rendered.
4. Add the onion and cook until lightly browned for 3 to 5 minutes. Add the

garlic and cook for a minute. Bacon, Egg & Brussels Sprout Hash

5. Add the sliced Brussels sprouts, mustard, chicken stock (or water) and season with salt and pepper. Stir through and cover with a lid. Reduce the heat to medium-low and cook for 8 to 10 minutes, or until the Brussels sprouts are tender.
6. Remove the lid. Using a spatula, create four small wells and crack in the eggs. Cook until the whites are opaque and cooked through while the egg yolks are still runny. Optionally, you can cover the skillet with a lid to cook faster. Bacon, Egg & Brussels Sprout Hash
7. Eat immediately while still warm.

135. Keto Chicken Salad

Made for: Lunch | Prep Time: 20 minutes | Servings: 02
Per Serving: Kcal: 581, Protein: 38g, Fat: 43g, Net Carb: 3g

INGREDIENTS:
- 2 boneless chicken breasts, skin on (285 g/10 oz)
- 6 thin-cut slices bacon or 3 regular slices (90 g/ 3.2 oz)
- 1 large avocado, sliced (200 g/7.1 oz)
- 4 cups (120g) mixed leafy greens of choice
- 4 tbsp Keto Ranch Dressing (60 ml/2 fl oz) or use dairy-free Ranch Dressing
- ghee or duck fat for greasing
- salt and pepper, to taste

INSTRUCTIONS:
1. Preheat the oven to 200 °C/400 °F. Start by crisping up the chicken breasts. Season the chicken breasts with salt and pepper from all sides. Grease a small skillet with ghee or duck fat. Place the chicken breasts, skin side down, on the hot pan.
2. Without moving it, cook the chicken on high until golden brown and crispy, for 5-6 minutes. Then, flip the chicken on the other side, cook for 30 seconds. Transfer the skillet into the oven.
3. Cook the chicken for 10-15 minutes. It's done when an instant read thermometer inserted into the thickest part reads 74 °C/ 165 °F.
4. If you want to bake the bacon in the oven, spread the slices over a baking sheet lined with parchment paper.
5. Bake bake for 10 minutes until crispy and golden brown. Alternatively, you can

crisp up the bacon separately on a frying pan.
6. Once the chicken is cooked, transfer to a cutting board and let it rest for 5 minutes.
7. Slice the avocado and the cooked chicken. Assemble the salad: start with the leafy greens, and then add avocado, crispy bacon and sliced chicken.
8. Top each salad with 2 tablespoons of Ranch Dressing.
9. This salad is best served immediately. You can always keep some cooked chicken and crisped up bacon in the fridge and reheat or simply use cold.

136. Taco Stuffed Avocados

Made for: Lunch | Prep Time: 15 minutes | Servings: 02
Per Serving: Kcal: 518, Protein: 22g, Fat: 43g, Net Carb: 8g

INGREDIENTS:
- 2 ripened avocados, cut in half and pit removed
- ¾ cup (170g) Keto Super Taco Meat
- ¼ cup (60g) diced fresh tomatoes, or salsa
- ½ cup (56g) shredded Mexican or cheddar cheese, divided

INSTRUCTIONS:
1. Preheat oven to 400 degrees.
2. Place Keto Super Taco Meat (or other taco meat of your choice), tomatoes, and ¼ cup cheese to a medium bowl and stir together.
3. Divide the filling between the avocado halves and stuff filling into the halves.
4. Sprinkle with remaining cheese and place on a baking sheet. Tip: Use a muffin pan instead of a regular baking sheet to keep the avocados from tipping in the oven.
5. Bake for 8-10 minutes, or until cheese is melted. Serve warm. To eat, scoop out with a spoon or fork.

137. Baked Egg Banquet

Made for: Lunch | Prep Time: 20 minutes | Servings: 02
Per Serving: Kcal: 498, Protein: 40g, Fat: 36g, Net Carb: 2g

INGREDIENTS:
- 2 large eggs.
- 3 oz minced beef.
- 2 oz cheddar cheese (grated).

INSTRUCTIONS:
1. Preheat oven at 400 degrees.
2. Put the minced beef into a baking dish; make two holes in the mince and crack in the eggs.
3. Sprinkle the cheese over the top.
4. Bake for 10-15 minutes or until the eggs are cooked.

138. Sandwich Lunchbox

Made for: Lunch | **Prep Time:** 15 minutes | **Servings:** 02
Per Serving: Kcal: 1009, Protein: 56g, Fat: 112g, Net Carb: 4g

INGREDIENTS:
- 12 Slices Genoa Salami
- 12 Slices Ham
- 12 slices Pepperoni
- 12 Slices Provolone
- 6 tbsp Mayo
- 1/2 cup (37.5g) Shredded Lettuce
- 40 black olives
- 2 apples

INSTRUCTIONS:
1. Lay ingredients on cutting board and roll sandwich up. Secure with a toothpick.
2. Place your ingredients into your EasyLunchboxes. Cover and refrigerate until ready to use. Use within 3 days.

139. Keto Sandwich

Made for: Lunch | **Prep Time:** 25 minutes | **Servings:** 04
Per Serving: Kcal: 295, Protein: 25g, Fat: 16g, Net Carb: 3g

INGREDIENTS:
- 2 slices keto bread
- 1/2 cup (112g) guacamole
- 1 small tomato sliced
- 1/4 cup (10.5g) baby spinach loosely packed
- 1 slice cheese optional

INSTRUCTIONS
1. Lightly toast your keto bread of choice.
2. Spread one piece of toasted bread with avocado, then add the tomato, baby spinach, and cheese. Place the second piece of bread on to, slice in half and serve.

140. Paleo Lamb Meatballs

Made for: Lunch | **Prep Time:** 20 minutes | **Servings:** 02
Per Serving: Kcal: 485, Protein: 135g, Fat: 24g, Net Carb: 6g

INGREDIENTS:
- 1-lb ground lamb
- One egg
- 2 tsp Organic Italian spice blend
- 1 tsp cumin powder
- 1 tsp coriander powder
- 3 tsp dried oregano
- 3 tsp whole fennel seeds
- 1 Tbsp fresh parsley, generous amount, minced
- ¼ tsp sea salt
- ¼ tsp coarse black pepper

INSTRUCTIONS:
1. Preheat oven to 400 degrees. Prepare a baking pan with parchment paper.
2. In a medium bowl, combine lamb, egg, and spices blend well with your hands. Separate and roll into four even balls. Say a positive affirmation or word while forming the meatballs.
3. Place on the baking sheet and bake for 20 minutes. Enjoy immediately or store in an airtight container for up to 5 days.

141. Keto Tuna Salad

Made for: Lunch | **Prep Time:** 5 minutes | **Servings:** 02
Per Serving: Kcal: 450, Protein: 26g, Fat: 32g, Net Carb: 5g

INGREDIENTS:
- 10 oz. canned tuna (drained)
- 1 large avocado
- 1 celery rib
- 2 cloves fresh garlic
- 3 tablespoon mayonnaise
- 1 small red onion
- 1 tablespoon freshly squeezed lemon juice
- 1/4 cucumber
- 1 handful parsley
- 1/4 teaspoon salt
- pepper to taste

INSTRUCTIONS:
1. Rinse and dry the vegetables. Finely chop the cucumber, onion, and celery. Mince the garlic.
2. Set aside half of the parsley, then add the rest of the ingredients to a large bowl.
3. Mix everything together until the avocado is well-mashed and all the ingredients have been coated. Add salt and pepper to taste.
4. Garnish with remaining parsley before serving.

142. Egg & Bacon Sandwich

Made for: Lunch | Prep Time: 15 minutes | Servings: 01
Per Serving: Kcal: 490, Protein: 28g, Fat: 39g, Net Carb: 6g

INGREDIENTS:
- Cooking spray.
- Two large eggs.
- 1 tbsp coconut flour.
- 1 tbsp butter (salted).
- ¼ tsp baking powder.
- One slice cheddar cheese.
- Two slices of bacon (grilled)

INSTRUCTIONS:
1. Place butter in the microwave for 30 seconds or until melted.
2. Let the butter cool slightly. Mix in 1 egg, coconut flour, and baking powder; microwave for one and a half minutes.
3. Allow bread to cool and slice to make two equally thin slices.
4. Using the cooking spray, fry the remaining egg to your preference. Grill the bread until toasted and crunchy.
5. Assemble the sandwich placing a slice of toast on the bottom, cheese, bacon, and fried egg; top with remaining toast.

143. Pancakes With Almond Flour

Made for: Lunch | Prep Time: 15 minutes | Pancakes: 06
Per Pancake: Kcal: 177, Protein: 7g, Fat: 14g, Net Carb: 2g

INGREDIENTS:
- 2 eggs
- 1/3 cup (60ml) unsweetened coconut milk
- 1 tsp vanilla extract
- 1 ¼ cup (140g) almond flour
- 1 tsp baking powder
- keto syrup and blueberries, for serving

INSTRUCTIONS:
1. To start, gather all of your ingredients one one place.
2. Then in a bowl, beat eggs, milk, and vanilla.
3. Add almond flour and baking powder.
4. Stir the flour in until the batter is smooth.
5. Heat a large non-stick skillet and pour ¼ cup of the keto batter into the skillet.
6. Cook the pancakes until bubbles appear on the surface. Lift and flip the pancakes and cook for 30 seconds.
7. Serve warm, drizzled with syrup and topped with blueberries.

144. Low Carb Lunch Ideas

Made for: Lunch | Prep Time: 5 minutes | Servings: 01
Per Serving: Kcal: 382, Protein: 36g, Fat: 21g, Net Carb: 2g

INGREDIENTS:
- ½ avocado, cubed
- 4 slices deli turkey, rolled and sliced
- ½ cup (75g) grape tomatoes halved
- 1 slice Provolone or Mozzarella cheese, cubed
- ¼ cup (45g) pitted black olives
- 1 tablespoon basil pesto

INSTRUCTIONS:
1. To a glass lunch container, add the avocado, deli turkey, tomatoes, Provolone cheese, and olives, making alternate rows of each.
2. Pack the pesto into a mini sauce container. Prior to serving, drizzle the pesto over the salad.

145. Charming Cream Cheese

Made for: Lunch | Prep Time: 10 minutes | Servings: 01
Per Serving: Kcal: 333, Protein: 22g, Fat: 28g, Net Carb: 2g

INGREDIENTS:
- 2 large eggs
- 2 oz cream cheese.
- 1 tsp granulated sugar substitute.
- ½ tsp ground cinnamon.

INSTRUCTIONS:
1. Blend all ingredients until smooth. Allow resting for 2 minutes.
2. Grease a large frying pan and pour in ¼ of the mixture.
3. Cook for 2 minutes until golden, flip and cook for an additional minute.
4. Repeat the process until all mixture has gone.

146. Keto turkey with cheese

Made for: Lunch | Prep Time: 15 minutes | Servings: 01
Per Serving: Kcal: 601, Protein: 44g, Fat: 45g, Net Carb: 5g

INGREDIENTS:
- 2 tbsp butter, divided
- 1½ lbs turkey breast tenderloin
- 1 cup heavy whipping cream
- 6 oz. (¾ cup) cream cheese
- 1 tbsp tamari soy sauce

- salt and pepper, for seasoning
- 1½ oz. small capers (non-pareil), strained

INSTRUCTIONS:
1. Preheat the oven to 350°F (175°C).
2. Over medium heat, melt one-third of the butter in a large oven-proof frying pan. Generously season the turkey tenderloin with salt and pepper, and then fry for about 8-10 minutes, until golden brown on all sides.
3. Carefully move the hot pan with tenderloin, onto the middle oven rack. Roast uncovered for about 10 minutes, or until the tenderloin reaches an internal temperature of at least 165°F (74°C). Place on a serving dish and tent with foil.
4. Add another third of the butter, along with any turkey drippings into a small saucepan. Over medium heat, stir until the butter has melted. Add the cream and cream cheese. Stir together and bring to a light boil. Lower the heat and simmer uncovered, until thickened. Stir in the soy sauce, season with salt and pepper, and set aside.
5. Melt the remaining butter in a small frying pan, over medium-high heat. Quickly sauté the capers until crispy.
6. Slice the turkey into 1/2" (15 cm) slices. Place on a serving platter, and top with the creamy cream cheese sauce and fried capers.

147. Bacon & Avocado

Made for: Lunch | **Prep Time:** 25 minutes | **Servings:** 02
Per Serving: Kcal: 544, Protein: 23g, Fat: 46g, Net Carb: 1g

INGREDIENTS:
- 6 slices bacon.
- Two avocados.
- Two small onions (diced).
- 2 tbsp lime juice.
- 2 tbsp garlic powder.
- Cooking spray.

INSTRUCTIONS:
1. Preheat the oven at 180 degrees.
2. Spray a baking tray with cooking spray, cook the bacon 15-20 minutes until crispy.
3. Remove seeds from avocados; in a massive bowl, mash the avocado flesh with a fork.
4. Add onions, garlic, and lime juice; mash until well combined.

5. Allow the crispy bacon to cool and place one slice on a plate; top with 2 tbsp of avocado guacamole. Place another bacon slice on top and add another 2 tbsp of guacamole and top with bacon. Repeat to make another sandwich.

148. Cheesy Chicken Fritters

Made for: Lunch | **Prep Time:** 25 minutes | **Servings:** 04
Per Serving: Kcal: 389, Protein: 47g, Fat: 21g, Net Carb: 6g

INGREDIENTS:
- 1.5 lb (700g) skinless, boneless chicken breast
- Two medium eggs
- 1/3 cup (37.33g) almond flour
- 1 cup shredded mozzarella cheese
- 2 Tbsp fresh basil - finely chopped
- 2 Tbsp chives - chopped
- 2 Tbsp parsley - chopped
- 1/2 tsp (77.5g) garlic powder
- a pinch of sea salt and new ground black pepper - or to taste
- 1 Tbps olive oil

INSTRUCTIONS:
1. Place the chicken breast on a chopping board and using a sharp knife, chop it into tiny pieces, then place them in a large mixing bowl.
2. Into the large bowl, stir in almond flour, eggs, mozzarella, basil, chives, parsley, garlic powder, salt, and pepper. Mix well to combine.
3. Heat oil in a large non-stick pan, over medium-low heat. With an ice cream scoop or a large spoon, scoop into the chicken mixture and transfer it to the pan, then slightly flatten to create a pancake. Don't overcrowd the pan, cook the pancakes in batches, about 4 per shipment.
4. Fry until golden brown on both sides, about 6-8 minutes. Keep in mind that you need to cook them at medium-low temp. Otherwise, they will burn on the outside but won't get well prepared on the inside.

149. Garlic Butter Chicken

Made for: Lunch | **Prep Time:** 25 minutes | **Servings:** 04
Per Serving: Kcal: 899, Protein: 62g, Fat: 72g, Net Carb: 2g

INGREDIENTS:
- 4 chicken breasts (defrosted).

- 6 oz butter (room temperature).
- One garlic clove (crushed).
- 3 tbsp olive oil.
- 1 tsp lemon juice.
- ½ tsp salt.
- ½ tsp garlic powder.

INSTRUCTIONS:
1. Mix butter, garlic powder, garlic clove, lemon juice, and salt. When well combined, set aside.
2. In a large frying pan, heat the oil and fry chicken breasts until thoroughly cooked through and golden brown.
3. Place chicken on a plate and smoothly smother each chicken breast with a garlic butter mixture.

150. Lunch Meat Roll Ups

Made for: Lunch | **Prep Time:** 5 minutes | **Servings:** 02
Per Serving: Kcal: 415, Protein: 23g, Fat: 35g, Net Carb: 3g

INGREDIENTS:
- 4 slices lunch meat
- 4 slices cheese
- sea salt and black pepper
- garnishes of your choice, if desired shredded lettuce, herb cream cheese, guacamole

INSTRUCTIONS:
1. Lay your lunch meat slices on a work surface and top with a slice of cheese.
2. Note: This would be a good time to herb spread cream cheese, guacamole or dressing of your choice on top.
3. Starting at the bottom, roll your lunch meat up around the cheese until you have a log.
4. Continue rolling up your meat and cheese roll ups until you reach your desired amount. Sprinkle with sea salt and black pepper.
5. Serve with a dark, leafy green salad or bowl of bone broth.

151. Halloumi and greens salad

Made for: Lunch | **Prep Time:** 25 minutes | **Servings:** 02
Per Serving: Kcal: 456, Protein: 18g, Fat: 42g, Net Carb: 5g

INGREDIENTS:
- 2 handfuls salad leaves
- 1/2 tomato, cut into wedges

- fresh herbs, of your choice (e.g. coriander)
- 1/2 avocado, stoned and chopped
- 1 to 2 tablespoons salad dressing, of your choice
- 1 to 2 teaspoons olive oil
- 3 to 4 slices halloumi cheese

INSTRUCTIONS:
1. Onto a plate, add the salad leaves, tomato, herbs, and avocado. Drizzle with dressing of your choice.
2. Warm the oil in a pan over a high heat. Add the sliced halloumi and cook on each side for about 90 seconds, turning once, until golden brown. Remove from the pan, chop quickly and add to the salad. Serve immediately while the cheese is still hot!

152. Fried Chicken with Lemon

Made for: Lunch | **Prep Time:** 25 minutes | **Servings:** 02
Per Serving: Kcal: 190, Protein: 22g, Fat: 10g, Net Carb: 2g
INGREDIENTS:
- 2 skinless, boneless chicken breast fillets
- 1 lemon
- salt and freshly ground black pepper to taste
- 1 tablespoon olive oil
- 1 teaspoon dried oregano
- 2 sprigs fresh parsley, for garnish

INSTRUCTIONS:
1. Cut lemon in half, and squeeze juice from 1/2 the lemon on chicken. Season with salt to taste. Let sit while you heat oil in a small frying pan over medium low heat.
2. When oil is hot, put chicken in frying pan. As you pan fry the chicken, add juice from other 1/2 lemon, pepper to taste and oregano. Cook for 5 to 10 minutes each side, or until juices run clear. Serve with parsley for garnish.

153. Creamy Chicken Curry

Made for: Lunch | **Prep Time:** 25 minutes | **Servings:** 04
Per Serving: Kcal: 374, Protein: 34g, Fat: 27g, Net Carb: 2g

INGREDIENTS:
- 24 oz chicken thighs (lean & defrosted).
- One ¼ cup (57g) of coconut milk.
- ⅓ cup (50g) red onion (diced).
- 4 tsp curry paste.
- Cooking spray.

INSTRUCTIONS:

1. Preheat the oven at 200 degrees.
2. Rub chicken with 2 tsp of curry paste. Set aside for 15-20 minutes.
3. Spray a large frying pan with cooking spray, fry onions and add in remaining 2 tsp curry paste and fry 3-4 minutes.
4. Place chicken thighs in the pan with onions and sear for 3-4 minutes. Turn the chicken over, reduce heat, and pour in coconut milk. Simmer for 7-8 minutes.
5. Pour the curry mixture into a large ovenproof dish and bake for 15-20 minutes.

154. Broccoli Cheese Baked

Made for: Lunch | Prep Time: 30 minutes | Servings: 04
Per Serving: Kcal: 61, Protein: 6g, Fat: 6g, Net Carb: 1g

INGREDIENTS:

- 2 cups broccoli (florets).
- Two eggs.
- One cup cheddar cheese (grated).
- ½ cup (30g) spinach.
- ¼ cup (37.5g) onions (diced).
- ¼ cup (22.5g) parmesan (grated).
- ⅓ cup (80g) sour cream.
- One lemon zest.

INSTRUCTIONS:

1. Preheat the oven at 180 degrees.
2. Place broccoli in a microwave-safe bowl with ¼ cup of water. Microwave for 3 minutes on high or until broccoli is tender.
3. Chop broccoli florets into small pieces and place in a large bowl. Add all other ingredients and mix well until thoroughly combined.
4. Line an ovenproof dish with greaseproof paper and pour in the mixture.
5. Bake for 20-25 minutes until puffed and browned.
6. Cool for 10 minutes and cut into 24 square bites.

155. Cheese & Bacon

Made for: Lunch | Prep Time: 30 minutes | Servings: 04
Per Serving: Kcal: 207, Protein: 10g, Fat: 18g, Net Carb: 3g

INGREDIENTS:

- 1 cauliflower head (florets).
- 8 oz bacon (in strips).
- 3 oz butter.
- ⅔ cup (160g) parmesan (grated).

- ⅓ cup (37.5g) mozzarella (grated).
- ½ tsp black pepper.

INSTRUCTIONS:

1. Preheat the oven at 200 degrees.
2. Bring a large pan of water to the boil, add cauliflower, and cook for 7-8 minutes until tender.
3. Drain the water and add butter and pepper. Blend until cauliflower is a smooth puree.
4. In a frying pan, fry bacon until crispy. Add half of the bacon and all juice to the puree, along with half of the parmesan.
5. Stir well and pour into an ovenproof dish.
6. Sprinkle over the remaining bacon, parmesan, and mozzarella.
7. Bake for 15-20 minutes until the cheese is melted and golden.

156. Cabbage Stir Fry

Made for: Lunch | Prep Time: 10 minutes | Servings: 01
Per Serving: Kcal: 380, Protein: 4g, Fat: 43g, Net Carb: 2g

INGREDIENTS:

- 5 oz cabbage (cut in long strips).
- 2 oz butter.
- Two bacon slices (diced).

INSTRUCTIONS:

1. In a large frying pan, melt half of the butter and fry the bacon until crispy.
2. Add the remaining butter and stir in the cabbage; cook until cabbage begins to change colour.

157. Golden Zucchini

Made for: Lunch | Prep Time: 25 minutes | Servings: 01
Per Serving: Kcal: 692, Protein: 28g, Fat: 64g, Net Carb: 5g

INGREDIENTS:

- 1 zucchini/courgette.
- Two garlic cloves.
- 8 oz of goat's cheese (crumbled).
- 1 ½ oz baby spinach.
- 4 tbsp olive oil.
- 2 tbsp marinara sauce (unsweetened).

INSTRUCTIONS:

1. Preheat the oven at 190 degrees.
2. Slice the zucchini lengthwise in half. Using a small spoon, scrape out the seeds and put in a small bowl.

3. Finely slice the garlic cloves and fry for 1-2 minutes until lightly browned. Stir in spinach and zucchini seeds and cook until soft.
4. Place the two zucchini halves on a baking tray and spread over the marinara sauce. Top with garlic mixture and sprinkle over the goats' cheese.
5. Bake for 15-20 minutes until zucchini is tender and cheese is golden brown.

158. Salmon traybake

Made for: Lunch | **Prep Time:** 30 minutes | **Servings:** 04
Per Serving: Kcal: 438, Protein: 34g, Fat: 25g, Net Carb: 9g

INGREDIENTS:
- 2 red onions, cut into wedges
- 2 red peppers, sliced into strips
- 1 yellow pepper, sliced into strips
- 1 courgette, halved lengthways and thickly sliced
- 1 garlic bulb, halved across the middle
- 2 medium tomatoes, halved
- 3 tbsp olive oil, plus extra to drizzle
- 270g (1.8 cup) cherry tomatoes on the vine
- 4 good-quality sustainable salmon fillets (about 150g each)
- Squeeze of lemon juice
- Handful of fresh basil leaves

INSTRUCTIONS:
1. Preheat the oven to 200°C/fan180°C/gas 6. Tumble the onions, peppers, courgette, garlic and medium tomatoes into a shallow roasting tray. Pour over 3 tbsp olive oil, season with sea salt and ground black pepper, then gently toss to coat. Roast for 20 minutes.
2. Add the vine tomatoes to the tray and lay the salmon fillets on top. Season, then drizzle with a little more oil and a squeeze of lemon juice. Return to the oven for 10-12 minutes until the salmon is just cooked through and the vegetables are tender. Scatter with fresh basil leaves to serve.

159. Steak & aubergine salad

Made for: Lunch | **Prep Time:** 25 minutes | **Servings:** 04
Per Serving: Kcal: 455, Protein: 23g, Fat: 30g, Net Carb: 10g

INGREDIENTS:

- 1 aubergine, halved lengthways, cut into thin slices
- 2 tbsp flour
- 3 ½ tbsp olive oil
- 1 sirloin steak
- 100g (4/3 cup) lamb's lettuce
- 50g (1/2 cup) feta, cut into cubes

For the dressing
- 1 green chilli, halved and chopped
- ½ lemon, juiced
- ½ small pack coriander, plus extra leaves to serve
- ½ small pack mint, plus extra leaves to serve

INSTRUCTIONS:
1. Dust the aubergine slices in the flour, mixed with some seasoning. Heat 2 tbsp of the olive oil in a large frying pan until shimmering. Add the aubergine to the pan and fry for a few mins on each side until collapsing and soft, then set aside. Turn up the heat, season the steak, then add to the pan and fry for 2 mins on each side for rare (longer if you want it medium). Set aside to rest for 5 mins, then slice.
2. Blitz the remaining olive oil in a blender or small food processor with the rest of the dressing ingredients and a splash of water. When ready to serve, mix half the dressing with the lamb's lettuce, then tip onto a plate. Top with the crispy aubergine and steak, crumble over the feta, then drizzle over the remaining dressing. Scatter over the remaining herbs and serve.

160. Coconut Fish Curry

Made for: Lunch | **Prep Time:** 30 minutes | **Servings:** 04
Per Serving: Kcal: 354, Protein: 22g, Fat: 23g, Net Carb: 5g

INGREDIENTS:
- 1 tbsp sunflower oil, vegetable oil or coconut oil
- 1 onion, chopped
- 1 large garlic clove, crushed
- 1 tsp turmeric
- 1 tsp garam masala
- 1 tsp chilli flakes
- 400ml can coconut milk
- 390g pack fish pie mix
- 200g (3/2 cup) frozen peas
- 1 lime, cut into wedges
- yogurt and rice, to serve

INSTRUCTIONS:

1. Heat the oil in a large saucepan over a medium heat, add the onion and a big pinch of salt. Gently fry until the onion is translucent, so around 10 mins, then add the garlic and spices. Stir and cook for another minute, adding a splash of water to prevent them sticking. Tip in the coconut milk and stir well, then simmer for 10 mins.
2. Tip the fish pie mix and the frozen peas into the pan and cook until the peas are bright green and the fish is starting the flake, so around 3 mins. Season and add lime juice to taste. Ladle into bowls and serve with yogurt and rice.

161. Chicken and Broccoli

Made for: Lunch | **Prep Time:** 25 minutes | **Servings:** 04
Per Serving: Kcal: 354, Protein: 22g, Fat: 23g, Net Carb: 5g

INGREDIENTS:

- Four boneless skinless chicken breast halves (6 ounces each)
- 1/2 teaspoon garlic salt
- 1/4 teaspoon pepper
- One tablespoon olive oil
- 4 cups (340g) fresh broccoli florets
- 1 cup (96g) chicken broth
- One tablespoon all-purpose flour
- One tablespoon snipped fresh dill
- 1 cup (250ml) 2% milk

INSTRUCTIONS:

1. Sprinkle chicken with garlic salt and pepper. In a large skillet, heat oil over medium heat; brown chicken on both sides. Remove from pan.
2. Add broccoli and broth to the same skillet; bring to a boil. Reduce heat; simmer, covered, until broccoli is just tender, 3-5 minutes. Using a slotted spoon, remove broccoli from the pan, reserving broth. Keep broccoli warm.
3. In a small bowl, mix flour, dill, and milk until smooth; stir into the broth in the pan. Bring to a boil, stirring constantly; cook and stir until thickened, 1-2 minutes. Add chicken; cook, covered, over medium heat until a thermometer inserted in chicken reads 165°, 10-12 minutes. Serve with broccoli.

162. Roasted cauliflower with tomato

Made for: Lunch | **Prep Time:** 40 minutes | **Servings:** 02

Per Serving: Kcal: 480, Protein: 14g, Fat: 34g, Net Carb: 4g

INGREDIENTS:

- 1 cauliflower, cut into florets
- 2 tsp nigella seeds
- 2 tbsp vegetable oil
- 3 tsp garam masala
- 2 garlic cloves, crushed
- 2cm piece ginger, grated
- 500g passata
- 2 tbsp cashew nut butter
- 50ml double cream/whipping cream
To serve
- brown rice or naan bread
- ½ bunch coriander, chopped

INSTRUCTIONS:

1. Heat oven to 200C/180C fan/gas 6. Toss the cauliflower florets with the nigella seeds, 1 tbsp of the oil and 2 tsp of the garam masala. Spread out onto a roasting tray and cook for 35-40 mins until starting to soften and char, tossing halfway through.
2. Meanwhile, heat the rest of the oil in a small pan. Add the garlic, ginger, passata and the remaining garam masala and leave to simmer, uncovered, for 10-15 mins.
   Stir in the cashew nut butter and cream, then season to taste.
3. Serve the sauce over the brown rice or naan bread, top with the roasted cauliflower and garnish with the coriander.

163. Easy chicken curry

Made for: Lunch | **Prep Time:** 45 minutes | **Servings:** 02
Per Serving: Kcal: 612, Protein: 48g, Fat: 46g, Net Carb: 2g

INGREDIENTS:

- 2 tbsp sunflower oil
- 1 onion, thinly sliced
- 2 garlic cloves, crushed
- thumb-sized piece of ginger, grated
- 6 chicken thighs, boneless and skinless
- 3 tbsp medium spice paste (tikka works well)
- 400g (2 cup) can chopped tomatoes
- 100g (1/3 cup) Greek yogurt
- 1 small bunch of coriander, leaves chopped
- 50g (1/2 cup) ground almonds
- naan breads or cooked basmati rice, to serve

INSTRUCTIONS:

1. Heat the oil in a flameproof casserole dish or large frying pan over a medium heat. Add the onion and a generous pinch of salt and fry for 8-10 mins, or until the onion has turned golden brown and sticky. Add the garlic and ginger, cooking for a further minute.
2. Chop the chicken into chunky 3cm pieces, add to the pan and fry for 5 mins before stirring through the spice paste and tomatoes, along with 250ml water. Bring to the boil, lower to a simmer and cook on a gentle heat uncovered for 25-30 mins or until rich and slightly reduced. Stir though the yogurt, coriander and ground almonds, season and serve with warm naan or fluffy basmati rice.

164. Garden salmon salad

Made for: Lunch | **Prep Time:** 15 minutes | **Servings:** 02
Per Serving: Kcal: 434, Protein: 30g, Fat: 31g, Net Carb: 1g

INGREDIENTS:

- 2 courgettes
- 100g (1 cup) fresh shelled peas
- 8 radishes, halved
- 3 tbsp rapeseed oil
- 1 large lemon, zested and juiced
- 2 tbsp fat-free natural yogurt
- 75g pea shoots
- 4 poached salmon fillets, skin removed and flaked into large chunks
- 2 tbsp mixed seeds
- 1/2 small bunch dill, fronds picked

INSTRUCTIONS:

1. Cut the courgettes into long thin strips using a peeler, and discard the soft, seeded core. Toss the courgette ribbons, peas and radishes together in a large bowl. Whisk the oil, lemon zest and juice, and yogurt together, then toss with the veg.
2. Put the pea shoots, dressed veg and large flakes of salmon on a large platter. Finish with a good grinding of black pepper, and scatter over the mixed seeds and dill to serve.

165. Perk You Up Porridge

Made for: Lunch | **Prep Time:** 20 minutes | **Servings:** 02
Per Serving: Kcal: 216, Protein: 8g, Fat: 17g, Net Carb: 5g

INGREDIENTS:

- 2 tbsp almond flour.
- 2 tbsp sesame seeds (ground).
- 2 tbsp flaxseed (ground).
- ½ cup of almond milk (unsweetened).

INSTRUCTIONS:

1. Mix almond flour, sesame seeds, and flax seeds in a bowl.
2. Stir in the almond milk and microwave for one minute.
3. Stir again and microwave for an additional minute.

166. Greek bouyiourdi

Made for: Lunch | **Prep Time:** 30 minutes | **Servings:** 02
Per Serving: Kcal: 490, Protein: 16g, Fat: 45g, Net Carb: 2g

INGREDIENTS:

- 3 large ripe tomatoes
- 1 garlic clove, crushed
- 200g (3/2 cup) block feta
- 1 large mild green chilli, or 1 green pepper, sliced
- 1 tsp roughly chopped oregano leaves
- 4 tbsp olive oil
- warmed pitta breads, to serve

INSTRUCTIONS:

1. Cut 1 tomato through the middle, then cut two slices from the centre and set aside. Scoop the seeds from the rest of the tomato, then grate the flesh, discarding the skin. Deseed and grate the rest of the tomatoes in the same way, then mix the grated flesh with the garlic. Season and spoon into a 16cm baking dish.
2. Heat the oven to 200C/180C fan/gas 6. Nestle the feta block in the garlicky tomatoes, then top with the sliced tomatoes, the chilli, oregano, olive oil and a pinch of sea salt. Cover the dish and bake for 15 mins, then uncover and bake for a further 15 mins. Serve warm with the pitta breads on the side for dunking.

167. Blueberry Whirl Mousse

Made for: Lunch | **Prep Time:** 40 minutes | **Servings:** 02
Per Serving: Kcal: 510, Protein: 6g, Fat: 56g, Net Carb: 3g

INGREDIENTS:

- Two cups thick whipping cream.
- 3 oz blueberries (frozen & defrosted).

- 2 oz chopped walnuts.
- ½ lemon zest.
- ¼ tsp vanilla extract.

INSTRUCTION:
1. In a bowl, whisk the cream, vanilla, and lemon zest until soft peaks are formed.
2. Stir in the walnuts until thoroughly combined.
3. Slightly crush the blueberries and gently swirl into the mousse.
4. Cover the bowl and place it in the refrigerator for 3-4 hours until mousse thickens.

168.   Strawberry & Blueberry

Made for: Lunch | **Prep Time:** 10 minutes | **Servings:** 02
Per Serving: Kcal: 150, Protein: 6g, Fat: 16g, Net Carb: 4g

INGREDIENTS:
- 8 oz strawberries (frozen & defrosted).
- 8 oz blueberries (frozen & defrosted).
- One cup of Greek yoghurt (full fat).
- ½ cup (116g) thick whipping cream/double cream.
- 1 tsp orange extract.

INSTRUCTIONS:
1. Place all ingredients into a blender and mix until thoroughly combined.
2. Pour into a bowl and freeze for 40-60 minutes.

169.   Baked Salsa Chicken

Made for: Lunch | **Prep Time:** 30 minutes | **Servings:** 02
Per Serving: Kcal: 170, Protein: 9g, Fat: 7g, Net Carb: 5g

INGREDIENTS:
- 4 chicken breasts boneless and skinless
- 1 tsp chili powder or taco seasoning
- 1 pinch salt and pepper
- 2 cups chunky salsa no sugar added
- 2 cups cheddar cheese shredded
- 2 tbsp chopped cilantro optional

INSTRUCTIONS:
1. Preheat oven to 375°F and heat large skillet over high heat.
2. Season chicken breasts with chili powder, salt and pepper.
3. Spray skillet with cooking spray and transfer chicken to skillet. Cook chicken for 2 minutes per side, or until just browned.

4. Place chicken into a 9x9 baking dish, cover in salsa and then sprinkle cheese on top.
5. Bake for 30 minutes, or until cheese is bubbly and internal temperature of the chicken is 165 degrees.
6. Top with fresh chopped cilantro if desired.

170.   Coconut Curls

Made for: Lunch | **Prep Time:** 35 minutes | **Servings:** 02
Per Serving: Kcal: 133, Protein: 3g, Fat: 15g, Net Carb: 2g

INGREDIENTS:
- Four egg yolks.
- One cup of shredded coconut.
- One cup of dark chocolate chips (unsweetened).
- ¾ cup (87.75g) walnuts (chopped).
- ¼ cup (60ml) of coconut oil.
- 3 tbsp swerve.
- 3 tbsp butter.

INSTRUCTIONS:
1. Preheat the oven at 175 degrees.
2. In a large bowl, mix egg yolks, coconut oil, butter, and swerve. Gradually stir in the chocolate chips, coconut, and walnuts.
3. Line a baking tray with greaseproof paper.
4. Using a tablespoon, place spoonful by a spoonful of the mixture on the tray.
5. Bake for 15-20 minutes until golden brown.

171.   Vegan banana cupcakes

Made for: Lunch | **Prep Time:** 35 minutes | **Servings:** 12 cups
Per cup: Kcal: 160, Protein: 3g, Fat: 6g, Net Carb: 5g

INGREDIENTS:
- 2 large bananas (about 225g), blackened and peeled
- 50ml vegetable or sunflower oil
- 65g (1/3 cup) light brown sugar
- 150g (4/3 cup) plain flour
- 2 tsp baking powder
- 2 tsp cinnamon
- 50g (1/3 cup) dried fruit and seed mix
- 2 tbsp oats
- 2 tbsp mixed seeds

INSTRUCTIONS:
1. Heat the oven to 180C/160C fan/gas 4. Mash the bananas in a medium bowl with

a fork, then mix in the oil and sugar until combined.
2. Add the flour, baking powder, cinnamon and dried fruit and seed mix. Mix until well combined.
3. Line a cupcake tray with 10-12 cupcake cases (the amount you need will depend on how big the bananas are) and fill them ¾ full of the mixture. Sprinkle with the oats and mixed seeds.
4. Bake for 25 mins, or until a skewer inserted into the middle of a muffin comes out clean. Leave to cool on a wire rack.

172. Vegan brownies

Made for: Lunch | **Prep Time:** 40 minutes | **Makes:** 12
Per Serving: Kcal: 314, Protein: 5g, Fat: 16g, Net Carb: 5g

INGREDIENTS:
- 2 tbsp ground flaxseed
- 200g (4/3 cup) dark chocolate, roughly chopped
- ½ tsp coffee granules
- 80g vegan margarine, plus extra for greasing
- 125g (1 cup) self-raising flour
- 70g (1/2 cup) ground almonds
- 50g (1/2 cup) cocoa powder
- ¼ tsp baking powder
- 250g (2 cup) golden caster sugar
- 1½ tsp vanilla extract

INSTRUCTIONS:
1. Heat oven to 170C/150C fan/gas 3½. Grease and line a 20cm square tin with baking parchment. Combine the flaxseed with 6 tbsp water and set aside for at least 5 mins.
2. In a saucepan, melt 120g chocolate, the coffee and margarine with 60ml water on a low heat. Allow to cool slightly.
3. Put the flour, almonds, cocoa, baking powder and ¼ tsp salt in a bowl and stir to remove any lumps. Using a hand whisk, mix the sugar into the melted chocolate mixture, and beat well until smooth and glossy, ensuring all the sugar is well dissolved. Stir in the flaxseed mixture, vanilla extract and remaining chocolate, then the flour mixture. Spoon into the prepared tin.
4. Bake for 35-45 mins until a skewer inserted in the middle comes out clean with moist crumbs. Allow to cool in the

tin completely, then cut into squares. Store in an airtight container and eat within three days.

173. Goan mussels

Made for: Lunch | **Prep Time:** 30 minutes | **Servings:** 04
Per Serving: Kcal: 292, Protein: 14g, Fat: 23g, Net Carb: 4g

INGREDIENTS:
- 1kg fresh mussel
- sunflower oil, for frying
- 1 onion, chopped
- thumb-sized piece ginger, grated
- 4 garlic cloves, crushed
- 2 green chillies, chopped
- 1 tsp black mustard seed
- ½ tsp ground turmeric
- 2 tsp ground cumin
- 2 tsp ground coriander
- 400ml coconut milk
- coriander sprigs, to serve
- lime wedges, to serve

INSTRUCTIONS:
1. Remove the beards, then wash the mussels well in cold water. Refresh the water and repeat until it is clear. Discard any mussels that are broken or stay open when tapped.
2. Heat the oil in a flameproof casserole. Fry the onion until very lightly brown, then add the ginger, garlic, chillies, spices, a good pinch of salt and a grinding of pepper. Cook for 2-3 mins until fragrant and toasted. Pour in the coconut milk and bring to the boil, then simmer for a few mins to get everything mixed together.
3. Tip the mussels into the dish, cover, turn up the heat to maximum and boil for 3-4 mins until the mussels have just opened. Scatter over the coriander sprigs and serve with lime wedges for squeezing over.

174. Soy & butter salmon

Made for: Lunch | **Prep Time:** 30 minutes | **Servings:** 04
Per Serving: Kcal: 307, Protein: 21g, Fat: 23g, Net Carb: 1g

INGREDIENTS:
- 2 tbsp butter
- 4 x 100g skinless salmon fillets
- 2 tbsp low-salt soy sauce
- 1 tbsp honey
- 1 tbsp sesame seeds

- 2 sliced spring onions
- For the cucumber salad
- 1 cucumber, finely sliced
- few drops sesame oil

INSTRUCTIONS:
1. Heat the barbecue. If you are using coals, wait until they turn white. If you are indoors, heat a griddle pan. Cut four pieces of foil that will easily wrap a piece of salmon and lay them on the work surface. Spread a little butter onto the centre of each piece of foil to stop the salmon sticking. Lay the salmon on top. Mix the soy with the honey and divide it between the parcels, pouring it over the salmon. Dot any remaining butter on top and then fold the foil around the salmon tightly to make a parcel.
2. Put the parcels on the barbecue or griddle and cook for 5-10 mins. Check one parcel to see how it's getting along but be careful – it will be hot. Once the salmon is cooked, open the parcels and scatter some sesame and spring onion into each.
3. Mix the cucumber with a few drops of sesame oil and season with a little salt. Serve the salmon with the cucumber salad.

175. Almond Cheesecake

Made for: Lunch | **Prep Time:** 25 minutes | **Servings:** 04
Per Serving: Kcal: 281, Protein: 8g, Fat: 29g, Net Carb: 3g

INGREDIENTS:
- 24 oz cream cheese.
- Four large eggs.
- 1 cup (150g) stevia.
- ⅓ cup (80g) sour cream.
- ½ tsp almond extract.

INSTRUCTIONS:
1. Preheat the oven at 175 degrees.
2. In a bowl, whisk the cream cheese until smooth, then gently add in stevia, sour cream, and almond extract, mix until well combined.
3. Add the eggs one by one and whisk until a thick, creamy mixture is formed.
4. Grease a springform pan, pour in the mixture, and bake for 45-50 minutes until puffed and lightly browned.
5. Remove from the oven and allow to sit at room temperature for an hour.
6. Place in the refrigerator for 5-6 hours.

176. Egg and avocado

Made for: Lunch | **Prep Time:** 15 minutes | **Servings:** 01
Per Serving: Kcal: 594, Protein: 29g, Fat: 47g, Net Carb: 5g

INGREDIENTS:
- 3 eggs, lightly beaten
- 60ml (¼ cup) low fat milk
- 1/3 cup (40g) grated cheddar cheese
- 3 teaspoons olive oil
- 1/2 small avocado, diced
- 1 small tomato, thinly sliced
- 2 teaspoons lemon juice
- 1 tablespoon chopped fresh chives
- Basil, to serve

INSTRUCTIONS:
1. Preheat grill to high. Whisk eggs and milk in a medium bowl. Season with salt and pepper
2. Heat 2 tsp oil in a non-stick 20cm frying pan. Pour in egg mixture and cook over medium heat for 3-4 minutes until almost set. Sprinkle omelette with cheese and place under hot grill for a few minutes until puffed and golden
3. Toss avocado and tomato with lemon juice and remaining teaspoon of oil. Sprinkle avocado mixture and half the herbs over one-half of omelette. Fold omelette in half and slide onto a warm plate to serve. Scatter with remaining herbs

177. Lemon & Lime Pancakes

Made for: Lunch | **Prep Time:** 25 minutes | **Servings:** 04
Per Serving: Kcal: 273, Protein: 9g, Fat: 28g, Net Carb: 4g

INGREDIENTS:
- 4 eggs.
- 2 cups (224g) almond flour.
- ¼ cup (62.5ml) of water.
- 8 tbsp butter (melted).
- 2 tbsp swerve.
- 1 tbsp coconut oil.
- 1 tsp baking powder.
- One lime zest.
- One lemon zest.

INSTRUCTIONS:
1. Place all ingredients in a blender and blend until well combined.
2. Allow resting for 10-15 minutes.
3. In a frying pan, heat a little oil, pour in ⅓ cup of the butter mixture.
4. Cook for 2-3 minutes on each side until

golden brown.

5. Repeat the process until all of the batters have gone.

178. Baked eggs

Made for: Lunch | **Prep Time:** 15 minutes | **Servings:** 04
Per Serving: Kcal: 327, Protein: 18g, Fat: 16g, Net Carb: 10g

INGREDIENTS:

- 120g baby (4 cup) spinach leaves
- 100g (1/2 cup) semi-dried tomatoes, chopped
- 70g (1/2 cup) Danish feta cheese, crumbled
- 2 tablespoons roughly chopped fresh basil
- 4 shallots, thinly sliced
- 1 tablespoon olive oil
- 4 eggs
- Wholegrain toasts (optional), to serve

INSTRUCTIONS:

1. Preheat the oven to 180°C/160°C. Lightly spray four 1-cup (250ml) capacity ovenproof ramekins with oil
2. Place spinach in a heatproof bowl. Pour ever enough boiling water to cover, set aside for 10 seconds then drain. Once cool enough to handle squeeze out excess water. Combine spinach, tomatoes, feta, basil and shallots in a medium bowl. Divide evenly between prepared dishes, and drizzle each with 1 teaspoon oil. Place dishes on a baking tray and crack an egg on top of each dish
3. Cover with foil and bake for 15 minutes or until egg is cooked to your liking. Season with black pepper. Serve with toast if you like.

179. Sage-Rubbed Salmon

Made for: Lunch | **Prep Time:** 25 minutes | **Servings:** 02
Per Serving: Kcal: 220, Protein: 19g, Fat: 16g, Net Carb: 1g

INGREDIENTS

- Two tablespoons minced fresh sage
- One teaspoon garlic powder
- One teaspoon kosher salt
- One teaspoon freshly ground pepper
- One skin-on salmon fillet (1-1/2 pounds)
- Two tablespoons olive oil

INSTRUCTIONS:

1. Preheat oven to 375°. Mix the first four ingredients; rub onto the flesh side of salmon. Cut into six portions.
2. In a large cast-iron skillet, heat oil over medium heat. Add salmon, skin side down; cook 5 minutes. Transfer skillet to oven; bake just until fish flakes easily with a fork, about 10 minutes.

180. Thai broccoli rice

Made for: Lunch | **Prep Time:** 25 minutes | **Servings:** 04
Per Serving: Kcal: 380, Protein: 15g, Fat: 26g, Net Carb: 2g

INGREDIENTS:

- 100g (1/2 cup) salted peanuts
- 1 head of broccoli, cut into florets and the stem cut in half
- 2 tbsp olive oil
- 1 red onion, finely diced
- 1 garlic clove, crushed
- 1 tbsp grated ginger
- 1 medium red chilli, deseeded and finely diced
- ½ small red cabbage, shredded
- 1 red pepper, deseeded and sliced into strips
- small pack coriander, roughly chopped
- **For the dressing**
- zest and juice 1 lime
- 2 tbsp tamari
- ½ tbsp golden caster sugar
- 2 tbsp olive oil

INSTRUCTIONS:

1. Heat a frying pan over a medium heat and add the peanuts. Toast evenly, regularly shaking the pan, then remove and set aside. Put the broccoli in a food processor and pulse until it looks like green couscous grains. Empty into a large bowl and set aside.
2. Heat the oil in a large frying pan and fry the onion, garlic, ginger and chilli until soft and aromatic. Add the broccoli rice to the pan and mix through, making sure everything is well coated. Sauté for 3-4 mins until al dente. Transfer to a large bowl and add the red cabbage, red pepper, half the coriander and half the toasted peanuts. Mix to combine.
3. To make the dressing, whisk the lime zest and juice, tamari, sugar and oil together until combined. Toss the dressing through the broccoli rice and transfer to a serving bowl or individual bowls. To serve, garnish with the remaining coriander and peanuts.

181. Mom's Roast Chicken

Made for: Lunch | **Prep Time:** 30 minutes | **Servings:** 02
Per Serving: Kcal: 405, Protein: 44g, Fat: 24g, Net Carb: 2g

INGREDIENTS:
- One broiler/fryer chicken (4 to 5 pounds)
- Two teaspoons kosher salt
- One teaspoon coarsely ground pepper
- Two teaspoons olive oil
- Minced fresh thyme or rosemary, optional

INSTRUCTIONS:
1. Rub outside of the chicken with salt and pepper. Transfer chicken to a rack on a rimmed baking sheet. Refrigerate, uncovered, overnight.
2. Preheat oven to 450°. Remove chicken from refrigerator while oven heats. Heat a 12-in. Cast-iron or ovenproof skillet in the oven for 15 minutes.
3. Place chicken on a work surface, neck side down. Cut through the skin where legs connect to the body. Press thighs down so joints pop and legs lie flat.
4. Carefully place chicken, breast side up, into hot skillet; press legs down so they lie flat on the bottom of the pan. Brush with oil. Roast until a thermometer inserted in the thickest part of the thigh reads 170°-175°, 35-40 minutes. Remove chicken from oven; let stand 10 minutes before carving. If desired, top with herbs before serving.

182. Keto Sausage Balls

Made for: Lunch | **Prep Time:** 35 minutes | **Balls:** 25
Per Ball: Kcal: 62, Protein: 2g, Fat: 5g, Net Carb: 1g

INGREDIENTS:
- 1 pound breakfast sausage
- 4 ounces cream cheese
- 1 cup (112g) shredded cheddar cheese
- 1/2 cup (56g) almond flour
- 1/2 teaspoon baking powder

INSTRUCTIONS:
1. Preheat oven to 375 degrees.
2. Combine all of the ingredients until well incorporated. I find this easiest in my stand mixer.
3. Lightly spray a large baking sheet or line with silicone baking mats

4. Roll the sausage balls into golf ball size balls. I had 25 each.
5. Bake 20-24 minutes.

183. Parmesan Chicken

Made for: Lunch | **Prep Time:** 25 minutes | **Servings:** 02
Per Serving: Kcal: 498, Protein: 40g, Fat: 32g, Net Carb: 4g

INGREDIENTS:
- 1/2 cup (120g) butter, melted
- Two teaspoons Dijon mustard
- One teaspoon Worcestershire sauce
- 1/2 teaspoon salt
- 1 cup dry bread crumbs
- 1/2 cup (45g) grated Parmesan cheese
- Six boneless skinless chicken breast halves (7 ounces each)

INSTRUCTIONS:
1. Preheat oven to 350°. In a shallow bowl, combine butter, mustard, Worcestershire sauce, and salt. Place bread crumbs and cheese in another shallow dish. Dip chicken in butter mixture, then in bread crumb mixture, patting to help coating adhere.
2. Place in an ungreased 15x10x1-in. Baking pan. Drizzle with any remaining butter mixture. Bake, uncovered, until a thermometer inserted in chicken reads 165°, 25-30 minutes.

184. Tuna & Cheese Oven Bake

Made for: Lunch | **Prep Time:** 25 minutes | **Servings:** 04
Per Serving: Kcal: 957, Protein: 44g, Fat: 85g, Net Carb: 5g

INGREDIENTS:
- 16 oz tuna (tinned in olive oil).
- 5 oz celery (finely chopped).
- 4 oz parmesan (grated).
- 1 cup (230g) mayonnaise.
- One green bell pepper (diced).
- One onion (diced).
- 2 oz butter.
- 1 tsp chilli flakes.

INSTRUCTIONS:
1. Preheat the oven at 200 degrees.
2. In a large frying pan, fry the celery, pepper, and onion until soft.
3. In a bowl, mix tuna, mayonnaise, parmesan, and chilli flakes until well combined.
4. Stir in the cooked vegetables; pour the mixture into an ovenproof dish.

5. Bake for 15-20 minutes or until golden brown.

185. Keto Shrimp Scampi

Made for: Lunch | **Prep Time:** 30 minutes | **Servings:** 04
Per Serving: Kcal: 321, Protein: 17g, Fat: 23g, Net Carb: 2g

INGREDIENTS:
- 2 Tbsp avocado oil
- 4 Tbsp butter, or ghee
- 1 lb raw shrimp, peeled and deviened
- 1 cup (96g) white wine, or chicken broth
- 4 cloves garlic, peeled and minced
- 2 tsp lemon zest
- 1/2 tsp onion powder, optional
- 1/2 tsp sea salt, to taste
- 1/4 tsp black pepper
- 3 to 4 medium-sized zucchini squash, spiralized
- 2 Tbsp fresh parsley, chopped

INSTRUCTIONS:
1. Heat the avocado oil and butter in a large skillet over medium-high heat. Stir together the oil and butter. Once the butter has melted and the skillet is hot, add the shrimp. Cook 2 minutes, flip and cook for another 1 minute. Add the white wine, garlic, lemon zest, onion powder, sea salt and black pepper.
2. Stir and allow mixture to come to a full boil. Continue cooking until sauce has thickened and reduced by a third of its original volume, about 5 minutes.
3. Add the zucchini noodles to the skillet and stir them into the sauce. Cover and cook 2 to 3 minutes, until noodles have softened but are still al dente.
4. Remove the lid and continue cooking, stirring occasionally, until noodles have reached desired done-ness and everything is well-coated in thick sauce.

186. Spicy Crab Pot Pie

Made for: Lunch | **Prep Time:** 20 minutes | **Servings:** 04
Per Serving: Kcal: 1106, Protein: 50g, Fat: 99g, Net Carb: 5g

INGREDIENTS:
- 4 large eggs (lightly whisked).
- 16 oz of crab meat (tinned & drained).
- 12 oz cheddar cheese (grated).
- 1 cup (230g) mayonnaise.
- One red onion (diced).
- 2 tbsp butter.
- 2 tsp paprika.

- ¼ tsp cayenne pepper.

INSTRUCTIONS:
1. Preheat the oven 180 degrees.
2. Heat the butter and fry the onion until tender.
3. In a large bowl, mix eggs, mayonnaise, crab, paprika, cayenne pepper, and ⅔ cheddar cheese; stir in the fried onions.
4. Pour the mixture into a greased ovenproof dish, sprinkle over the remaining cheddar cheese.
5. Bake for 30-35 minutes until firm and golden brown.

187. Garlic Bacon

Made for: Lunch | **Prep Time:** 20 minutes | **Servings:** 04
Per Serving: Kcal: 239, Protein: 9g, Fat: 21g, Net Carb: 6g

INGREDIENTS:
- 16 oz green beans (trimmed).
- Six garlic cloves (crushed).
- Six bacon rashers.
- 1 tbsp olive oil.
- 1 tbsp butter.
- ½ tsp salt.

INSTRUCTIONS:
1. In a large frying pan, fry the bacon until crispy and set aside.
2. Bring a large saucepan of water to the boil, add green beans and salt and cook for 5-7 minutes; drain and set aside.
3. In the same frying pan where the bacon was cooked, melt butter and olive oil, fry the garlic for 30 seconds until lightly browned. Crumble in the cooked, crispy bacon and add the green beans to the pan; saute for 1-2 minutes, stirring continuously.

188. Tomato & Leek Bake

Made for: Lunch | **Prep Time:** 30 minutes | **Servings:** 04
Per Serving: Kcal: 627, Protein: 34g, Fat: 51g, Net Carb: 5g

INGREDIENTS:
- 12 large eggs.
- One cup of thick cream/single cream.
- ½ leek (thinly sliced).
- 7 oz cheddar cheese (grated).
- 3 oz cherry tomatoes (halved).
- 1 oz parmesan (grated).
- 1 tsp onion powder.
- ½ tsp black pepper.

INSTRUCTIONS:

1. Preheat the oven at 200 degrees.
2. Grease a large ovenproof dish and sprinkle in the diced leeks.
3. In a large bowl, whisk together eggs, cheddar cheese, onion powder, and black pepper.
4. Pour the egg mixture over the leeks; add cherry tomatoes and parmesan to the top.
5. Bake for 40-45 minutes until completely set.

189. Shakshuka

Made for: Lunch | **Prep Time:** 20 minutes | **Servings:** 02
Per Serving: Kcal: 322, Protein: 15g, Fat: 24g, Net Carb: 3g

INGREDIENTS:

- Two tablespoons olive oil
- One medium onion, chopped
- One garlic clove, minced
- One teaspoon ground cumin
- One teaspoon pepper
- 1/2 to 1 teaspoon chilli powder
- 1/2 teaspoon salt
- One teaspoon Sriracha chilli sauce or hot pepper sauce, optional
- Two medium tomatoes, chopped
- Four large eggs
- Chopped fresh cilantro
- Whole pita pieces of bread, toasted

INSTRUCTIONS:

1. In a large cast-iron or another heavy skillet, heat oil over medium heat. Add onion; cook and stir until tender, 4-6 minutes. Add garlic, seasonings, and, if desired, chilli sauce; cook 30 seconds longer. Add tomatoes; cook until mixture is thickened, stirring occasionally, 3-5 minutes.
2. With the back of a spoon, make four wells in the vegetable mixture; break an egg into each well. Cook, covered until egg whites are completely set and yolks begin to thicken but are not hard, 4-6 minutes. Sprinkle with cilantro; serve with pita bread.

190. Brekkie bakes for lunch

Made for: Lunch | **Prep Time:** 30 minutes | **Servings:** 01
Per Serving: Kcal: 601, Protein: 38g, Fat: 60g, Net Carb: 6g

INGREDIENTS:

- 1 tablespoon olive oil

- 4 chipolatas
- 4 small Swiss brown mushrooms
- 125g (1/3 cup) packets vine ripened cherry tomatoes
- 1 rindless rashers bacon, cut into large pieces
- 2 eggs
- 10g (1/4 cup) baby spinach leaves, to serve
- Toasted bread, to serve
- Tomato chutney, optional, to serve

INSTRUCTIONS:

1. Preheat oven to 180°C. Heat oil in a large ovenproof frying pan over a medium heat. Add chipolatas and cook for 8 minutes, turning throughout cooking until browned on all sides
2. Add mushrooms, tomatoes, bacon and eggs. Cover pan with a lid or foil and place in oven. Bake for 17 minutes. Add the spinach and cook for a further 3 minutes or until eggs are cooked to your liking and spinach has wilted slightly. Serve with toast and chutney, if you like

191. Aubergine & Olive Feast

Made for: Lunch | **Prep Time:** 15 minutes | **Servings:** 04
Per Serving: Kcal: 849, Protein: 33g, Fat: 77g, Net Carb: 5g

INGREDIENTS:

- 10 oz halloumi (cut into slices).
- 1 aubergine (cut into bite size pieces).
- 3 oz butter.
- Twelve olives (pitted).
- 1 tsp paprika.
- 1 tsp chilli flakes.

INSTRUCTIONS:

1. Melt the butter in a large frying pan.
2. Place the aubergine chunks and olives in one half and halloumi in the other.
3. Season with paprika and chilli; cook for 8-10 minutes, occasionally turning to ensure halloumi is golden brown on both sides and aubergine is cooked through.

192. Kick-the-Boredom

Made for: Lunch | **Prep Time:** 20 minutes | **Servings:** 04
Per Serving: Kcal: 529, Protein: 31g, Fat: 40g, Net Carb: 6g

INGREDIENTS:
- 16 oz minced beef (frozen & defrosted).
- 1 ½ cups (300g) canned chopped tomatoes.
- 3 oz cheddar cheese (grated).
- Two garlic cloves (crushed).
- One red onion (diced).
- ½ red pepper (diced).
- ½ yellow pepper (diced).
- 2 tsp tomato puree.
- 2 tsp coriander.
- 1 tsp chilli powder.

INSTRUCTIONS:
1. Preheat the oven at 180 degrees.
2. In a large frying pan, fry the onions and garlic cloves until tender. Stir in the beef and fry until browned and cooked through.
3. Add chopped tomatoes, red and yellow peppers, tomato puree, coriander, and chilli powder; fry 6-7 minutes until bubbling.
4. Pour into an ovenproof dish and sprinkle cheese on top.
5. Bake for 25-30 minutes.

193. Chicken Enchilada Casserole

Made for: Lunch | **Prep Time:** 20 minutes | **Servings:** 04
Per Serving: Kcal: 745, Protein: 68g, Fat: 50g, Net Carb: 6g

INGREDIENTS
- 2 pounds cooked chicken, (shredded or cubed)
- 1 (4 ounce) can green diced chiles
- 1 cup (260g) keto-friendly red enchilada sauce
- 2 cups (225g) shredded cheese, divided (I used Colby-Jack)
- 2 tablespoons taco seasoning

INSTRUCTIONS:
1. Preheat oven to 375 degrees.
2. Add all of the ingredients to a mixing bowl except 1 cup of the shredded cheese. Mix everything together until combined.
3. Spread the mixture into an 8x8 casserole dish. Then, top with the remaining shredded cheese.

4. Bake uncovered for 15 minutes, or until the cheese is melted. Top with your favorite keto-friendly toppings and enjoy!

194. Mushroom Soufflé Omelette

Made for: Lunch | **Prep Time:** 30 minutes | **Servings:** 04
Per Serving: Kcal: 459, Protein: 20g, Fat: 37g, Net Carb: 4g

INGREDIENTS:
- 1 tablespoon olive oil
- 400g (5 cup) Swiss brown mushrooms, sliced
- Salt and pepper
- 4 eggs
- 2 tablespoons milk
- ¼ teaspoon table salt
- 20g (1/8 cup) melted butter
- ¼ cup (22.5g) finely grated parmesan
- ¼ cup crème fraiche
- Finely grated parmesan, extra, to serve
- 2 tablespoons finely chopped chives

INSTRUCTIONS:
1. Heat oil in a large 25cm non-stick frying pan over medium-high heat. Add the mushrooms, season with salt and pepper and cook for 6-7 minutes or until golden. Remove, cover and keep warm. Wipe out the pan.
2. Separate eggs, placing egg yolks into a small bowl and egg whites into a large bowl. Add milk to egg yolks and whisk with a fork. Using a hand beater, whisk egg whites and the ¼ teaspoon salt until stiff peaks form.
3. Heat the frying pan over medium heat. Brush with butter to grease. Using a large metal spoon, gently fold the egg yolks into the egg whites.
4. Pour half the mixture into the pan and cook for 4-5 minutes, or until golden and the eggs are just set. Spoon over half the crème fraiche, parmesan and mushrooms and carefully fold the omelette in half. Cook for 1 minute or until almost set.
5. Transfer to a serving plate (omelette will continue cooking once removed from heat). Repeat using remaining eggs, crème fraiche, cheese and mushrooms. Sprinkle with chives, extra parmesan and pepper to serve.

195. Tuna Sushi Bites

Made for: Lunch | **Prep Time:** 20 minutes | **Servings:** 02
Per Serving: Kcal: 250, Protein: 22g, Fat: 20g, Net Carb: 3g

INGREDIENTS:
- 1 medium cucumber.
- ½ can tuna (in olive oil).
- ½ medium avocado (sliced).
- 1 tsp chilli sauce.
- ¼ tsp black pepper.
- ¼ tsp of cayenne pepper.

INSTRUCTIONS:
1. Thinly slice the cucumber (lengthways) until the outer skin has gone. Thinly slice the unskinned cucumber until you have six long strips.
2. In a bowl, mix the tuna, chilli sauce, black pepper, and cayenne pepper until well combined.
3. Take a slice of a cucumber and spread the mixture over, leaving half an inch at each end.
4. Place two pieces of avocado on each cucumber slice and carefully roll.
5. Secure each roll with a toothpick.

196. Mexican Salmon Fillets

Made for: Lunch | **Prep Time:** 20 minutes | **Servings:** 04
Per Serving: Kcal: 451, Protein: 33g, Fat: 34g, Net Carb: 7g

INGREDIENTS:
- 4 salmon fillets (frozen & defrosted).
- Two avocados (chopped into small cubes).
- 4 tsp cajun seasoning.
- One jalapeno (finely diced).
- One onion (finely diced).
- 1 tbsp olive oil.
- 1 tbsp lime juice (fresh).
- 1 tbsp fresh coriander (finely diced).

INSTRUCTIONS:
1. Season both sides of the salmon in cajun seasoning.
2. Heat the oil in a frying pan; fry the salmon until browned, flip and repeat for the other side until salmon easily flakes with a fork.
3. Mix the avocados, onion, jalapenos, lime, and coriander until well combined.
4. Serve salmon and avocado mix together on a plate.

197. Classic Bacon and eggs

Made for: Lunch | **Prep Time:** 30 minutes | **Servings:** 4
Per Serving: Kcal: 270, Protein: 16g, Fat: 20g, Net Carb: 2g

INGREDIENTS
- Four eggs
- 2½ oz. bacon, in slices
- cherry tomatoes (optional)
- fresh parsley (optional)

INSTRUCTIONS
1. Fry the Bacon in a pan on medium-high heat until crispy. Put aside on a plate. Leave the rendered fat in the pan.
2. Use the same pan to fry the eggs. Place it over medium heat and crack your eggs into the bacon grease. You can also crack them into a measuring cup and carefully pour into the pan to avoid splattering of hot grease.
3. Cook the eggs any way you like them. For sunny side up, leave the eggs to fry on one side and cover the pan with a lid to make sure they get cooked on top; for eggs cooked over easy, flip the eggs over after a few minutes and cook for another minute. Cut the cherry tomatoes in half and fry them at the same time—salt and pepper to taste.

198. Chicken Drumsticks

Made for: Lunch | **Prep Time:** 30 minutes | **Drumsticks:** 05
Per D.stick: Kcal: 160, Protein: 12g, Fat: 13g, Net Carb: 0.4g

INGREDIENTS
- 10 chicken drumsticks (~ 1.2 kg/ 2.6 lbs), weight includes bones, will yield about 50% meat
- 1/4 cup ghee or butter, you can make your own ghee (56/ 2 oz)
- 1 tbsp paprika
- 2 tsp gluten-free baking powder or use a mixture of 1/2 tsp baking soda + 1 tsp cream of tartar
- 1 tsp sea salt

INSTRUCTIONS:
1. Preheat the oven to 200 °C/400 °F (fan assisted), or 220 °C/425 °F (conventional). Start by pat drying the chicken drumsticks with a paper towel.
2. Using your fingers, rub the ghee or butter under the skin. To do this, simply pull up the skin of the chicken and massage the fat into the flesh. Spread

any remaining ghee on top of the skin.
3. Mix the spices for the rub: paprika, baking powder and salt. Cover the drumsticks in the rub and place on a baking sheet lined with parchment paper. For even better results, place the drumsticks on a rack.
4. Place in the oven and bake for 30-40 minutes until the skin is crispy and the meat is cooked through.
5. Enjoy!

199. Mexican scrambled eggs

Made for: Lunch | **Prep Time:** 25 minutes | **Servings:** 2
Per Serving: Kcal: 338, Protein: 21g, Fat: 24g, Net Carb: 5g

INGREDIENTS
- ½ oz. butter
- ½ scallion, finely chopped
- One pickled jalapeño, finely chopped
- ½ tomato, finely chopped
- Three eggs
- 1½ oz. shredded cheese
- salt and pepper

INSTRUCTIONS
1. In a large frying pan, melt the butter over medium-high heat.
2. Add scallions, jalapeños, and tomatoes, and fry for 3-4 minutes.
3. Beat the eggs and pour ithem iinto the pan—scramble for 2 minutes. Add cheese and seasonings.

200. Goat cheese salad with balsamico butter

Made for: Lunch | **Prep Time:** 15 minutes | **Servings:** 2
Per Serving: Kcal: 824, Protein: 37g, Fat: 73g, Net Carb: 3g

INGREDIENTS
- 10 oz. goat cheese
- ¼ cup pumpkin seeds
- 2 oz. butter
- 1 tbsp balsamic vinegar
- 3 oz. baby spinach

INSTRUCTION
1. Preheat the oven to 400°F (200°C).
2. Put slices of goat cheese in a greased baking dish and bake in the oven for 10 minutes.
3. While the goat cheese is in the oven, toast pumpkin seeds in a dry frying pan over fairly high temperature until they get some color and start to pop.

4. Lower the heat, add butter and let simmer until it turns a golden-brown color and a pleasant nutty scent. Add balsamic vinegar and let boil for a few more minutes. Turn off the heat.
5. Spread out baby spinach on a plate. Place the cheese on top and add the balsamico butter.

201. Keto Pancakes

Made for: Lunch | **Prep Time:** 10 minutes | **Servings:** 04
Per Serving: Kcal: 192, Protein: 9g, Fat: 16g, Net Carb: 3g

INGREDIENTS
- 2 large eggs room temperature
- 1 teaspoon coconut oil melted
- 1/4 cup (60ml) milk of choice I used unsweetened coconut milk
- 1 cup (112g) almond flour
- 1/2 teaspoon baking powder
- 1 teaspoon granulated sweetener of choice optional

INSTRUCTIONS
1. In a mixing bowl, whisk together the eggs, coconut oil, and milk until combined. In a separate bowl, mix the almond flour and baking powder.
2. Gently fold through the dry ingredients into the wet ingredients until combined.
3. Grease a large non-stick pan and place it over medium heat. Once hot, pour 1/4 cup spoonfuls of the batter onto the pan and immediately cover it. Cook the pancakes for 3-4 minutes, or until the edges begin to bubble. Remove the lid and carefully flip the pancakes, and cook for a further 1-2 minutes, covered. Repeat the process until all the batter has been cooked.
4. Serve the pancakes immediately.

202. Keto Oatmeal

Made for: Lunch | **Prep Time:** 10 minutes | **Servings:** 01
Per Serving: Kcal: 381, Protein: 9g, Fat: 27g, Net Carb: 0.4g

INGREDIENTS
- Two tablespoons Golden Flaxseed Meal
- Two tablespoons Coconut Flour
- Two tablespoons Chia Seeds
- 1/2 cup (120ml) Unsweetened Almond Milk
- Two tablespoons Heavy Cream
- 2-3 tablespoons Sugar-Free Syrup
- One teaspoon Vanilla Essence

INSTRUCTIONS

1. Place the dry ingredients into a small saucepan and mix together.
2. Add the remaining ingredients.
3. Place the saucepan over medium heat and whisk the ingredients together for about 10 minutes until it has thickened and is warmed through.
4. Pour into a bowl and top with your favourite toppings - we recommend extra Sugar-Free Syrup and chopped Pecans.

203. Keto tuna plate

Made for: Lunch | Prep Time: 15 minutes | Servings: 02
Per Serving: Kcal: 931, Protein: 52g, Fat: 76g, Net Carb: 3g

INGREDIENTS

- 4 eggs
- 2 oz. baby spinach
- 10 oz. tuna in olive oil
- 1 avocado
- ½ cup (120g) mayonnaise
- salt and pepper

INSTRUCTION

1. Begin by cooking the eggs. Lower them carefully into boiling water and boil for 4-8 minutes depending on whether you like them soft or hard boiled.
2. Cool the eggs in ice-cold water for 1-2 minutes when they're done; this will make it easier to remove the shell.
3. Place eggs, spinach, tuna and avocado on a plate. Serve with a hearty dollop of mayonnaise and perhaps a wedge of lemon. Season with salt and pepper.

204. Strawberry Avocado Smoothie

Made for: Lunch | Prep Time: 15 minutes | Servings: 02
Per Serving: Kcal: 106, Protein: 1g, Fat: 7g, Net Carb: 4g

INGREDIENTS

- 1 lb Frozen strawberries
- 1 1/2 cups (360ml) Almond Breeze Original Almond Milk (regular or vanilla)
- One large Avocado
- 1/4 cup Besti Powdered Allulose (or other powdered sweeteners of choice - adjust the amount to taste)

INSTRUCTION

1. Puree all ingredients in a blender, until

smooth. Adjust sweetener to taste as needed.

205. Keto Cheese Crackers

Made for: Lunch | Prep Time: 20 minutes | Servings: 2
Per Serving: Kcal: 131, Protein: 6g, Fat: 11g, Net Carb: 2g

INGREDIENTS

- 210 g almond meal (2 cups)
- 80 g cheddar cheese I use Mersey Valley Vintage
- 1 egg
- 1 tablespoon Everything but the Bagel Seasoning
- Salt flakes to sprinkle over top

INSTRUCTIONS

1. Preheat oven to 180°C. (fan-forced)
2. Place all ingredients, except salt flakes into a food processor and pulse until dough comes together.
3. Roll dough out between 2 large pieces of baking paper until 2-3mm thick.
4. Using a pizza wheel cut into small crackers. Season with salt flakes and lift onto a large baking tray.
5. Bake 13-18 minutes. Some of the crackers on the outside may need to be removed earlier than those in the centre. Tap the crackers with the very tip of your finger to check that they are firm. Remove from oven and allow to cool on tray for 1-2 minutes before transferring to cooling rack. Cool completely before storing in an airtight container.

206. Green Keto Smoothie

Made for: Lunch | Prep Time: 5 minutes | Servings: 02
Per Serving: Kcal: 141, Protein: 4g, Fat: 10g, Net Carb: 4g

INGREDIENTS

- 1 oz. kale leaves
- 1/2 avocado (peeled and stone removed)
- One stick celery (chopped)
- 2 oz. cucumber (peeled)
- 1 cup (240g) unsweetened almond milk (or regular milk)
- 1 tbsp. peanut butter (you can use any nut butter you like)
- 2 tbsp. freshly squeeze lemon juice

INSTRUCTION

1. Add all of the ingredients to a high-speed blender.

2. Pulse to combine, stopping to scrape down the sides if necessary.
3. Serve immediately garnished with fresh mint or store in the fridge for later that day.

207. Fried Tomatoes

Made for: Lunch | **Prep Time:** 5 minutes | **Servings:** 01
Per Serving: Kcal: 320, Protein: 0g, Fat: 36g, Net Carb: 0g

INGREDIENTS
- 1 tsp rapeseed oil
- Three tomatoes halved
- Four large eggs
- 1 tbsp chopped parsley
- 1 tbsp chopped basil

INSTRUCTIONS
1. Heat the oil in a small nonstick frying pan, then cook the tomatoes cut-side down until starting to soften and colour. Meanwhile, beat the eggs with the herbs and plenty of freshly ground black pepper in a small bowl.
2. Scoop the tomatoes from the pan and put them on two serving plates. Pour the egg mixture into the pan and stir gently with a wooden spoon, so the egg that sets on the base of the pan moves to enable the uncooked egg to flow into space. Stop stirring when it's nearly cooked to allow it to put into an omelette. Cut into four and serve with the tomatoes.

208. Chicken Nuggets

Made for: Lunch | **Prep Time:** 25 minutes | **Servings:** 02
Per Serving: Kcal: 550, Protein: 60g, Fat: 27g, Net Carb: 8g

INGREDIENTS
- 2 chicken breasts, cut into cubes
- 1/2 cup (56 g) coconut flour
- 1 egg
- 2 Tablespoons (20 g) garlic powder
- 1 teaspoon (5 g) salt (or to taste)
- 1/4-1/2 cup (60-120 ml) ghee for shallow frying

INSTRUCTION
1. Cube the chicken breasts if you haven't done so already.
2. In a bowl, mix together the coconut flour, garlic powder, and salt. Taste the mixture to see if you'd like more salt.

3. In a separate bowl, whisk 1 egg to make the egg wash.
4. Place the ghee in a saucepan on medium heat (or use a deep fryer).
5. Dip the cubed chicken in the egg wash and then drop into the coconut flour mixture to coat it with the "breading."
6. Carefully place some of the "breaded" chicken cubes into the ghee and fry until golden (approx. 10 minutes). Make sure there's only a single layer of chicken in the pan so that they can all cook in the oil. Turn the chicken pieces to make sure they get cooked uniformly. Depending on the size of the pan, you might need to do this step in batches.
7. Place the cooked chicken pieces onto paper towels to soak up any excess oil.

209. Peanut Butter Smoothie

Made for: Lunch | **Prep Time:** 10 minutes | **Servings:** 02
Per Serving: Kcal: 172, Protein: 5g, Fat: 15g, Net Carb: 4g

INGREDIENTS
- 1 cup (240ml) Unsweetened Almond Milk
- Two tablespoons Peanut butter no added sugar, no added oil
- Three tablespoons Erythritol erythritol or xylitol or monk fruit
- 1/4 cup (58g) heavy cream/double cream or canned coconut cream if dairy-free
- 1 cup () crushed ice or more for a frothy/ice smoothie
- One tablespoon unsweetened cocoa powder

INSTRUCTION
1. In a blender add all the ingredients, the order doesn't matter.
2. Blend on high speed until smooth. If you want a frothier/icy smoothie to add a few more ice cubes, blend again until smooth.

210. Egg and Ham Rolls

Made for: Lunch | **Prep Time:** 25 minutes | **Servings:** 04
Per Serving: Kcal: 158, Protein: 12g, Fat: 13g, Net Carb: 1g

INGREDIENTS
- 1 4 slices of ham
- One cucumber, sliced thin
- Four eggs whisked well
- 2 Tablespoons (30 ml) avocado oil, to cook with

INSTRUCTIONS

1. Add one teaspoon of avocado oil to a frying pan on low to medium heat and spread it around with a paper towel.
2. Add 1/4 cup of whisked eggs to the pan and roll it around to spread it thin.
3. Place a lid on top of the frying pan and let it cook until the base of the egg wrap is cooked (approx. 2-3 minutes). Carefully place on a plate and let cool.
4. Repeat in batches with the rest of the egg mixture to make egg wraps.
5. Create rolls with the egg wraps, slices of ham, and cucumber slices

211. Keto salmon and spinach plate

Made for: Lunch | Prep Time: 15 minutes | Servings: 02
Per Serving: Kcal: 791, Protein: 37g, Fat: 70g, Net Carb: 2g

INGREDIENTS

- 12 oz. salmon, boneless fillets, in portion pieces
- 2 tbsp butter for frying
- 3 oz. room tempered butter, for serving
- ½ red bell pepper
- 2 oz. baby spinach
- salt and pepper

INSTRUCTION

1. Fry the salmon in butter over medium heat, a few minutes on each side. Lower the heat towards the end. Season with salt and pepper.
2. Put the salmon, butter and vegetables on a plate and serve.

212. Keto Flu Smoothie

Made for: Lunch | Prep Time: 5 minutes | Servings: 01
Per Serving: Kcal: 141, Protein: 2g, Fat: 11g, Net Carb: 5g

INGREDIENTS

- 1/2 cup Kale
- Two large Strawberries
- 50 grams of Avocado
- 1/2 cup (85g) Cucumber, with peel
- 1/2 cup (120g) Unsweetened Almond Milk
- 1 tsp Stevia
- 1 tsp Vanilla Extract
- 1/2 tsp Pink Himalayan Salt

INSTRUCTION

1. Add all ingredients to a blender. Blend until smooth. Chill or pour over ice.

213. Blueberry Smoothie

Made for: Lunch | Prep Time: 5 minutes | Servings: 01
Per Serving: Kcal: 101, Protein: 2g, Fat: 7g, Net Carb: 5g

INGREDIENTS

- ¼ cup (35g) blueberries frozen
- 1 cup (240ml) almond milk unsweetened
- 1 oz (30g) avocado circa ¼ small avocado
- ¼ tsp vanilla extract
- 1 tsp powdered sweetener optional

INSTRUCTIONS

1. Place all ingredients in a blender and blend until smooth.
2. Taste and add optional sweetener if required.

214. Keto Smoothie Recipe

Made for: Lunch | Prep Time: 5 minutes | Servings: 01
Per Serving: Kcal: 353, Protein: 4g, Fat: 36g, Net Carb: 6g

INGREDIENTS

- 1 1/4 cups (285g) Thai Kitchen Coconut Milk
- 1 tsp low-carb sweetener — or more
- 1/4 avocado
- 1/2 cup blackberries
- 1 tsp chia seeds
- 2 tsp unsweetened cocoa powder
- 1 tsp peanut or almond butter

INSTRUCTION

1. Add all ingredients to a blender. Blend until smooth. Chill or pour over ice.

215. Basil Chicken Saute

Made for: Lunch | Prep Time: 25 minutes | Servings: 02
Per Serving: Kcal: 322, Protein: 23g, Fat: 24g, Net Carb: 2g

INGREDIENTS

- 1 chicken breast (0.5 lb or 225 g), minced or chopped very small
- 2 cloves of garlic, minced
- 1 chili pepper, diced (optional)
- 1 cup (1 large bunch) basil leaves, finely chopped
- 1 Tablespoon (15 ml) tamari sauce
- 2 Tablespoons (30 ml) avocado or coconut oil to cook in
- Salt, to taste

INSTRUCTION

1. Add oil to a frying pan and saute the garlic and pepper.

2. Then add in the minced chicken and saute until the chicken is cooked.
3. Add the tamari sauce and salt to taste. Add in the basil leaves and mix it in.

216. Crispy Chicken Drumsticks

Made for: Lunch | **Prep Time:** 45 minutes | **Servings:** 02
Per Serving: Kcal: 630, Protein: 72g, Fat: 29g, Net Carb: 4g

INGREDIENTS
- 10 chicken drumsticks
- 1-2 (15-30 g) Tablespoons salt
- 3 Tablespoons (24 g) curry powder (or onion powder)
- 3 Tablespoons (30 g) garlic powder
- 1/2 Tablespoon (7 ml) of coconut oil for greasing baking tray (optional)

INSTRUCTION
1. Preheat oven to 450 F (230 C). Grease a large baking tray with coconut oil.
2. Mix the salt and spices together in a bowl.
3. Coat each drumstick with the mixture, place on the baking tray, and bake for 40 minutes.

217. Keto Lava Cake

Made for: Lunch | **Prep Time:** 15 minutes | **Servings:** 02
Per Serving: Kcal: 460, Protein: 11g, Fat: 43g, Net Carb: 3g

INGREDIENTS
- 2 oz unsweetened chocolate (55g), at least 85% cocoa solids
- 1 tbsp super-fine almond flour
- 2 oz butter unsalted, plus more for greasing ramekins
- 2 eggs
- 3.5 tbsp powdered sweetener

INSTRUCTIONS
1. Heat oven to 175 Celsius/350 Fahrenheit.
2. Grease 2 ramekins with butter.
3. Melt the chocolate and butter and stir to combine.
4. Beat your eggs well - best with a mixer.
5. Add to the chocolate/butter mix together with almond flour and sweetener and stir. You'll get a dough-like consistency that is pourable.
6. Pour into 2 ramekins.
7. Bake 9 minutes until the top is set but still jiggly. Do not over-bake!
8. Turnout onto plates and serve with a dusting of powdered sweetener and

pomegranate seeds or a couple of raspberries. A mint leaf would round off the look nicely!

218. Keto mackerel and egg plate

Made for: Lunch | **Prep Time:** 15 minutes | **Servings:** 02
Per Serving: Kcal: 689, Protein: 35g, Fat: 60g, Net Carb: 4g

INGREDIENTS
- 4 eggs
- 2 tbsp butter for frying
- 8 oz. canned mackerel in tomato sauce
- 2 oz. lettuce
- ½ red onion
- ¼ cup olive oil
- salt and pepper

INSTRUCTION
1. Fry the eggs in butter, just the way you want them – sunny side up or over easy.
2. Put lettuce, thin slices of red onion and mackerel on a plate together with the eggs. Season to taste with salt and pepper. Drizzle olive oil over the salad and serve.

219. Spinach & Eggs

Made for: Lunch | **Prep Time:** 15 minutes | **Servings:** 01
Per Serving: Kcal: 419, Protein: 13g, Fat: 40g, Net Carb: 1g

INGREDIENTS
- 2 large eggs.
- ½ cup (20g) baby spinach.
- 2 tbsp mayonnaise.
- 1 tbsp butter.
- Pinch salt and pepper.

INSTRUCTIONS
1. Melt butter in a large frying pan and crack in the eggs.
2. As the eggs are frying, spoon over the melted butter from the pan until the yolk begins to have a white tint.
3. Place spinach on a plate with the mayonnaise, season with salt and pepper; place eggs next to spinach.

220. Guacamole Burgers

Made for: Lunch | **Prep Time:** 40 minutes | **Servings:** 04
Per Serving: Kcal: 601, Protein: 44g, Fat: 45g, Net Carb: 3g

INGREDIENTS
- 1-1.5 lbs (454-731 g) ground beef

- 4 eggs
- Coconut oil to cook with
- 1 cup (220 g) guacamole

INSTRUCTION

1. With your hands, mold the ground beef into 4 patties.
2. Cook the 4 burger patties, either in a skillet with a bit of coconut oil or on a grill.
3. Once the burgers are cooked through, place to the side.
4. Fry the eggs (preferably in coconut oil) in a skillet.
5. Place 1 fried egg on top of each burger and then top with guacamole.

221. Broccoli Beef Stir-Fry

Made for: Lunch | **Prep Time:** 25 minutes | **Servings:** 02
Per Serving: Kcal: 400, Protein: 22g, Fat: 30g, Net Carb: 6g

INGREDIENTS

- 2 cups (225g) broccoli florets
- 1/2 lb (225g) beef, sliced thin and precooked (you can use leftover Slow Cooker Asian Pot Roast (see page 70 for recipe))
- 3 cloves of garlic, minced
- 1 teaspoon (1 g) fresh ginger, grated
- 2 Tablespoons (30 ml) tamari sauce or to taste
- Avocado oil to cook in

INSTRUCTION

1. Place 2 Tablespoons of avocado oil into a skillet or saucepan on medium heat. Add the broccoli florets into the skillet.
2. When the broccoli softens to the amount you want (I like it soft, but some people like it crunchier), add in the beef slices.
3. Saute for 2 minutes and then add in the garlic, ginger, and tamari sauce.
4. Serve immediately.

222. Bacon & Egg

Made for: Lunch | **Prep Time:** 15 minutes | **Servings:** 04
Per Serving: Kcal: 274, Protein: 17g, Fat: 24g, Net Carb: 1g

INGREDIENTS

- 8 large eggs.
- 5 oz bacon (slices).
- Handful of cherry tomatoes (halved).

INSTRUCTIONS

1. In a large frying pan, fry bacon rashers until crispy. Set aside, leaving bacon fat in the pan.
2. Crack the eggs into the frying pan and fry eggs to your preferred taste.
3. When eggs are nearly cooked, throw in the cherry tomatoes and fry until lightly browned.

223. Fried salmon with asparagus

Made for: Lunch | **Prep Time:** 15 minutes | **Servings:** 02
Per Serving: Kcal: 591, Protein: 28g, Fat: 52g, Net Carb: 2g

INGREDIENTS

- 8 oz. green asparagus
- 3 oz. butter
- 9 oz. salmon, boneless fillets, in pieces
- salt and pepper

INSTRUCTION

1. Rinse and trim the asparagus.
2. Heat up a hearty dollop of butter in a frying pan where you can fit both the fish and vegetables.
3. Fry the asparagus over medium heat for 3-4 minutes. Season with salt and pepper. Gather everything in one half of the frying pan.
4. If necessary, add more butter and fry the pieces of salmon for a couple of minutes on each side. Stir the asparagus every now and then. Lower the heat towards the end.
5. Season the salmon and serve with the remaining butter.

224. Salmon with lemon & butter

Made for: Lunch | **Prep Time:** 25 minutes | **Servings:** 02
Per Serving: Kcal: 573, Protein: 31g, Fat: 49g, Net Carb: 1g

INGREDIENTS

- 1 tbsp olive oil
- 2 lbs salmon, boneless fillets
- 1 tsp sea salt
- ground black pepper
- 7 oz. butter
- 1 lemon

INSTRUCTION

1. Preheat the oven to 400°F (200°C).
2. Grease a large baking dish with olive oil. Place the salmon, with the skin-side down, in the prepared baking dish. Generously season with salt and pepper.

3. Slice the lemon thinly and place on top of the salmon. Cover with half of the butter in thin slices.
4. Bake on middle rack for about 20–30 minutes, or until the salmon is opaque and flakes easily with a fork.
5. Heat the rest of the butter in a small sauce pan until it starts to bubble. Remove from heat and let cool a little. Gently add some lemon juice.
6. Serve with lemon butter and a side dish of your choice. See below for suggestions.

225. Tuna Lunch Bowl

Made for: Lunch | **Prep Time:** 15 minutes | **Servings:** 01
Per Serving: Kcal: 860, Protein: 45g, Fat: 42g, Net Carb: 6g

INGREDIENTS
- 1 tuna steak (120 g/4.2 oz) - or use tinned, drained tuna
- 1 tsp sesame seeds
- pinch of sea salt
- 1 tsp ghee, butter or virgin coconut oil
- 1/2 avocado, sliced (100 g/3.5 oz)
- 10 pitted black olives (30 g/1.1 oz)
- 1 tbsp mayonnaise (15 g/0.5 oz) - you can make your own mayo
- 1/2 medium cucumber, sliced (70 g/ 2.5 oz)
- 6 quail's eggs or 1 large egg
- 1/4 small red onion, finely sliced (15 g/ 0.5 oz)
- 10 walnut halves (20 g/0.7 oz)
- 1 tbsp extra virgin olive oil (15 ml)
- large handful of watercress (50 g/ 1.8 oz)

INSTRUCTION
1. Preheat the oven to 180 °C/ 355 °F (fan assisted) 200 °C/ 400 °F (conventional). Wash and dry the watercress.
2. Place the walnuts on a baking tray and roast in the oven for 6-8 minutes until golden. Remove from the oven and allow to cool.
3. Coat the tuna with sesame seeds, ghee and a pinch of salt. If using tinned tuna, simply sprinkle the sesame seeds over the salad in the end.
4. Heat a griddle pan and fry the tuna to your liking - 1 1/2 minutes per side for pink, up to 3 minutes per side for well done. Remove from the heat and allow to cool slightly before slicing.
5. Boil the quail eggs for 2-3 minutes (or about 10 minutes for large eggs). Plunge into cold water before peeling.

6. Slice the rest of ingredients.
7. Place the watercress in bowl and add olives, halved quail eggs, avocado, walnuts and drizzle with 1 tbsp of olive oil and top with 1 tbsp of mayonnaise. Optionally, garnish with ground black pepper.
8. Tastes the best when served fresh, but can be stored in the fridge for 1 day.

226. Rosemary Baked Salmon

Made for: Lunch | **Prep Time:** 35 minutes | **Servings:** 02
Per Serving: Kcal: 632, Protein: 63g, Fat: 18g, Net Carb: 0g

INGREDIENTS
- 2 salmon filets (fresh or defrosted)
- 1 Tablespoon (2 g) fresh rosemary leaves
- 1/4 cup (60 ml) olive oil
- 1 teaspoon (5 g) salt (optional or to taste)

INSTRUCTION
1. Preheat oven to 350 F (175 C).
2. Mix the olive oil, rosemary, and salt together in a bowl.
3. Place one salmon filet at a time into the mixture and rub mixture onto the filet.
4. Wrap each filet in a piece of aluminum foil with some of the remaining mixture.
5. Bake for 25-30 minutes.

227. Cheese Egg Wrap

Made for: Lunch | **Prep Time:** 15 minutes | **Servings:** 02
Per Serving: Kcal: 413, Protein: 24g, Fat: 33g, Net Carb: 4g

INGREDIENTS
- 3 large eggs.
- 5 oz bacon (cooked and diced).
- 1 oz cheddar cheese (grated).
- 1 tbsp tomato sauce (low carb).

INSTRUCTIONS
1. In a large bowl, whisk the eggs until smooth.
2. Heat a large non-stick frying pan and slowly pour in half of the egg mixture; ensuring it reaches the edge of the pan.
3. Cook until the edges begin to brown and crisp, flip and cook the other side for an additional 30-40 seconds. Repeat with remaining egg mixture.
4. Spread the cooked egg with tomato sauce and fill with cheese and bacon; roll into an egg wrap.

228. Bacon Muffins

Made for: Lunch | **Prep Time:** 25 minutes | **Servings:** 2
Per Serving: Kcal: 300, Protein: 11g, Fat: 28g, Net Carb: 4g

INGREDIENTS

- 3 cups (360 g) almond flour
- 1 cup (100 g) bacon bits
- 1/2 cup (120 ml) ghee
- 4 eggs, whisked
- 2 teaspoons (2 g) lemon thyme
- 1 teaspoon (4 g) baking soda

INSTRUCTIONS

1. Preheat oven to 350 F (175 C).
2. Melt the ghee in a mixing bowl.
3. Add in the rest of the ingredients except the bacon bits to the mixing bowl.
4. Mix everything together well.
5. Lastly, add in the bacon bits.
6. Line a muffin pan with muffin liners. Spoon the mixture into the muffin pan (to around 3/4 full).
7. Bake for 18-20 minutes until a toothpick comes out clean when you insert it into a muffin.

229. Keto turkey plate

Made for: Lunch | **Prep Time:** 5 minutes | **Servings:** 2
Per Serving: Kcal: 650, Protein: 22g, Fat: 59g, Net Carb: 7g

INGREDIENTS

- 6 oz. deli turkey
- 1 avocado, sliced
- 2 oz. lettuce
- 3 oz. cream cheese
- 4 tbsp olive oil
- salt and pepper

INSTRUCTION

1. Divide the ingredients relevant to the serving number and place an equal amount of turkey, avocado, lettuce, and cream cheese on each plate.
2. Drizzle olive oil over the vegetables and season to taste with salt and pepper.

230. Keto California Omelet

Made for: Lunch | **Prep Time:** 20 minutes | **Servings:** 02
Per Serving: Kcal: 651, Protein: 48g, Fat: 35g, Net Carb: 4g

INGREDIENTS

- 6 large eggs, whisked
- 1/4 tsp lemon juice

- 1/4 tsp hot sauce (you can make your own Sriracha Sauce)
- 1/4 tsp sea salt
- 3 tbsp butter, ghee or duck fat (43 g/1.5 oz)
- 10-12 pieces cooked shrimp, peeled and deveined (115 g/4 oz)
- 2 tbsp minced parsley or cilantro
- 1/4 cup (37g) minced red bell pepper
- 1 medium green onion, sliced (15 g/ 0.5 oz)
- 1 large avocado, sliced (200 g/7.1 oz)

INSTRUCTIONS

1. In a small bowl whisk the eggs, lemon juice, hot sauce, and salt together. You can make one large omelet and eat half per serving, or make 2 regular omelets.
2. Heat the butter in a large nonstick pan over medium-low heat. Once melted pour in the whisked eggs. Cook lifting the edges with a spatula and tilting the pan to allow uncooked egg to run under the omelet until set but still moist on top. If you're making 2 smaller omelets, cook them in batches.
3. Arrange the shrimp, parsley, bell pepper, green onion, avocado and bacon across the top of the omelet. Gently fold in half and cook another 2-3 minutes until cooked through.
4. Serve immediately.

Keto Dinner Recipes

231. Keto mushroom omelet

Made for: Dinner | **Prep Time:** 20 minutes | **Servings:** 02
Per Serving: Kcal: 230, Protein: 16g, Fat: 21g, Net Carb: 2g

INGREDIENTS

- 6 eggs
- 2 oz. butter, for frying
- 2 oz. shredded cheese
- ½ yellow onion, chopped
- 8 large mushrooms, sliced
- salt and pepper

INSTRUCTIONS

1. Crack the eggs into a mixing bowl with a pinch of salt and pepper. Whisk the eggs with a fork until smooth and frothy.
2. Melt the butter in a frying pan, over medium heat. Add the mushrooms and onion to the pan, stirring until tender,

and then pour in the egg mixture, surrounding the veggies.
3. When the omelet begins to cook and get firm, but still has a little raw egg on top, sprinkle cheese over the egg.
4. Using a spatula, carefully ease around the edges of the omelet, and then fold it over in half. When it starts to turn golden brown underneath, remove the pan from the heat and slide the omelet on to a plate.

232. Almond Butter Choco

Made for: Dinner | **Prep Time:** 5 minutes | **Servings:** 01
Per Serving: Kcal: 190, Protein: 4g, Fat: 5g, Net Carb: 3g

INGREDIENTS
- 1 cup (240 ml) coconut milk or almond milk
- 2 Tablespoons (10 g) unsweetened cacao powder (or 1 scoop CoBionic Indulgence for added collagen)
- 1 Tablespoon (16 g) almond butter
- 1 teaspoon (5 ml) vanilla extract

INSTRUCTIONS
1. Place all the ingredients into a blender and blend well.

233. Keto Egg & Vegetable Skillet

Made for: Dinner | **Prep Time:** 20 minutes | **Servings:** 02
Per Serving: Kcal: 404, Protein: 17g, Fat: 32g, Net Carb: 8g

INGREDIENTS
- 3 tbsp ghee or virgin avocado oil (45 ml) - I used my Golden Ghee
- 1/2 small yellow onion, sliced (35 g/1.2 oz)
- 1 clove garlic, minced
- 1/2 small cauliflower, riced (240 g/8.5 oz)
- 2 cups (100g) shredded kale
- 1/2 tsp ground cumin
- 1/2 tsp sea salt, or to taste
- 1/4 tsp black pepper
- 2 tbsp chopped parsley or herbs of choice
- 4 large eggs

INSTRUCTIONS
1. Grease a skillet with 2 tbsp ghee (or avocado oil). Add sliced onion and cook for 3-5 minutes. Then add minced garlic and cook for just a minute.
2. Shred or tear the kale and remove the stalks.

3. Add the cauliflower rice (here's how to "rice" cauliflower). Add the remaining ghee and kale shredded or torn into small pieces.
4. Cover with a lid and cook for about 5 minutes. Remove the lid and cook for another 3-5 minutes, stirring frequently.
5. Take off the heat. Season with salt and pepper to taste and add fresh parsley.
6. Fry the eggs in another skillet or a non stick pan greased with the reamining ghee (or avocado oil).
7. Top with the fried eggs. Eat immediately. The cooked vegetables (without the fried egg topping) can be stored in the fridge for up to 4 days.

234. Chives Egg Muffins

Made for: Dinner | **Prep Time:** 35 minutes | **Servings:** 04
Per Serving: Kcal: 240, Protein: 12g, Fat: 22g, Net Carb: 3g

INGREDIENTS
- 6 eggs
- 1 cup kale, finely chopped
- 1/4 cup (17 g) chives, finely chopped
- 1/2 cup (120 ml) almond or coconut milk
- Salt and pepper to taste

INSTRUCTIONS
1. Preheat the oven to 350 F (175 C).
2. Whisk the eggs and add in the chopped kale and chives. Also add in the almond/coconut milk, salt, and pepper. Mix well.
3. Grease 8 muffin cups with coconut oil or line each cup with a prosciutto slice.
4. Divide the egg mixture between the 8 muffin cups. Fill only 2/3 of each cup as the mixture rises when it's baking.
5. Bake in oven for 30 minutes.
6. Let cool a few minutes and then lift out carefully with a fork. Note that the muffins will sink a bit.

235. Cauliflower Rice

Made for: Dinner | **Prep Time:** 20 minutes | **Servings:** 02
Per Serving: Kcal: 830, Protein: 36g, Fat: 74g, Net Carb: 7g

INGREDIENTS:

Cauliflower rice:
- 12 oz cauliflower head (grated).
- 1 ½ oz butter.
- ¼ tsp turmeric.
- ¼ tsp salt.

Steak:
- 1 large 1 inch thick steak (boneless).
- Two garlic cloves (crushed).
- 2 tbsp butter.

INSTRUCTIONS:
1. In a large frying pan, melt butter. Add cauliflower, salt, and turmeric.
2. Fry for 8-10 minutes or until the cauliflower has softened.
3. Towel dry the steak and rub on salt.
4. In a dry frying pan, sear the steak for 1 minute on each side.
5. Add in butter and garlic. Flip every 30 seconds for 8 minutes (medium-rare), spoon over garlic butter on every flip.
6. Cut steak into strips.

236. Barbecued bavette steak

Made for: Dinner | **Prep Time:** 20 minutes | **Servings:** 02
Per Serving: Kcal: 830, Protein: 36g, Fat: 74g, Net Carb: 7g

INGREDIENTS:
- 500g (2.5 cup) mixed heritage tomatoes
- 2 tbsp olive oil
- 500g bavette steak
- 2 red onions, cut into thick slices
- 200g jar grilled artichokes in oil, drained
- 150g feta, crumbled
- ½ bunch chives, roughly snipped

For the dressing
- 2 tbsp red wine vinegar
- 3 tbsp olive oil
- 1 tsp onion seeds
- 3 spring onions, trimmed and sliced

INSTRUCTIONS:
1. Make the dressing by whisking the vinegar, oil, onion seeds and spring onions together, then set aside. Slice the tomatoes, then arrange over a large serving platter and lightly season with salt. Drizzle over most of the oil and set aside.
2. Heat a barbecue or griddle pan to high and season the steak well. Cook for 2-3 mins on each side until charred but rare in the middle, then transfer to a warm plate to rest. Drizzle the remaining oil over the onions and grill until charred. Separate into rings and set aside.
3. Slice the steak and arrange the tomatoes over it. Drizzle with any resting juices. Scatter over the artichokes and charred onions, then the feta and chives.

To serve, drizzle over the dressing.

237. Oven-Baked Brie Cheese

Made for: Dinner | **Prep Time:** 15 minutes | **Servings:** 04
Per Serving: Kcal: 342, Protein: 15g, Fat: 31g, Net Carb: 1g

INGREDIENTS
- 9 oz. Brie cheese or Camembert cheese
- 1 garlic clove, minced
- 1 tbsp fresh rosemary, coarsely chopped
- 2 oz. pecans or walnuts, coarsely chopped
- 1 tbsp olive oil
- salt and pepper

INSTRUCTIONS
1. Preheat the oven to 400°F (200°C).
2. Place the cheese on a sheet pan lined with parchment paper or in a small non-stick baking dish.
3. In a small bowl, mix the garlic, herb and nuts together with the olive oil. Add salt and pepper to taste.
4. Place the nut mixture on the cheese and bake for 10 minutes or until cheese is warm and soft and nuts are toasted. Serve warm or lukewarm.

238. Keto smoked salmon

Made for: Dinner | **Prep Time:** 10 minutes | **Servings:** 02
Per Serving: Kcal: 1016, Protein: 33g, Fat: 97g, Net Carb: 1g

INGREDIENTS
- 12 oz. smoked salmon
- 1 cup (230g) mayonnaise
- 2 cups (60g) baby spinach
- 1 tbsp olive oil
- ½ lime (optional)
- salt and pepper

INSTRUCTIONS
1. Put salmon, spinach, a wedge of lime, and a hearty dollop of mayonnaise on a plate.
2. Drizzle olive oil over the spinach and season with salt and pepper.

239. Pancake Recipe

Made for: Dinner | **Prep Time:** 15 minutes | **Servings:** 02
Per Serving: Kcal: 257, Protein: 18g, Fat: 18g, Net Carb: 5g

INGREDIENTS
- 3 (3) Eggs

- 1/2 cup (105 g) cottage cheese
- 1/3 cup (37.33 g) Superfine Almond Flour
- 1/4 cup (62.5 g) Unsweetened Almond Milk
- 2 tablespoons (2 tablespoons) Truvia
- Vanilla extract
- 1 teaspoon (1 teaspoon) Baking Powder
- Cooking Oil Spray

INSTRUCTIONS

1. Place ingredients in a blender jar in the order listed. Blend until you have a smooth, liquid batter.
2. Heat a nonstick saucepan on medium-high heat. Spray with oil or butter.
3. Place 2 tablespoons of batter at a time to make small, dollar pancakes. This is a very liquid, delicate batter so do not try to make big pancakes with this one as they will not flip over as easily.
4. Cook each pancake until the top of the pancake has made small bubbles and the bubbles have disappeared, about 1-2 minutes.
5. Using a spatula, gently loosen the pancake, and then flip over.
6. Make the rest of the pancakes in this manner and serve hot.

240. Bacon & Spinach Bake

Made for: Dinner | Prep Time: 35 minutes | Servings: 04
Per Serving: Kcal: 660, Protein: 28g, Fat: 61g, Net Carb: 4g

INGREDIENTS

- 8 large eggs.
- 8 oz fresh spinach.
- 1 cup (232g) thick cream.
- 5 oz bacon (diced).
- 5 oz cheddar cheese (grated).
- 2 tbsp butter.

INSTRUCTIONS

1. Preheat the oven at 175 degrees.
2. In a large frying pan, melt the butter and fry the bacon until crispy. Add in the spinach and fry until wilted. Set aside.
3. In a large bowl, whisk together the eggs and cream.
4. Pour the egg mixture into an ovenproof dish; add bacon and spinach and top with cheese.
5. Bake for 25-30 minutes until completely set and golden brown.

241. Omelet Wrap with Salmon

Made for: Dinner | Prep Time: 15 minutes | Servings: 01
Per Serving: Kcal: 765, Protein: 36g, Fat: 66g, Net Carb: 2g

INGREDIENTS

- 3 large eggs
- 1/2 large avocado (100g/3.5 oz)
- 1/2 package smoked salmon (50 g/ 1.8 oz)
- 2 heaped tbsp full-fat cream cheese (64 g/ 2.3 oz)
- 2 tbsp freshly chopped chives
- 1 medium spring onion, chopped (15 g/ 0.5 oz)
- 1 tbsp ghee or butter
- sea salt & pepper, to taste

INSTRUCTIONS

1. Crack the eggs into a mixing bowl with a pinch of salt and pepper and beat them well with a whisk or fork. Keto Omelet Wrap with Salmon & Avocado
2. Mix the cream cheese with chopped chives. Slice the smoked salmon, peel and slice the avocado. Keto Omelet Wrap with Salmon & Avocado
3. Pour the eggs evenly in a hot pan greased with ghee. Cook over a medium-low heat. Don't rush it and don't try to cook it fast or the omelet will end up being too crispy and dry.
4. Use a spatula to bring in the egg from the sides towards to centre for the first 30 seconds. Cook for another minute or two. Make sure you don't cook the omelet for too long. The desired texture should be soft, fluffy and not too juicy. Keto Omelet Wrap with Salmon & Avocado
5. Slide the omelet onto a plate and spoon the cheese spread all over. Keto Omelet Wrap with Salmon & Avocado
6. Add the salmon, avocado, chopped spring onion and fold into a wrap. Keto Omelet Wrap with Salmon & Avocado
7. Serve immediately or store in the fridge for up to a day.

242. Bacon Wraps with Avocado

Made for: Dinner | Prep Time: 15 minutes | Servings: 02
Per Serving: Kcal: 459, Protein: 27g, Fat: 40g, Net Carb: 4g

INGREDIENTS

- 2 Almost Zero Carb Wraps
- 3 slices bacon cooked

- 2 large eggs
- 1/2 cup (60g) grated cheddar cheese
- 1/2 avocado sliced
- 1/4 cup (65g) salsa
- salt and pepper to taste

INSTRUCTIONS

1. Cook the bacon in the pan until crisp. Remove, cut in half and set aside. Pour out all but 2 teaspoons of bacon fat. Slice the avocado.
2. In a small bowl, beat the eggs and half of the cheddar cheese cheese with a fork. Cook the scrambled eggs to your liking and remove from the pan. Season with salt and pepper.
3. Place the wraps into the hot pan over medium heat (I had to overlap mine just a bit in the middle). Divide the scrambled eggs and place them on 1/2 of each wrap, not going past the middle. Add the avocado, bacon and remaining cheese. Add 1 tablespoon of water to the pan and cover quickly with a lid. Leave covered for 1-2 minutes or until the cheese has melted and the bottom of the wraps have browned a bit. Serve with salsa.

243. Broccoli and Cheddar muffin

Made for: Dinner | Prep Time: 25 minutes | Muffins: 12
Per Muffin: Kcal: 94, Protein: 6g, Fat: 6g, Net Carb: 1g

INGREDIENTS

- 1/2 tsp dried thyme
- 1/2 tsp garlic powder
- 1 1/2 cups (234g) broccoli steamed and chopped (or frozen and thawed)
- 2/3 cup (80g) grated cheddar cheese plus more for topping

INSTRUCTIONS

1. Whisk in garlic powder and thyme until combined. Stir in broccoli and cheddar. Divide evenly into muffin tins1 filling each about 2/3 full.
2. Sprinkle with more cheddar if desired. Bake in preheated oven for 12-15 minutes, or until set.

244. Low-Carb Keto Dinner

Made for: Dinner | Prep Time: 5 minutes | Servings: 01
Per Serving: Kcal: 450, Protein: 21g, Fat: 43g, Net Carb: 5g

INGREDIENTS

- 2 eggs
- 1 tbsp cream (skip if paleo)
- 1 tsp butter
- 3 slices bacon (50g)
- 1 large crimini mushroom (40g)
- 4 broccoli sticks (60g)
- 1/4 avocado (40g)
- pinch salt
- pinch black pepper

INSTRUCTIONS

1. Add some water to a pot and heat.
2. Add the broccoli sticks to the boiling water and cook for 2-3 minutes.
3. Add the bacon slices to a frying pan and cook on both sides until nice and crispy. Don't discard of the oil.
4. Slice the shiitake mushroom and avocado.
5. Take the broccoli out of the water and add them to the bacon grease along with the mushroom slices.
6. Fry in the bacon grease until nice and tender.
7. In a small bowl, whisk the eggs and cream together.
   *For this step you can either fry the eggs inside the grease or fry them in some ghee.
8. Scramble the eggs until desired thickness.
9. Add your fried eggs, avocado, broccoli, bacon and mushrooms to a plate. Sprinkle the salt & pepper over.

245. Keto Butter Recipe

Made for: Dinner | Prep Time: 5 minutes | Servings: 02
Per Serving: Kcal: 353, Protein: 4g, Fat: 36g, Net Carb: 7g

INGREDIENTS

- 1 1/4 cups (285g) Thai Kitchen Coconut Milk
- 1 tsp low-carb sweetener — or more
- 1/4 avocado
- 1/2 cup blackberries
- 1 tsp chia seeds
- 2 tsp unsweetened cocoa powder
- 1 tsp peanut or almond butter

INSTRUCTIONS

1. Add all ingredients to a blender. Blend until smooth. Chill or pour over ice.

246. Chia Seeds Bread

Made for: Dinner | **Pre. Time:** 25 minutes | **Makes:** 12 breads
Per Bread: Kcal: 148, Protein: 5g, Fat: 12g, Net Carb: 2g

INGREDIENTS

- 4 eggs
- 1/4 cup almond milk or water
- 1/2 teaspoon salt
- 1 cup (112g) almond flour
- 1/4 cup (60g) melted butter
- 2 teaspoons baking soda
- 1/2 cup (86g) chia seeds

INSTRUCTIONS

1. Add everything into a bowl and stir well until you got an even mass.
2. Pour everything into a baking tin which is laid out with baking sheets.
3. Bake at 350°F for 30 minutes or until golden brown. Have an eye on it!

247. Delicious Keto Salad

Made for: Dinner | **Prep Time:** 25 minutes | **Servings:** 1
Per Serving: Kcal: 318, Protein: 15g, Fat: 25g, Net Carb: 7g

INGREDIENTS

- 60g (1/2 cup) pack peppered smoked mackerel, torn into pieces
- 25g bag watercress
- 60g pack ready-cooked beetroot
- 25g bag honey-roasted mixed nuts
- For the dressing
- One small red onion, very thinly sliced
- 1 tbsp sherry vinegar
- pinch of sugar
- 1 tbsp extra virgin olive oil

INSTRUCTIONS

1. Mix together the onion, vinegar, sugar and a pinch of salt. Leave to pickle while you dice the beetroot and roughly chop the nuts.
2. Divide the watercress and smoked mackerel between six plates. Scatter over the beetroot and nuts, then top with a cluster of the pickled onions. Whisk the oil into the pickling vinegar, then drizzle the dressing around the outside of each plate.

248. Keto skillet pizza

Made for: Dinner | **Prep Time:** 30 minutes | **Servings:** 02
Per Serving: Kcal: 600, Protein: 32g, Fat: 50g, Net Carb: 4g

INGREDIENTS

- 6 oz. mozzarella cheese, shredded
- 4 oz. fresh sausage, cooked and crumbled
- 2 oz. pepperoni, sliced
- 2 oz. green bell peppers
- 1 tsp Italian seasoning
- 4 tbsp unsweetened tomato sauce

INSTRUCTIONS

1. Heat a 7" nonstick skillet over medium heat.
2. Sprinkle 3/4 of the cheese in the bottom of the skillet. The cheese will melt into a thin, solid layer.
3. Lower the heat and top the melted cheese with sausage, bell pepper, remaining cheese and pepperoni. Cook on low heat for 3-4 minutes until the toppings are warmed.
4. Sprinkle the Italian seasoning over the pizza. The pizza is done when the cheese on top is melted and when the cheese "crust" is browned.
5. Remove from heat and let cool for 5 minutes before serving.
6. Remove the pizza from the skillet and onto a plate. Use a pizza cutter to cut the pizza into slices. Serve with tomato sauce for dipping.

249. Bacon & Broccoli Wrap

Made for: Dinner | **Prep Time:** 5 minutes | **Servings:** 02
Per Serving: Kcal: 258, Protein: 15g, Fat: 19g, Net Carb: 4g

INGREDIENTS

- One large egg.
- One cup (156g) broccoli (chopped).
- One onion (sliced).
- One slice of bacon.
- ¼ cup (50g) tomatoes (chopped).
- 2 tbsp cheddar cheese.
- 1 tbsp milk.
- 1 tsp avocado oil.
- Pinch salt and pepper.

INSTRUCTIONS

1. Fry bacon until crispy and remove from pan. Add broccoli and cook for 3 minutes until soft, mix in tomatoes and pour into a bowl.
2. In a separate bowl, mix egg, milk, onion, and salt and pepper. Add oil to a large frying
3. pan over medium heat; pour in the egg mixture, covering the frying pan's base.

Cook for 2 minutes until the bottom has set, flip and cook the other side.
4. Place egg wrap on a plate, fill the bottom half with broccoli mixture, top with bacon, and roll into a wrap.

250. Coconut Milk Shake

Made for: Dinner | **Prep Time:** 15 minutes | **Servings:** 01
Per Serving: Kcal: 224, Protein: 16g, Fat: 44g, Net Carb: 0.2g

INGREDIENTS
- ½ avocado
- ½ cups (120g) Unsweetened Coconut Milk
- 5 drops stevia
- 5 Ice Cubes

INSTRUCTIONS
1. Add all the ingredients to the blender.
2. Blend until smooth.

251. Salmon and Avocado

Made for: Dinner | **Prep Time:** 5 minutes | **Servings:** 02
Per Serving: Kcal: 680, Protein: 28g, Fat: 62g, Net Carb: 1g

INGREDIENTS
- 7 ounces. Smoked salmon
- Two avocados
- 1/2 cup (115g) mayonnaise
- Salt and Pepper

INSTRUCTIONS
1. Split the avocado in half, remove the pit, and scoop out avocado pieces with a spoon. Place on a plate.
2. Add salmon and a hearty dollop of mayonnaise to the plate.
3. Top with freshly ground black pepper and a sprinkle of sea salt.

252. Strawberry Pancakes

Made for: Dinner | **Prep Time:** 15 minutes | **Servings:** 04
Per Serving: Kcal: 320, Protein: 14g, Fat: 36g, Net Carb: 4g

INGREDIENTS
- Four large eggs.
- 1 cup (240g) of thick cream.
- 7 oz cottage cheese.
- 2 oz fresh strawberries.
- 2 oz butter.
- 1 tbsp psyllium husk (powder).

INSTRUCTIONS
1. Mix cottage cheese, eggs, and psyllium husk until well combined. Allow resting for 10 minutes.
2. Heat butter in a large frying pan and fry each pancake on medium heat for 3-4 minutes on each side.
3. In a bowl, whip the cream until peaks are formed.
4. Serve the pancakes topped with cream and fresh strawberries.

253. Super Cheese Omelets

Made for: Dinner | **Prep Time:** 15 minutes | **Servings:** 01
Per Serving: Kcal: 511, Protein: 24g, Fat: 43g, Net Carb: 5g

INGREDIENTS:
- Three large mushrooms (sliced).
- Three large eggs.
- 1 oz cheddar cheese (grated).
- 1 oz butter.
- ¼ onion (finely sliced).
- Pinch salt and Pepper.

INSTRUCTIONS:
1. In a bowl, whisk together the eggs, salt, and Pepper.
2. In a large frying pan, melt the butter and fry onions and mushrooms until tender. Pour in the egg mixture so that it surrounds the onions and mushrooms.
3. As the sides begin to firm and it is still slightly runny in the middle, sprinkle on the cheese.
4. Continue cooking until the egg mixture is completely formed and cooked through.

254. Chicken with Lemon

Made for: Dinner | **Prep Time:** 60 minutes | **Servings:** 04
Per Serving: Kcal: 680, Protein: 28g, Fat: 62g, Net Carb: 1g

INGREDIENTS
- 1½ lbs (680g) chicken whole
- salt and Pepper
- 1 tsp barbecue seasoning dry rub
- 2½ oz. butter sliced
- ½ lemon, cut into wedges
- One yellow onion cut into wedges
- 2 tbsp water
- ½ tsp butter for greasing the baking dish

INSTRUCTIONS
1. Preheat the oven to 350°F (175°C). Grease a deep baking dish with butter.
2. Prepare the chicken by drying it thoroughly with paper towels—Season

the entire chicken with salt and pepper, including the cavity. Don't skimp on the salt! Next, rub the outside of the chicken with the barbecue seasoning, and then place it in the baking dish.

3. Surround the chicken with the onion and lemon wedges, and then evenly place the butter slices on top of the chicken.
4. Move the baking dish to the lower oven rack, and bake for 1½ hours or more, depending on the size of the chicken. Frequently baste the chicken with drippings, and if necessary, add water. If testing the chicken for readiness with a kitchen thermometer, insert it into the thickest part of the thigh, avoiding the bone. The chicken is ready when the temperature reads 165°F (75°C).

255. Keto chicken garam masala

Made for: Dinner | Prep Time: 35 minutes | Servings: 04
Per Serving: Kcal: 732, Protein: 33g, Fat: 65g, Net Carb: 6g

INGREDIENTS
- 1½ lbs (450g) boneless chicken thighs, sliced
- One red bell pepper, thinly sliced
- 3 tbsp coconut oil
- 2½ tbsp garam masala seasoning
- 2 tsp turmeric
- Two garlic cloves, finely chopped
- 1 tsp salt
- 1¼ cups (370g) coconut cream or heavy whipping cream
- 3 tbsp fresh cilantro, roughly chopped

INSTRUCTIONS
1. Place a large skillet over medium-high heat and add the coconut oil.
2. When the oil is hot, add the garam masala, turmeric and garlic into the pan. Fry for a minute while stirring, making sure it doesn't get burned.
3. Add the chicken and salt, then stir thoroughly—Fry for about 3 minutes before adding the bell pepper. Continue frying for about 2 minutes. Add the coconut cream and let it simmer, uncovered, over medium heat for 10 minutes.
4. Garnish with cilantro and serve.

256. Salmon with lemon and butter

Made for: Dinner | Prep Time: 35 minutes | Servings: 02

Per Serving: Kcal: 572, Protein: 30g, Fat: 51g, Net Carb: 2g

INGREDIENTS
- ½ tbsp olive oil
- 1 lb salmon
- ½ tsp sea salt
- ground black pepper
- 3½ oz. butter
- ½ lemon

INSTRUCTIONS
1. Preheat the oven to 400°F (200°C).
2. Grease a large baking dish with olive oil. Place the salmon, with the skin-side down, in the prepared baking dish. Generously season with salt and pepper.
3. Slice the lemon thinly and place on top of the salmon. Cover with half of the butter in thin slices.
4. Bake on middle rack for about 20–30 minutes, or until the salmon is opaque and flakes easily with a fork.
5. Heat the rest of the butter in a small saucepan until it starts to bubble. Remove from heat and let cool a little. Gently add some lemon juice.
6. Serve with lemon butter and a side dish of your choice. See below for suggestions.

257. Lamb & lettuce pan-fry

Made for: Dinner | Prep Time: 25 minutes | Servings: 04
Per Serving: Kcal: 465, Protein: 30g, Fat: 37g, Net Carb: 3g

INGREDIENTS
- 25g (1/8 cup) butter
- Four lamb neck fillets, cut into chunks
- Two handfuls frozen peas
- 150ml chicken stock
- 3 Baby Gem lettuces, cut into quarters

INSTRUCTIONS
1. Heat the butter in a frying pan until sizzling, then add the lamb. Season with salt, if you like, and pepper, then cook for 6-7 mins until browned on all sides. Scatter in the peas, pour in the stock, then bring up to a simmer and gently cook until the peas have defrosted. Add the lettuce to the pan and simmer for a few mins until just starting to wilt, but still vibrant green. Serve scooped straight from the pan, with buttered

258. Tomatoes and Cheese

Made for: Dinner | **Prep Time:** 20 minutes | **Servings:** 02
Per Serving: Kcal: 435, Protein: 26g, Fat: 35g, Net Carb: 2g

INGREDIENTS:

- Six large eggs
- 1/2 medium or yellow-white onion (55 g/ 1.9 oz)
- 2/3 cup crumbled soft cheese like feta
- 2/3 cup cherry tomatoes, halved (100 g/ 3.5 oz)
- 1 tbsp ghee or duck fat (15 ml)
- 2 tbsp freshly chopped herbs such as chives or basil
- sea salt and ground pepper, to taste

INSTRUCTIONS:

1. Preheat the oven (or ideally grill if you have it) to 200 °C/ 400 °F (fan assisted), or 220 °C/ 425 °F (conventional). Peel and slice the onion. Place on a hot pan greased with ghee and cook until lightly browned.
2. Crack the eggs into a bowl and season with salt and Pepper. Add finely chopped herbs (I used chives) and whisk well.
3. When the onion is browned, pour in the eggs and cook until you see the edges turning opaque.
4. Top with the crumbled cheese and halved cherry tomatoes. Place under the broiler and cook for 5-7 minutes or until the top is cooked.
5. Remove from the oven and set aside to cool down. Serve immediately or store in the fridge for up to 5 days. You can freeze the frittata fr up to 3 months.

259. Keto Carrot Cake

Made for: Dinner | **Prep Time:** 20 minutes | **Servings:** 02
Per Serving: Kcal: 443, Protein: 14g, Fat: 40g, Net Carb: 5g

INGREDIENTS:

- ¾ cup (84g) almond flour.
- ½ cup (55g) carrot (grated).
- One large egg.
- 2 tbsp cream cheese.
- 2 tbsp walnuts (finely chopped).
- 2 tbsp butter (melted).
- 2 tbsp erythritol.
- 1 tbsp thick cream.
- 2 tsp cinnamon.
- 1 tsp mixed spice.
- 1 tsp baking powder.

INSTRUCTIONS:

1. In a bowl, mix almond flour, cinnamon, baking powder, erythritol, walnuts, and mixed spice.
2. Mix in the egg, butter, thick cream, and carrot until well combined.
3. Grease 2 microwave-safe ramekins and split the mixture evenly between the two.
4. Microwave on high for 5 minutes.
5. Spread cream cheese on the top.

260. Chicken, broccoli & beetroot salad

Made for: Dinner | **Prep Time:** 30 minutes | **Servings:** 02
Per Serving: Kcal: 640, Protein: 58g, Fat: 36g, Net Carb: 6g

INGREDIENTS

- 250g (3/2 cup) thin-stemmed broccoli
- 2 tsp rapeseed oil
- 3 skinless chicken breasts
- 1 red onion, thinly sliced
- 100g (2.5 cup) bag watercress
- 2 raw beetroots (about 175g), peeled and julienned or grated
- 1 tsp nigella seeds
- For the avocado pesto
- small pack basil
- 1 avocado
- ½ garlic cloves, crushed
- 25g (1/5 cup)) walnut halves, crumbled
- 1 tbsp rapeseed oil
- juice and zest 1 lemon

INSTRUCTIONS

1. Bring a large pan of water to the boil, add the broccoli and cook for 2 mins. Drain, then refresh under cold water. Heat a griddle pan, toss the broccoli in 1/2 tsp of the rapeseed oil and griddle for 2-3 mins, turning, until a little charred. Set aside to cool. Brush the chicken with the remaining oil and season. Griddle for 3-4 mins each side or until cooked through. Leave to cool, then slice or shred into chunky pieces.
2. Next, make the pesto. Pick the leaves from the basil and set aside a handful to top the salad. Put the rest in the small bowl of a food processor. Scoop the flesh from the avocado and add to the food processor with the garlic, walnuts, oil, 1 tbsp lemon juice, 2-3 tbsp cold water and some seasoning. Blitz until smooth, then transfer to a small serving dish. Pour the remaining lemon juice over the sliced onions and leave for a few mins.

3. Pile the watercress onto a large platter. Toss through the broccoli and onion, along with the lemon juice they were soaked in. Top with the beetroot, but don't mix it in, and the chicken. Scatter over the reserved basil leaves, the lemon zest and nigella seeds, then serve with the avocado pesto.

261. Broccoli Bacon Salad

Made for: Dinner | **Prep Time:** 40 minutes | **Servings:** 02
Per Serving: Kcal: 512, Protein: 20g, Fat: 50g, Net Carb: 5g

INGREDIENTS
- 1 lb (454g) broccoli florets
- Four small red onions or two large ones, sliced
- 20 slices of bacon, chopped into small pieces
- 1 cup (240ml) coconut milk
- Salt to taste

INSTRUCTIONS
1. Cook the bacon first, and then cook the onions in the bacon fat.
2. Blanche the broccoli florets (or you can use them raw or soften them by boiling them first).
3. Toss the bacon pieces, onions, and broccoli florets together with the coconut milk and salt to taste. Serve at room temperature.

262. Spring roast chicken

Made for: Dinner | **Prep Time:** 60 minutes | **Servings:** 04
Per Serving: Kcal: 439, Protein: 55g, Fat: 40g, Net Carb: 3g

INGREDIENTS
- 8 chicken thighs, on the bone, skin on
- 2 tbsp olive oil
- 1 lemon, zested and cut into wedges
- 4 shallots, thickly sliced
- 4 rosemary sprigs
- small pack tarragon
- 450g (3.3 cup) asparagus spears, trimmed
- 2 courgettes, thickly sliced on the diagonal
- 250g (2 cup) peas (preferably fresh, not frozen)
- 100g (1 cup) feta, crumbled

INSTRUCTIONS
1. Heat oven to 200C/180C fan/gas 6. Put the chicken thighs in a large shallow roasting tin, season and toss with the olive oil, lemon zest and wedges, shallots, rosemary and tarragon. Arrange the chicken thighs, skin-side up, and roast for 40-50 mins until the skin is crisp and golden.
2. Meanwhile, bring a large pan of water to the boil and cook the asparagus for 3 mins or until tender, adding the courgettes and peas for the final minute.
3. Drain the vegetables and toss in with the chicken, coating well with the cooking juices. Crumble over the feta and serve.

263. Fried Chicken and Paprika Sauce

Made for: Dinner | **Prep Time:** 35 minutes | **Servings:** 02
Per Serving: Kcal: 300, Protein: 10g, Fat: 9g, Net Carb: 4g

INGREDIENTS
- One tablespoon coconut oil
- Three and ½ pounds chicken breasts
- 1 cup (96g) chicken stock
- One and ¼ cups yellow onion, chopped
- One tablespoon lime juice
- ¼ cup (24g) of coconut milk
- Two teaspoons paprika
- One teaspoon red pepper flakes
- Two tablespoons green onions, chopped
- Salt and black pepper to the taste

INSTRUCTIONS
1. Heat up a pan with the oil over medium-high heat, add chicken, cook for 2 minutes on each side, transfer to a plate and leave aside.
2. Reduce heat to medium, add onions to the pan and cook for 4 minutes.
3. Add stock, coconut milk, pepper flakes, paprika, lime juice, salt and pepper and stir well.
4. Return chicken to the pan, add more salt and pepper, cover pan and cook for 15 minutes.
5. Divide between plates and serve.

264. Chicken with Cheese Sauce

Made for: Dinner | **Prep Time:** 45 minutes | **Servings:** 04
Per Serving: Kcal: 339, Protein: 12g, Fat: 11g, Net Carb: 4g

INGREDIENTS
- 1 lb. (450g) boneless chicken thigh
- ½ teaspoon black pepper
- 1 cup (112g) almond flour
- One egg
- ½ cup (108g) extra virgin olive oil, to fry
- 1 cup (60g) almond yogurt

- 1 cup (120g) grated cheddar cheese
- Two teaspoons mustard

INSTRUCTIONS

1. Cut the boneless chicken thigh into slices, then set aside.
2. Crack the egg, then place in a bowl.
3. Season the egg with black pepper, then stirs until incorporated.
4. Dip the sliced chicken in the beaten egg, then roll in the almond flour. Make sure that the chicken is completely coated with almond flour.
5. Preheat a frying pan over medium heat, then pour olive oil into the pan.
6. Once the oil is hot, put the chicken in the frying pan and fry until both sides of the chicken are lightly golden brown, and the chicken is thoroughly cooked.
7. Place the crispy chicken on a serving dish.
8. In the meantime, place almond yogurt, grated cheddar cheese, and mustard in a saucepan, then bring to a simmer over low heat.
9. Stir the sauce until incorporated, then remove from heat.
10. Drizzle the cheese sauce over the chicken, then serve.
11. Enjoy warm!

265. Keto turkey with sauce

Made for: Dinner | **Prep Time:** 25 minutes | **Servings:** 02
Per Serving: Kcal: 815, Protein: 40g, Fat: 60g, Net Carb: 6g

INGREDIENTS

- 1 tbsp butter
- ¾ lb turkey breast
- 1 cup (240g) crème fraîche or heavy whipping cream
- 3½ oz. Cream cheese
- ½ tbsp tamari soy sauce
- salt and pepper
- ¾ oz. small capers

INSTRUCTIONS

1. Preheat the oven to 350°F (175°C).
2. Melt half of the butter over medium heat, in a large ovenproof frying pan. Season the turkey generously and fry until golden brown all around.
3. Finish off the turkey breasts in the oven when the turkey is cooked through and has an internal temperature of at least 165°F (74°C), place on a plate, and tent with foil.

4. Pour turkey drippings into a small saucepan. Add cream and cream cheese. Stir and bring to a light boil. Lower the heat and let simmer until thickened. Add soy sauce, season with salt and pepper.
5. Heat remaining butter in a medium frying pan over high heat. Quickly sauté the capers until crispy.
6. Serve turkey with sauce and fried capers.

266. Baked cod with goat's cheese

Made for: Dinner | **Prep Time:** 15 minutes | **Servings:** 02
Per Serving: Kcal: 200, Protein: 26g, Fat: 8g, Net Carb: 1g

INGREDIENTS

- 1 tsp rapeseed oil
- 1 garlic clove, grated
- 200g spinach (6 cup)
- 2 x 125g skinless cod fillets
- 25g soft goat's cheese (1/4 cup)
- 2 tomatoes, each sliced into 3
- a few thyme leaves, to serve

INSTRUCTIONS

1. Heat oven to 200C/180C fan/gas 6. Heat the oil in a non-stick pan, add the garlic and fry very briefly to soften it. Tip in the spinach and stir until wilted. Spoon into the base of two gratin dishes, then top with the cod. Spread over some of the goat's cheese and arrange the tomatoes on top.
2. Snip over a few thyme leaves, then bake for 10 mins until the fish flakes easily when tested. Serve in the dishes.

267. Chicken and Snap

Made for: Dinner | **Prep Time:** 20 minutes | **Servings:** 04
Per Serving: Kcal: 228, Protein: 20g, Fat: 11g, Net Carb: 6g

INGREDIENTS:

- Two tablespoons vegetable oil
- One bunch scallions, thinly sliced
- Two garlic cloves, minced
- One red bell pepper, thinly sliced
- 2½ cups (147g) snap peas
- 1¼ cups (175g) boneless skinless chicken breast, thinly sliced
- Salt and freshly ground Black Pepper
- Three tablespoons soy sauce
- Two tablespoons rice vinegar
- Two teaspoons Sriracha (optional)

- Two tablespoons sesame seeds, plus more for finishing
- Three tablespoons chopped fresh cilantro, plus more for finishing

INSTRUCTIONS:
1. In a large sauté pan, heat the oil over medium heat. Add the scallions and garlic, and sauté until fragrant, about 1 minute. Add the bell pepper and snap peas and sauté until just tender, 2 to 3 minutes.
2. Add the chicken and cook until it is golden and fully cooked, and the vegetables are tender 4 to 5 minutes.
3. Add the soy sauce, rice vinegar, Sriracha (if using), and sesame seeds; toss well to combine. Allow the mixture to simmer for 1 to 2 minutes.
4. Stir in the cilantro, then garnish with a sprinkle of extra cilantro and sesame seeds. Serve immediately.

268. Creamy chicken stew

Made for: Dinner | **Prep Time:** 20 minutes | **Servings:** 04
Per Serving: Kcal: 228, Protein: 20g, Fat: 11g, Net Carb: 6g

INGREDIENTS:
- 3 leeks, halved and finely sliced
- 2 tbsp olive oil, plus extra if needed
- 1 tbsp butter
- 8 small chicken thighs
- 500ml chicken stock
- 1 tbsp Dijon mustard
- 75g crème fraîche
- 200g frozen peas
- 3 tbsp dried or fresh breadcrumbs
- small bunch of parsley, finely chopped

INSTRUCTIONS:
1. Tip the leeks and oil into a flameproof casserole dish on a low heat, add the butter and cook everything very gently for 10 mins or until the leeks are soft.
2. Put the chicken, skin-side down, in a large non-stick frying pan on a medium heat, cook until the skin browns, then turn and brown the other side. You shouldn't need any oil but if the skin starts to stick, add a little. Add the chicken to the leeks, leaving behind any fat in the pan.
3. Add the stock to the dish and bring to a simmer, season well, cover and cook for 30 mins on low. Stir in the mustard, crème fraîche and peas and bring to a

simmer. You should have quite a bit of sauce.
4. When you're ready to serve, put the grill on. Mix the breadcrumbs and parsley, sprinkle them over the chicken and grill until browned.

269. Garlic Chicken

Made for: Dinner | **Prep Time:** 25 minutes | **Servings:** 04
Per Serving: Kcal: 694, Protein: 48g, Fat: 49g, Net Carb: 10g

INGREDIENTS:

Cauliflower mash:
- One large cauliflower head (chopped).
- One cup (96g) of chicken stock.
- 3 tbsp butter (cubed).
- 1 tsp salt.
- 1 tsp fresh thyme (chopped).

Garlic chicken:
- 32 oz chicken drumsticks.
- Six garlic cloves (finely chopped).
- ½ cup (32g) fresh parsley (chopped).
- 2 oz butter.
- Juice of 1 lemon.
- 2 tbsp olive oil.

INSTRUCTIONS:
1. Preheat oven at 450 degrees.
2. Place the chicken in a greased ovenproof dish.
3. Drizzle olive oil and lemon juice on the chicken and top with garlic and parsley.
4. Bake for 40-45 minutes or until chicken is thoroughly cooked through and browned. Cauliflower mash:
5. In a large pan, bring chicken stock and salt to boil.
6. Add cauliflower, bring back to boil, reduce heat and simmer for 15-20 minutes, or until cauliflower is tender.
7. Take cauliflower from the pan and add to a blender with 3 tbsp of the stock.
8. Add the butter and thyme; blend until smooth and well combined.

270. Salmon, avocado & cucumber salad

Made for: Dinner | **Prep Time:** 20 minutes | **Servings:** 04
Per Serving: Kcal: 458, Protein: 23g, Fat: 38g, Net Carb: 2g

INGREDIENTS:
- 4 skinless salmon fillets, approx 100g each
- 3 avocados

- 1 cucumber
- 400g bag mixed salad leaves

For the dressing
- 4 tbsp chopped mint
- grated zest 1 and juice o limes
- 2 tsp clear honey
- 3 tbsp olive oil, plus a little extra for the salmon

INSTRUCTIONS:
1. Season the salmon, then rub with oil. Mix the dressing ingredients together. Halve, stone, peel and slice the avocados. Halve and quarter the cucumber lengthways, then cut into slices. Divide salad, avocado and cucumber between four plates, then drizzle with half the dressing.
   Heat a non-stick pan. Add the salmon and fry for 3-4 mins on each side until crisp but still moist inside. Put a salmon fillet on top of each salad and drizzle over the remaining dressing. Serve warm.

271. Roast salmon

Made for: Dinner | **Prep Time:** 65 minutes | **Servings:** 04
Per Serving: Kcal: 397, Protein: 35g, Fat: 27g, Net Carb: 1g

INGREDIENTS:
- 40g (1/8 cup) preserved lemon, flesh and pith removed
- 100ml gin
- 1kg side organic farmed or wild salmon (tail end)
- 50g (1/8 cup)) sea salt
- 50g (1/4 cup) golden caster sugar
- 1 tsp thyme leaves
- 1 tsp chilli flakes
- ½ small bunch dill, washed

For the preserved lemon roasting oil
- 30g preserved lemons, seeds removed
- 4 tbsp olive oil

INSTRUCTIONS:
1. In a food processor, blitz together the lemon and gin. Lay your salmon skin-side down in a roasting tin and pour over the lemon and gin mix. Combine the salt, sugar, thyme and chilli flakes, then spoon over the salmon. Cover with cling film and chill for at least 2 hrs.
2. Heat oven to 160C/140C fan/gas 3. Thirty mins before you want to cook the

salmon, remove it from the fridge and allow it to come to room temperature. To make the roasting oil, blitz the preserved lemons and olive oil. Gently rinse the cure from the salmon and pat dry with kitchen paper. Lay it skin-side down in an oiled roasting tray and pour over the roasting oil, rubbing it all over the fish. Cover the tin tightly with foil and roast for 15 mins.
3. Remove the foil and return the fish to the oven for a further 10 mins. Take out of the oven and rest for 5 mins, then scatter over freshly torn dill, to serve

272. Mighty Meaty Moussaka

Made for: Dinner | **Prep Time:** 25 minutes | **Servings:** 04
Per Serving: Kcal: 742, Protein: 43g, Fat: 59g, Net Carb: 10g

INGREDIENTS:
- 20 oz minced beef.
- One medium aubergine (thinly sliced)
- One onion (finely chopped).
- Two garlic cloves (crushed).
- ½ cup (112g) tomato puree.
- 4 tbsp olive oil.
- 1 tbsp paprika powder.
- 1 tsp salt.
- ½ tsp black pepper.
- ½ tsp cinnamon (ground).

Cheese sauce:
- 7 oz swiss cheese (grated).
- 3 oz cream cheese.
- ½ cup (116g) of thick cream.
- One garlic clove (crushed).
- ¼ tsp salt.

INSTRUCTIONS:
1. Preheat oven at 350 degrees.
2. In a large frying pan, fry the auberge slices until golden brown and softened. Set to one side.
3. In the same pan, cook the minced beef until browned. Add onion, garlic, and spices; pour in the tomato puree and simmer for 5 minutes.
4. In a pan, mix the cheese sauce ingredients (only using half of the swiss cheese). Stirring continuously, Simmer until sauce thickens.
5. Pour meat sauce into an ovenproof dish, layer the auberges on top and pour on the cheese sauce. Sprinkle the remaining swiss cheese on top.
6. Bake for 20-25 minutes or until cheese turns golden brown.

273. Creamy Keto Chicken

Made for: Dinner | **Prep Time:** 25 minutes | **Servings:** 04
Per Serving: Kcal: 758, Protein: 40g, Fat: 64g, Net Carb: 5g

INGREDIENTS:
- 32 oz chicken thighs (boneless and skinless).
- 16 oz cauliflower (florets).
- 7 oz cheddar cheese (grated).
- 4 oz cherry tomatoes (halved).
- 1 ½ oz butter.
- One leek (chopped).
- ¾ cup (180g) sour cream.
- ½ cup (112g) of cream cheese (softened).
- 3 tbsp pesto.
- 3 tbsp lemon juice (fresh).
- ½ tsp black pepper.

INSTRUCTIONS:
1. Preheat oven at 400 degrees.
2. In a large frying pan, melt the butter and fry chicken until cooked and golden brown.
3. In a bowl, mix sour cream, cream cheese, lemon juice, pesto, and Pepper until well combined.
4. Place chicken in a large ovenproof dish, pour cream cheese mixture on top.
5. Add cauliflower, leek, and tomatoes.
6. Bake in the oven for 25 minutes, remove and sprinkle cheese on top.
7. Bake for a further 10 minutes or until cheese is melted and golden brown.

274. Chicken Lettuce Wraps

Made for: Dinner | **Prep Time:** 20 minutes | **Servings:** 02
Per Serving: Kcal: 500, Protein: 42g, Fat: 28g, Net Carb: 5g

INGREDIENTS:
- 1 lb ground chicken
- 1 tbsp olive oil
- 2 tbsp red curry paste
- 1 tbsp ginger minced
- Four cloves garlic minced
- One red bell pepper sliced thinly
- Four green onions chopped
- 1 cup (90g) cabbage shredded or coleslaw mix
- 1/4 cup (64g) hoisin sauce
- 1/4 tsp salt or to taste
- 1/4 tsp pepper or to taste
- Five leaves basil chopped
- 1/2 head iceberg lettuce cut into half

INSTRUCTIONS:
1. Add olive oil to a large skillet and heat until oil is boiling. Add ground chicken and cook until no longer pink and starts to brown, break it up with a wooden spoon as necessary. It should take about 3 minutes.
2. Add red curry paste, ginger, garlic, peppers, coleslaw mix, and stir-fry for another 3 minutes. Add hoisin sauce and green onions, and toss. Remove from heat then add basil and toss. Transfer cooked chicken to a bowl.
3. Serve by placing spoonful's of chicken into pieces of lettuce, fold lettuce over like small tacos, and eat.

275. Spicy Salmon with Salsa

Made for: Dinner | **Prep Time:** 15 minutes | **Servings:** 02
Per Serving: Kcal: 445, Protein: 35g, Fat: 32g, Net Carb: 7g

INGREDIENTS:
- 4 salmon fillets.
- 1 tbsp olive oil.
- 4 tsp cajun seasoning.
- Two avocados (chopped into small chunks).
- One jalapeno (finely chopped).
- One red onion (finely chopped).
- 1 tbsp lime juice (fresh).
- 1 tbsp fresh coriander (finely chopped).

INSTRUCTIONS:
1. Season both sides of salmon with Cajun seasoning.
2. Heat the oil in a large frying pan and fry the salmon until extremely golden brown; turn and repeat for the other side.
3. Mix the avocados, jalapenos, onion, coriander, and lime until well combined.
4. Serve with salmon.

276. Cashew Chicken

Made for: Dinner | **Prep Time:** 25 minutes | **Servings:** 04
Per Serving: Kcal: 386, Protein: 22g, Fat: 24g, Net Carb: 5g

INGREDIENTS:
- Three raw chicken thighs boneless, skinless
- 2 tbsp coconut oil (for cooking)
- 1/4 cup (35g) raw cashews
- 1/2 medium Green Bell Pepper
- 1/2 tsp ground ginger
- 1 tbsp rice wine vinegar

- 1 1/2 tbsp liquid aminos
- 1/2 tbsp chilli garlic sauce
- 1 tbsp minced garlic
- 1 tbsp Sesame Oil
- 1 tbsp Sesame Seeds
- 1 tbsp green onions
- 1/4 medium white onion
- Salt + Pepper

INSTRUCTIONS:
1. Heat a pan over low heat and toast the cashews for 8 minutes or until they start to lightly brown and become fragrant. Remove and set aside.
2. Dice chicken thighs into 1-inch chunks. Cut onion and Pepper into equally large pieces.
3. Increase heat to high and add coconut oil to the pan.
4. Once the oil is up to temperature, add in the chicken thighs and allow them to cook through (about 5 minutes).
5. Once the chicken is fully cooked, add in the Pepper, onions, garlic, chilli garlic sauce, and seasonings (ginger, salt, Pepper). Allow cooking on high for 2-3 minutes.
6. Add liquid amino, rice wine vinegar, and cashews. Cook on high and allow the liquid to reduce down until it is a sticky consistency, there should not be excess liquid in the pan upon completing cooking.
7. Serve in a bowl, top with sesame seeds and drizzle with sesame oil. Enjoy!

277. Garlic Chicken Kebab

Made for: Dinner | **Prep Time:** 25 minutes | **Servings:** 04
Per Serving: Kcal: 276, Protein: 33g, Fat: 14g, Net Carb: 1g

INGREDIENTS:
- 32 oz chicken breast (cut into 1 inch cubes).
- Four garlic cloves (crushed).
- One lemon (zested and juiced).
- ½ cup (120g) of almond milk.
- ¼ cup (60g) olive oil.
- ¼ cup (15g) fresh parsley (finely chopped).
- ½ tsp salt.
- ¼ tsp black pepper.
- 1 tbsp mixed herbs (dried).

INSTRUCTIONS:
1. Heat the grill to high. Heat the oil in a medium-sized, non-stick frying pan,

add the mushrooms and fry over a high heat for 3 mins. Squeeze the sausagemeat out of their skins into nuggets, add to the pan and fry for a further 5 mins until golden brown. Add the garlic and asparagus and cook for another 1 min.
2. Whisk the eggs, soured cream, mustard and tarragon in a jug. Season well, then pour the egg mixture in to the pan. Cook for 3-4 mins, then grill for a further 1-2 mins or until the top has just set with a slight wobble in the middle. Serve with the salad leaves, if you like.

278. Antipasto Meat Sticks

Made for: Dinner | **Prep Time:** 15 minutes | **Servings:** 02
Per Serving: Kcal: 250, Protein: 15g, Fat: 28g, Net Carb: 1g

INGREDIENTS:
- 4 slices salami.
- Four slices sandwich ham.
- Four slices pepperoni.
- 4 slices cheddar cheese.
- Four slices mozzarella.
- One handful lettuce (chopped)
- 2 tbsp olive oil.
- 1 tbsp apple cider vinegar.
- 1 tbsp mayonnaise.
- ½ tsp mixed herbs (dried).

INSTRUCTIONS:
1. In 4 separate piles, layer the meat slices from biggest to smallest.
2. Spread with mayonnaise and add the cheese slices.
3. Sprinkle on lettuce.
4. Roll each pile into a tight sausage shape; secure with a toothpick.
5. In a dish, add olive oil, vinegar, and herbs to use as a dip for antipasto sticks.

279. Tarragon, mushroom & sausage frittata

Made for: Dinner | **Prep Time:** 20 minutes | **Servings:** 02
Per Serving: Kcal: 433, Protein: 25g, Fat: 32g, Net Carb: 1g

INGREDIENTS:
- 1 tbsp olive oil
- 200g (3/2 cup) chestnut mushrooms, sliced
- 2 Poultry sausage
- 1 garlic clove, crushed
- 100g (1/2 cup) fine asparagus
- 3 large eggs

- 2 tbsp half-fat soured cream
- 1 tbsp wholegrain mustard
- 1 tbsp chopped tarragon
- mixed rocket salad, to serve (optional)

INSTRUCTIONS:
1. Heat the grill to high. Heat the oil in a medium-sized, non-stick frying pan, add the mushrooms and fry over a high heat for 3 mins. Squeeze the sausagemeat out of their skins into nuggets, add to the pan and fry for a further 5 mins until golden brown. Add the garlic and asparagus and cook for another 1 min.
2. Whisk the eggs, soured cream, mustard and tarragon in a jug. Season well, then pour the egg mixture in to the pan. Cook for 3-4 mins, then grill for a further 1-2 mins or until the top has just set with a slight wobble in the middle. Serve with the salad leaves, if you like.

280. Healthy Lunchtime Ham

Made for: Dinner | **Prep Time:** 20 minutes | **Servings:** 02
Per Serving: Kcal: 459, Protein: 33g, Fat: 31g, Net Carb: 5g

INGREDIENTS:
- 5 iceberg lettuce leaves.
- Four slices sandwich ham.
- 4 slices cheddar cheese.
- ¼ cup (56g) guacamole.
- One tomato (sliced).
- ½ red onion (finely sliced.

INSTRUCTIONS:
1. Layer lettuce leaves onto a sheet of cling film. Ensure the leaves overlap with each other.
2. Layer the ham and cheese onto the leaves.
3. Do the same with tomato and onion and finally top with guacamole.
4. Using the clingfilm (as if you were using a sushi mat), roll the lettuce tightly to make the wrap.
5. When completely rolled, cut the wrap in half.

281. Chunky Salsa Tacos

Made for: Dinner | **Prep Time:** 20 minutes | **Servings:** 02
Per Serving: Kcal: 306, Protein: 15g, Fat: 22g, Net Carb: 3g

INGREDIENTS:
- Two large avocados (cut into small chunks).

- One tomato (cut into chunks).
- ½ red onion (roughly chopped).
- ¼ cup (15g) fresh coriander (finely chopped).
- One garlic clove (finely chopped).
- 3 tbsp lime juice (fresh).
- 1 tbsp jalapeno (finely chopped).
- ½ tsp salt.
- ½ tsp black pepper.

INSTRUCTIONS:
1. Preheat oven at 400 degrees.
2. Line a baking tray with greaseproof paper.
3. Make six piles of cheese with a large gap between them.
4. Bake for 10 minutes until cheese is melted and golden brown. Allow to slightly cool.
5. Place a large wire rack over the sink. Carefully place each melted cheese piece on the shelf and allow the edges to hang down between the wire rack bars.
6. Let cool completely.
7. Add all of the ingredients from the filling list to a bowl and mix well until combined.
8. Take each cheesy taco shell and add the filling.

282. Tasty Salted Turnip Fries

Made for: Dinner | **Prep Time:** 20 minutes | **Servings:** 02
Per Serving: Kcal: 219, Protein: 2g, Fat: 22g, Net Carb: 5g

INGREDIENTS:
- 16 oz turnips.
- 6 tbsp olive oil.
- 2 tsp onion powder.
- ½ tsp paprika.
- 1 tsp salt.

INSTRUCTIONS:
1. Preheat oven at 400 degrees.
2. Wash and peel the turnips; cut into ½ inch strips.
3. In a large bowl, toss the turnips in 2 tbsp of olive oil, salt, onion powder, and paprika.
4. Add remaining oil to a baking tray and heat in the oven for 5 minutes.
5. Bake for 25-30 minutes or until fries are golden brown and crispy.

283. Prawn, coconut & tomato curry

Made for: Dinner | **Prep Time:** 30 minutes | **Servings:** 04
Per Serving: Kcal: 335, Protein: 19g, Fat: 26g, Net Carb: 1g

INGREDIENTS:
- 2 tbsp vegetable oil
- 1 medium onion, thinly sliced
- 2 garlic cloves, sliced
- 1 green chilli, deseeded and sliced
- 3 tbsp curry paste
- 1 tbsp tomato purée
- 200ml vegetable stock
- 200ml coconut cream
- 350g raw prawn
- coriander sprigs and rice, to serve

INSTRUCTIONS:
1. Heat the oil in a large frying pan. Fry the onion, garlic and half the chilli for 5 mins or until softened. Add the curry paste and cook for 1 min more. Add the tomato purée, stock and coconut cream.
2. Simmer on medium heat for 10 mins, then add the prawns. Cook for 3 mins or until they turn opaque. Scatter on the remaining green chillies and coriander sprigs, then serve with rice.

284. Eggs with Asparagus

Made for: Dinner | **Prep Time:** 30 minutes | **Servings:** 02
Per Serving: Kcal: 301, Protein: 14g, Fat: 26g, Net Carb: 2g

INGREDIENTS:
- 2 pounds asparagus
- 1-pint cherry tomatoes
- Four eggs
- Two tablespoons olive oil
- Two teaspoons chopped fresh thyme
- Salt and Pepper to taste

INSTRUCTIONS:
1. Preheat the oven to 400°F. Grease a baking sheet with non-stick cooking spray.
2. Arrange the asparagus and cherry tomatoes in an even layer on the baking sheet. Drizzle the olive oil over the vegetables; season with the thyme and salt and Pepper to taste.
3. Roast in the oven until the asparagus is nearly tender and the tomatoes are wrinkled, 10 to 12 minutes.
4. Crack the eggs on top of the asparagus; season each with salt and Pepper.
5. Return to the oven and bake until the egg whites are set but the yolks are still jiggly, 7 to 8 minutes more.
6. To serve, divide the asparagus, tomatoes, and eggs among four plates.

285. Hot chicken with sausages

Made for: Dinner | **Prep Time:** 30 minutes | **Servings:** 01
Per Serving: Kcal: 587, Protein: 39g, Fat: 38g, Net Carb: 4g

INGREDIENTS:
- 1 tbsp olive oil
- 2 good-sized skin-on chicken thighs
- 1 (about 100g) spicy sausage
- 1-2 roasted red peppers from a jar, depending on their size (Peppadew are good in this)
- 1 red onions, halved and cut into crescent moon-shaped slices
- 100g (1/2 cup)) can cherry tomatoes
- 1/2 tsp chilli flakes
- 2 garlic cloves, grated to a purée
- 1 tbsp sherry vinegar
- 1 rosemary sprigs, leaves picked from 1, the others left whole
- 30ml chicken stock

INSTRUCTIONS:
1. Heat oven to 200C/180C fan/gas 6. Heat half the oil in a big shallow casserole dish in which the thighs can lie in a single layer – one 30cm across is ideal, if you use a bigger dish the sauce may evaporate. Quickly brown the chicken on both sides – you don't want to cook the chicken through, just get some colour on it – then remove from the pan. Do the same with the sausages in the remaining oil, colouring them all over. Cut the sausages on the diagonal into three or four pieces. Drain the peppers of their brine and cut into broad strips.
2. Add the onions and tomatoes to the dish or roasting tin with the chilli, garlic, seasoning, sherry vinegar, rosemary and sausages. Heat the stock and add that too. Mix everything together. Arrange so that the chicken is on top. Bake in the oven for 30 mins, stirring the 'sauce' that forms around the vegetables halfway through.
3. When 30 mins is up, add the peppers and cook for another 10 mins. The chicken should be cooked through with a thick sauce around it.

286. Overnight Oats

Made for: Dinner | Prep Time: 10 minutes | Servings: 02
Per Serving: Kcal: 533, Protein: 15g, Fat: 70g, Net Carb: 3g

INGREDIENTS:
- 1 cup (80g) organic rolled oats
- 2 ½ cups (350g) Strawberry Cashew Milk
- 1 Tablespoon Chia seeds
- 1 Tablespoon Whole flax seeds

INSTRUCTIONS:
1. Place rolled oats, chia seeds, and flax seeds in a large bowl. Poor in 2 ½ cups of strawberry cashew milk (or preferred dairy, nut or seed milk) and stir well to combine. Cover and store in the fridge for 1 hour or overnight.
2. Check consistency and add additional Strawberry Cashew Milk as desired. Portion into individual containers. Add fresh strawberries, cashews, chia seeds, flax seeds, or extra Strawberry Cashew Milk as toppings. Enjoy immediately or store in airtight containers for up to 5 days.

287. Curry Marinated Halloumi

Made for: Dinner | Prep Time: 30 minutes | Servings: 01
Per Serving: Kcal: 605, Protein: 25g, Fat: 55g, Net Carb: 3g

INGREDIENTS:
- 125 g halloumi (4.4 oz)
- 1 tsp curry spice mix
- 1 tbsp extra virgin olive oil (15 ml)
- 1/2 tbsp ghee or butter, or more olive oil (10 ml)
- Optional: fresh herbs such as cilantro to serve

INSTRUCTIONS:
1. Slice the halloumi into about eight 1 1/4 cm (1/2 inch) slices. Mix the olive oil and spice mix together to form a paste. Brush both sides of each halloumi slice with the paste.
2. Place in the fridge to marinate at least 15 minutes, but preferably a few hours.
3. Add the butter/ghee/oil to a large frypan and heat over medium heat.
4. Add the halloumi and cook 3-4 minutes on each side until browned.
5. Remove and serve immediately. If eaten as a main dish, serve alongside steamed or roasted vegetables. Halloumi should always be eaten warm. You can store

these in the fridge for up to 3 days and reheat before serving.

288. Simple Keto Chili

Made for: Dinner | Prep Time: 30 minutes | Servings: 04
Per Serving: Kcal: 424, Protein: 21g, Fat: 33g, Net Carb: 5g

INGREDIENTS:
- 1 tbsp ghee or butter (15 ml)
- 1 small yellow onion, finely diced (70 g/2.5 oz)
- 1 large stick celery, diced (64 g/2.3 oz)
- 2 cloves garlic, minced
- 450 g ground beef (1 lb)
- 1 medium red bell pepper, diced (120 g/4.2 oz)
- 1 tsp medium chilli powder, or to taste
- 1 tsp ground cumin
- 1 tsp dried oregano
- 1 tin chopped tomatoes (400 g/14.1 oz)
- 2 tbsp unsweetened tomato paste (30 g/1.1 oz).
- sea salt and ground black pepper, to taste
- 2 tbsp chopped cilantro (coriander), plus more for topping
- 2 tbsp extra virgin olive oil (30 ml)
- Optional: sour cream or full-fat yogurt, sliced avocado and/or lime wedges

INSTRUCTIONS:
1. Heat the ghee in a non stick frying pan or cast iron skillet. Add the onion and celery and fry on a medium heat for 2 - 3 minutes until soft. Add the garlic for a further 30 seconds.
2. Add the beef and fry for a further 4 to 5 minutes, breaking the meat up with a wooden spatula as it cooks.
3. Add the chopped red pepper, spices, tomatoes, tomato puree, seasoning and chopped cilantro. Simmer for 10 - 15 minutes until thick.
4. Check seasoning and adjust to taste. If it gets too dry, add some water or stock and stir through. When cooked, drizzle with olive oil.
5. Optionally, serve with sour cream and more fresh coriander. Serve with cauliflower rice, zucchini noodles or roasted vegetables of choice.
6. Store in the fridge in an airtight container for up to 4 days, or freezer for up to 3 months.

289. Spicy Kick-Start

Made for: Dinner | **Prep Time:** 20 minutes | **Servings:** 02
Per Serving: Kcal: 689, Protein: 35g, Fat: 59g, Net Carb: 4g

INGREDIENTS:
- 4 large eggs.
- 8 oz can of mackerel in tomato sauce.
- ½ red onion (finely sliced).
- ¼ cup (60g) olive oil.
- 2 oz lettuce.
- 2 tbsp butter.
- Salt and pepper.

INSTRUCTIONS:
1. Melt butter in a frying pan and cook the eggs to your preference.
2. On a serving plate, place lettuce and top with onion. Add the eggs and mackerel to the plate.
3. Drizzle olive oil over the lettuce and season with salt and pepper.

290. Keto-Classic Cereal

Made for: Dinner | **Prep Time:** 20 minutes | **Servings:** 04
Per Serving: Kcal: 207, Protein: 7g, Fat: 19g, Net Carb: 3g

INGREDIENTS:
- 1 cup (112g) almond flour.
- 2 tbsp water.
- 2 tbsp sunflower seeds.
- 1 tbsp coconut oil.
- 1 tbsp flaxseed meal.
- 1 tsp vanilla extract.
- 1 tsp cinnamon (ground).
- ¼ tsp salt.

INSTRUCTIONS:
1. Preheat oven at 350 degrees.
2. Add almond flour, sunflower seeds, flaxseed meal, cinnamon, and salt to a blender and blend until sunflower seeds are finely chopped.
3. Mix in the water and coconut oil and blend until a dough is formed.
4. Place dough on a piece of greaseproof paper and press flat. Place another piece of greaseproof paper on top and roll the dough until it is approximately 3mm in thickness.
5. Remove top paper and cut the dough into 1-inch squares.
6. Place the greaseproof paper (with the cut squares) on to a baking tray.
7. Bake in the oven for 10-15 minutes or until lightly browned and crisp.

8. Allow to cool and then separate the squares.
9. Serve with unsweetened almond milk.

291. Mushroom baked

Made for: Dinner | **Prep Time:** 15 minutes | **Servings:** 02
Per Serving: Kcal: 578, Protein: 30g, Fat: 47g, Net Carb: 6g

INGREDIENTS:
- 2 large deep cup (150g) mushrooms (stem removed).
- Four slices of bacon (cooked and chopped).
- Two large eggs.
- 1/10 cup (10g) parmesan (grated).
- Cooking spray.

INSTRUCTIONS:
1. Preheat oven at 375 degrees.
2. On a baking tray, spray the mushrooms with cooking spray and bake for 10 minutes.
3. Split the bacon and parmesan between the two mushrooms and bake for an additional 5 minutes.
4. Crack an egg into each mushroom and bake for an additional 10 minutes.

292. Cauliflower Hash

Made for: Dinner | **Prep Time:** 20 minutes | **Servings:** 04
Per Serving: Kcal: 556, Protein: 14g, Fat: 47g, Net Carb: 5g

INGREDIENTS:
- 16 oz cauliflower (head grated).
- Three large eggs.
- ½ onion (finely diced).
- 4 oz butter.
- 1 tsp salt.
- ¼ tsp black pepper.

INSTRUCTIONS:
1. Add all ingredients (except butter) to a large bowl and mix until well combined. Allow standing for 10 minutes.
2. Melt ¼ butter in a large frying pan. Add two scoops of the cauliflower mixture; flatten carefully until they are 3-4 inches in diameter.
3. Fry for 4-5 minutes on each side.
4. Repeat until all the mixture has gone.

293. Salmon Lemon Sauce

Made for: Dinner | **Prep Time:** 20 minutes | **Servings:** 04
Per Serving: Kcal: 400, Protein: 27g, Fat: 22g, Net Carb: 8g

INGREDIENTS:

- 4 (5 ounces) salmon fillets, skins removed
- salt and Pepper to taste
- 1 (12 ounces) container ricotta
- 1/2 cup (45g) Parmigiano Reggiano (parmesan), grated
- Two tablespoons basil, chopped
- Two teaspoons lemon zest
- salt and Pepper to taste
- 1/2 pound asparagus, trimmed
- One tablespoon butter
- 1/2 cup (46g) chicken broth
- Two tablespoons lemon juice
- Two teaspoons cornstarch

INSTRUCTIONS:

1. Season the salmon fillets with salt and Pepper to taste, lay them down with the skin side up, top with the mixture of the ricotta, parmesan, basil, lemon zest, salt and Pepper, several spears of asparagus and roll them up before placing them on a greased baking sheet with the seam side down.
2. Bake in a preheated 425F/220C oven until the salmon is just cooked, about 15-20 minutes.
3. Meanwhile, melt the butter in a small saucepan over medium heat, add the mixture of the broth, lemon juice, and corn starch and heat until it thickens, about 3-5 minutes.
4. Serve the salmon rolls topped with the lemon sauce and optionally garnish with more basil and lemon zest.

294. Cheese & Onion omelette

Made for: Dinner | Prep Time: 15 minutes | Servings: 02
Per Serving: Kcal: 516, Protein: 27g, Fat: 44g, Net Carb: 5g

INGREDIENTS:

- 4 large mushrooms.
- Three large eggs.
- ¼ onion (finely chopped).
- 1 oz cheddar cheese (grated).
- 1 oz butter.
- Salt and pepper.

INSTRUCTIONS:

1. Whisk the eggs until smooth; add salt and pepper.
2. Over medium heat, melt the butter in a large frying pan. Add onion and mushrooms and cook until lightly browned and softened. Pour the egg

mixture over the onions and mushrooms.
3. As the omelette is cooking and begins to firm, add the cheese.
4. Ease around the edges of the omelette with a spatula and fold in half.
5. Allow cooking until all is golden brown.

295. Hot & Spicy Chicken

Made for: Dinner | Prep Time: 25 minutes | Servings: 02
Per Serving: Kcal: 314, Protein: 17g, Fat: 23g, Net Carb: 6g

INGREDIENTS:

- 15 chicken wings.
- ½ cup (120g) chilli paste.
- ¼ cup (25g) erythritol
- ⅓ cup (94g) greek yogurt (full fat).
- ¼ cup (60g) mayonnaise.
- 2 tbsp soy sauce.
- 2 tbsp rice wine vinegar.
- 1 ½ tbsp lime juice (fresh).
- Pinch of salt.

INSTRUCTIONS:

1. Mix chilli paste, erythritol, soy sauce, and vinegar.
2. Add chicken wings to the sauce mixture and ensure each side is completely coated with the sauce.
3. Chill for 2-3 hours.
4. Preheat oven at 400 degrees.
5. Bake wings for 15 minutes, turn over and bake for an additional 15 minutes.
6. On a high heated grill, brown the chicken wings for 5-6 minutes.
7. Mix greek yoghurt, mayonnaise, lime juice, and salt. Use as a dipping sauce for the chicken wings.

296. Cauliflower Cheese Bake

Made for: Dinner | Prep Time: 15 minutes | Servings: 02
Per Serving: Kcal: 393, Protein: 15g, Fat: 33g, Net Carb: 7g

INGREDIENTS:

- 1 large cauliflower head.
- 8 oz thick cream.
- 4 oz cheddar (grated).
- 4 oz mozzarella (grated).
- 3 oz cream cheese (softened).
- 1 ½ tsp paprika.
- 1 tsp salt.
- ½ tsp black pepper.

INSTRUCTIONS:

1. Preheat oven at 375 degrees.

2. Cut cauliflower into 1-inch pieces and steam for 5 minutes until just becoming tender.
3. In a medium-sized pan, combine thick cream, cheddar, mozzarella, cream cheese, salt, pepper, and paprika. Over medium heat, I was stirring continuously, until a smooth sauce is formed.
4. Add the cauliflower to a baking dish and pour over the cheese sauce; stir to ensure all cauliflower is covered.
5. Bake for 30 minutes or until the top is bubbling and golden.

297. Carob Avocado Mousse

Made for: Dinner | **Prep Time:** 15 minutes | **Servings:** 04
Per Serving: Kcal: 859, Protein: 55g, Fat: 39g, Net Carb: 3g

INGREDIENTS:
- 2 Ripe bananas
- 2 Ripe avocados
- 2/3 Carob powder
- 3 tsp erythritol
- 1 tsp Vanilla extract
- 1/8 tsp Stevia (or to taste)

INSTRUCTIONS:
1. Using a small bowl, peel the banana and break into pieces. Smash well with a fork or potato masher. Add the avocados and do the same. Mix well till banana and avocado are incorporated. For a more smooth mousse texture, purée the mash with a hand blender or small food processor until smooth.
2. Add in the carob powder slowly, in three parts, and combine well.
3. Add erythritol and continue to blend.
4. Taste test, and add 1/8 teaspoon of stevia for additional sweetness to taste.
5. Transfer the mousse to individual bowls and serve. Store in the fridge until ready to eat, up to five days. Keeps well in the freezer for six months.

298. Avocado Egg Salad

Made for: Dinner | **Prep Time:** 15 minutes | **Servings:** 04
Per Serving: Kcal: 236, Protein: 11g, Fat: 21g, Net Carb: 3g

INGREDIENTS:
- Four large hard-boiled eggs, diced
- One avocado, diced
- Two green onions, sliced into thin rounds

- Four slices of low-sodium bacon, cooked to the desired crisp and crumbled
- ¼ cup (56g) nonfat plain yoghurt
- One tablespoon low-fat sour cream
- One whole lime, juiced
- One tablespoon snipped fresh dill
- 1/4 teaspoon salt
- 1/8 teaspoon fresh ground pepper
- dill and crumbled bacon, for garnish (optional)

INSTRUCTIONS:
1. To "boil" eggs, place each egg in the cavity of a muffin tin and hard "boil" in the oven for 30 minutes at 325F.
2. Remove from oven and transfer eggs to ice water; peel and dice.
3. In a salad bowl, combine diced eggs, avocado, green onions, and bacon; set aside.
4. In a mixing bowl, whisk together yoghurt, sour cream, lime juice, dill, salt, and pepper; whisk until well combined.
5. Add yoghurt mixture to the egg salad; stir until combined.
6. Garnish with dill and crumbled bacon.
7. Serve.
8. You can also spread the salad on four slices of bread; add tomatoes and lettuce to make a delicious egg salad sandwich.
9. Keep refrigerated.

299. Keto-Buzz Blueberry

Made for: Dinner | **Prep Time:** 25 minutes | **Servings:** 02
Per Serving: Kcal: 189, Protein: 12g, Fat: 13g, Net Carb: 4g

INGREDIENTS:
- Three large eggs.
- ½ cup (56g) almond flour.
- ¼ cup (60) of milk.
- ¼ cup (47.5g) of fresh blueberries.
- 2 tbsp coconut flour.
- 2 tbsp sweetener (granulated).
- 1 tsp cinnamon (ground).
- ½ tsp baking powder.

INSTRUCTIONS:
1. Add all ingredients (except blueberries) to a blender and mix until a thick batter is formed.
2. Add the blended mixture to a bowl and stir in blueberries.
3. Grease a large non-stick frying pan and allow the pot to get hot over medium heat.

4. Pour ¼ cup of the mixture into the hot pan, allow to cook for 2 - 3 minutes, or until the edges start to crisp and turn lightly browned. Flip and repeat.
5. Repeat the process using the remaining batter.

300. Perfect Mozzarella

Made for: Dinner | **Prep Time:** 15 minutes | **Servings:** 04
Per Serving: Kcal: 258, Protein: 16g, Fat: 18g, Net Carb: 5g

INGREDIENTS:
- 3 eggs.
- 8 oz mozzarella (grated).
- 4 oz bacon (grilled).
- 2 oz cream cheese.
- ⅔ cup (74.5g) almond flour.
- ½ cup (56g) cheddar cheese (grated).
- ⅓ cup (37g) coconut flour.
- 2 tsp baking powder.
- 1 tsp salt.

INSTRUCTIONS:
1. Preheat oven at 350 degrees.
2. Microwave the cream cheese and mozzarella for 60 seconds. Stir and microwave for an additional 60 seconds.
3. Put one egg, almond flour, coconut flour, baking powder, and salt into a blender and pour in the melted cheese mixture. Blend until a dough forms.
4. Split the dough into eight pieces. Flatten each piece to form a 5-inch circle, place on a baking tray lined with baking paper.
5. Scramble the remaining two eggs and divide between each circle; do the same with bacon and cheddar cheese.
6. Fold the edges in and seal the semi-circle using fingertips.
7. Bake for 20 minutes or until lightly browned.

301. Shredded with Chicken

Made for: Dinner | **Prep Time:** 15 minutes | **Servings:** 04
Per Serving: Kcal: 436, Protein: 67g, Fat: 66g, Net Carb: 5g

INGREDIENTS:
- 4 cups (300g) mixed salad greens or 5 oz container
- One fennel, fronds removed (1 cup shredded)
- ¼ red cabbage, shredded (1 cup shredded)
- 1/8 red onion (1/4 cup)
- ½ cup (32g) fresh herbs, such as mint, parsley, and cilantro
- Two chicken breasts
- 1 Tbsp Adobo Spice Mix
- Whipped Lemon Vinaigrette

INSTRUCTIONS:
1. Preheat grill on high. Season chicken evenly with a spice mix. Grill on medium-high for 10 minutes, turning halfway through. Set aside to cool.
2. Prepare the salad by rough chopping mixed greens and place equally in two salad bowls. Using a mandolin, shave fennel bulb on the first or mini-setting of your mandolin, along with the red onion. If slicing with a knife, slice ¼ inch thin or thinner. Slice fennel shreds in half and toss with greens.
3. Shave the red cabbage on the other mandolin setting for ¼ inch slices. Mix with greens and fennel. Add fresh mint, parsley, dill, or cilantro. Lightly toss with Whipped Lemon Vinaigrette. Finish with sliced chicken breast. Garnish with avocado, feta, or goat cheese if desired. Holds well for meal prep for five days.

302. Baked Jalapeno Poppers

Made for: Dinner | **Prep Time:** 25 minutes | **Servings:** 04
Per Serving: Kcal: 278, Protein: 18g, Fat: 47g, Net Carb: 1g

INGREDIENTS:
- 12 large jalapeños
- 12 oz. (340g) cream cheese - room temp
- 8 oz. (225g) shredded cheddar cheese
- 8 oz. (225g) bacon - cooked and crumbled
- 2-3 tbsp chopped chives
- 1/2 tsp garlic powder
- Sea salt and pepper - to taste

INSTRUCTIONS:
1. Preheat the oven to 360°F/180°C and line a large rimmed baking sheet with parchment paper.
2. Prepare the jalapeños: using a paring knife, cut each one in half, lengthwise. Carefully cut the ribs, then deseed and discard. Place the jalapeño halves on the prepared baking tray, cut side up.
3. In a mixing bowl, add cream cheese, shredded cheese, crumbled bacon, chives, garlic powder, and season with

salt and pepper to your taste. Mix until well combined.

4. Stuff each jalapeño with the cheese mixture, then place the baking tray in the preheated oven.
5. Bake for 15-20 minutes or until the peppers are tender and golden on tops.
6. Sprinkle with chives if desired and enjoy while hot!

303. Keto Bacon Wrapped

Made for: Dinner | **Prep Time:** 20 minutes | **Servings:** 02
Per Serving: Kcal: 321, Protein: 35g, Fat: 81g, Net Carb: 2g

INGREDIENTS:
- 1 lb (450g) extra-large raw shrimp - peeled, deveined, tail on
- sea salt and pepper - to taste
- 1/4 tsp chilli powder
- 1/4 tsp cayenne pepper
- 1 tsp smoked paprika
- 1 Tbsp fresh lemon juice
- 1 Tbsp olive oil
- 6-8 very thin slices of bacon - (about 12 oz. / 340g)

Keto white Sauce:
- 1 cup mayonnaise
- 1 Tbsp dijon mustard
- 2 tsp prepared horseradish
- 2 Tbsp apple cider vinegar
- 1 tsp garlic powder
- sea salt and pepper - to taste

INSTRUCTIONS:
1. Preheat the oven to 400°F (200°C) and line a large baking tray with parchment paper.
2. Place the raw shrimp into a bowl and sprinkle with seasonings. Drizzle olive oil and fresh lemon juice and gently toss to coat.
3. Cut the bacon strips in half and wrap each shrimp in one bacon half-slice. Insert a toothpick through the bacon to secure the wrap.
4. Arrange the shrimp in a single layer on the prepared pan. Roast the bacon-wrapped shrimp for 10-12 minutes, flipping it halfway.
5. Meanwhile, combine all sauce ingredients in a jug and whisk to emulsify. Refrigerate until ready to use.
6. Once the shrimp is done, carefully remove the toothpicks and transfer it to a serving plate.
7. Serve with white Keto sauce and Enjoy!

304. Roasted Chicken

Made for: Dinner | **Prep Time:** 25 minutes | **Servings:** 04
Per Serving: Kcal: 553, Protein: 37g, Fat: 39g, Net Carb: 9g

INGREDIENTS:
- Four chicken thighs
- 1½ pounds carrots, peeled and trimmed
- One large onion, peeled and cut into eighths
- One head of garlic
- Four tablespoons olive oil
- One tablespoon chopped fresh rosemary
- Kosher salt and freshly ground black pepper, to taste

INSTRUCTIONS:
1. Preheat the oven to 425°F.
2. Arrange the carrots and onion in a single layer on a greased baking sheet.
3. Slice the top of a head of garlic; discard the top, and place it on the tray.
4. Drizzle 2 tablespoons of olive oil over the vegetables; season with the rosemary, and salt and pepper.
5. Top with the chicken thighs. Rub each leg with one teaspoon olive oil; season with salt and pepper.
6. Roast in the oven until the chicken skin is golden, and the carrots are tender, 15 to 20 minutes.
7. To serve, divide the vegetables and chicken thighs among four plates.

305. Crispy Keto Cauliflower

Made for: Dinner | **Prep Time:** 10 minutes | **Servings:** 02
Per Serving: Kcal: 188, Protein: 15g, Fat: 12g, Net Carb: 4g

INGREDIENTS:
- 2 large eggs.
- 12 oz cauliflower rice (frozen).
- Olive oil for frying.
- ½ cup (50g) parmesan (grated).
- ½ tsp salt.
- ¼ tsp black pepper.
- ⅛ tsp paprika.

INSTRUCTIONS:
1. Microwave the cauliflower rice and allow it to soften.
2. Mix all ingredients, except the eggs, together with the rice until well combined.
3. When the mixture is thoroughly combined, stir in the eggs and mix well.

4. Heat olive oil in a large frying pan and scoop 1 heaped tbsp of mixture into the pan. Fry for 2 minutes on each side until crispy and golden brown.
5. Repeat the process until all mixture has gone.

306.   Tuna Stuffed Avocado

Made for: Dinner | **Prep Time:** 10 minutes | **Servings:** 02
Per Serving: Kcal: 476, Protein: 32g, Fat: 34g, Net Carb: 2g

INGREDIENTS:
- 1 avocado pitted
- 1 small can tuna (I prefer oil-packed tuna) drained
- 1 teaspoon mayo or more, to taste
- 1 teaspoon grainy mustard (I used Maille Old Style)
- Small squeeze of lime juice
- Chives chopped, to taste
- Salt & pepper to taste
- Sriracha drizzled, to taste

INSTRUCTIONS:
1. Cut your avocado in half and remove the pit.
2. In a small bowl, mix the tuna, mayo, mustard, lime juice, chives, and salt & pepper until combined. Give it a taste and adjust the ingredients as needed.
3. Spoon the tuna mixture equally into each avocado half.
4. Drizzle sriracha over top.
5. Eat immediately; I just use a small spoon and dig right in.

307.   Bacon Pancakes

Made for: Dinner | **Prep Time:** 20 minutes | **Servings:** 02
Per Serving: Kcal: 663, Protein: 23g, Fat: 61g, Net Carb: 4g

INGREDIENTS:
- 6 pieces bacon, diced
- 3 eggs
- 1/4 cup (60g) almond butter
- 2 tbsp grass-fed butter, melted

INSTRUCTIONS:
1. Heat a skillet over medium heat and add diced bacon. Cook, stirring occasionally, until the bacon is getting crispy, about 6-7 minutes. Remove and place on a paper towel lined plate and reserve bacon grease in the pan.
2. While the bacon is cooking, mix the eggs,

almond butter and butter together in a bowl.
3. When the bacon is finished, add it to the bowl and mix again.
4. In the same skillet you cooked the bacon in over medium-low heat, add a couple of large spoonfuls of the batter. Cook about 3-4 minutes on each side.

308.   Antipasto Salad Recipe

Made for: Dinner | **Prep Time:** 20 minutes | **Servings:** 04
Per Serving: Kcal: 462, Protein: 14g, Fat: 41g, Net Carb: 6g

INGREDIENTS:
- One large head or two hearts romaine chopped
- 4 ounces prosciutto cut in strips
- 4 ounces salami or pepperoni cubed
- 1/2 cup (84g) artichoke hearts sliced
- 1/2 cup (90g) olives mix of black and green
- 1/2 cup (120g) hot or sweet peppers pickled or roasted
- Italian dressing to taste

INSTRUCTIONS:
1. Combine all ingredients in a large salad bowl. Toss with dressing.

309.   Cheese & Tomato Salad

Made for: Dinner | **Prep Time:** 10 minutes | **Servings:** 04
Per Serving: Kcal: 216, Protein: 15g, Fat: 18g, Net Carb: 3g

INGREDIENTS:
- 8 oz mozzarella.
- 8 oz cherry tomatoes.
- 2 tbsp green pesto.

INSTRUCTIONS:
1. Rip the mozzarella into bite-size pieces and halve the tomatoes.
2. Stir in the pesto until well combined.

310.   Turkey Basil-Mayo

Made for: Dinner | **Prep Time:** 20 minutes | **Servings:** 04
Per Serving: Kcal: 142, Protein: 44g, Fat: 24g, Net Carb: 7g

INGREDIENTS:
- 1/2 cup (115g) gluten-free mayonnaise (I like Hellmann's Olive Oil Mayo)
- Six large basil leaves, torn
- One teaspoon lemon juice
- One garlic clove, chopped
- salt

- pepper

INSTRUCTIONS:
1. Combine ingredients in a small food processor then process until smooth. Alternatively, mince basil and garlic then whisk all ingredients together. It can be done a couple of days ahead of time.
2. Layout two large lettuce leaves, then layer on one slice of turkey and slather with Basil-Mayo. Layer on the second slice of turkey followed by the bacon and a few slices of both avocado and tomato. Season lightly with salt and pepper, then fold the bottom up, the sides in, and roll like a burrito. Slice in half then serves cold.

311. Healthy Egg Muffins

Made for: Dinner | **Prep Time:** 20 minutes | **Servings:** 04
Per Serving: Kcal: 312, Protein: 26g, Fat: 21g, Net Carb: 3g

INGREDIENTS:
- 1/2 lb (225g) pre-cooked ham, diced (can sub bacon or sausage)
- 1 bell pepper, finely diced
- 1/2 onion finely diced
- 10 eggs
- 1/2 tsp salt
- 1/2 tsp pepper
- 2 tsbp avocado oil or other fat of choice (I like bacon fat)

INSTRUCTIONS:
1. Preheat oven to 375° Fahrenheit.
2. Chop ham, bell pepper and onion as noted.
3. Crack eggs in a large bowl and whisk well. Add the chopped ingredients and 1/2 tsp each of salt and pepper and mix.
4. Grease muffin tin with fat/oil (make sure each section is covered well from top to bottom or the eggs will stick). Or you can use muffin tin liners.
5. Spoon the egg mixture into the muffin tin, filling them almost full (they will puff up while cooking).
6. Place in the oven and bake for 20 minutes. Remove and allow to cool slightly before serving. These can be refrigerated and keep well for 4-5 days (great for meal prep).

312. Chicken & Artichokes

Made for: Dinner | **Prep Time:** 15 minutes | **Servings:** 04
Per Serving: Kcal: 288, Protein: 22g, Fat: 20g, Net Carb: 4g

INGREDIENTS:
- Four boneless skinless chicken thighs (about 2 pounds)
- Two jars (7-1/2 ounces each) marinated quartered artichoke hearts, drained
- Two tablespoons olive oil
- One teaspoon salt
- 1/2 teaspoon pepper
- 1/4 cup (25g) shredded Parmesan cheese
- Two tablespoons minced fresh parsley

INSTRUCTIONS:
1. Preheat broiler. In a large bowl, toss chicken and artichokes with oil, salt, and pepper. Transfer to a broiler pan.
2. Broil 3 in. From heat 8-10 minutes or until a thermometer inserted in chicken reads 170°, turning chicken and artichokes halfway through cooking. Sprinkle with cheese. Broil 1-2 minutes longer or until cheese is melted. Sprinkle with parsley.

313. Cauliflower Rice Bowl

Made for: Dinner | **Prep Time:** 10 minutes | **Servings:** 04
Per Serving: Kcal: 198, Protein: 9g, Fat: 18g, Net Carb: 6g

INGREDIENTS:
- 2 cups (225g) cauliflower rice.
- ¼ cup (56g) tomato puree.
- 3 oz butter.
- 3 tsp onion (dried flakes).
- 2 tsp garlic (powder).
- ½ tsp chilli (flakes).
- ½ tsp black pepper.

INSTRUCTIONS:
1. In a large frying pan, add butter, garlic, and onions, cook for 2-3 minutes.
2. Add the cauliflower and black pepper, cook for 2-3 minutes until cauliflower begins to soften.
3. Add the tomato puree and chilli flakes; cook for an additional 4-5 minutes until cauliflower is cooked through.

314. Tomato & Pepper Tapas

Made for: Dinner | **Prep Time:** 20 minutes | **Servings:** 04
Per Serving: Kcal: 666, Protein: 29g, Fat: 59g, Net Carb: 5g

INGREDIENTS:

- 8 oz chorizo (sliced).
- 8 oz prosciutto.
- ½ cup (120g) mayonnaise.
- 4 oz cucumber (sliced).
- 4 oz cheddar cheese (cut into sticks).
- 2 oz red bell peppers (sliced).
- ½ tsp garlic powder.
- ½ tsp chilli flakes.

INSTRUCTIONS:

1. In a small bowl, mix mayonnaise, garlic, and chilli flakes until well combined.
2. Place the mayonnaise dip on a serving plate; arrange the meats, cheese, peppers, and cucumber around it.

315. Chicken & Goat Cheese

Made for: Dinner | **Prep Time:** 20 minutes | **Servings:** 02
Per Serving: Kcal: 251, Protein: 28g, Fat: 12g, Net Carb: 2g

INGREDIENTS:

- 1/2-pound (225g) boneless skinless chicken breasts, cut into 1-inch pieces
- 1/4 teaspoon salt
- 1/8 teaspoon pepper
- Two teaspoons olive oil
- 1 cup (125g) sliced fresh asparagus (1-inch pieces)
- One garlic clove, minced
- Three plum tomatoes, chopped
- Three tablespoons 2% milk
- Two tablespoons herbed fresh goat cheese, crumbled
- Hot cooked rice or pasta
- Additional goat cheese, optional

INSTRUCTIONS:

1. Toss chicken with salt and pepper. In a large skillet, heat oil over medium-high heat; saute chicken until no longer pink, 4-6 minutes. Remove from pan; keep warm.
2. Add asparagus to skillet; cook and stir over medium-high heat 1 minute. Add garlic; cook and stir 30 seconds. Stir in tomatoes, milk, and two tablespoons cheese; cook, covered, over medium heat until cheese begins to melt, 2-3 minutes. Stir in chicken. Serve with rice. If desired, top with additional cheese.

316. Meaty Cream Cheese

Made for: Dinner | **Prep Time:** 20 minutes | **Servings:** 04
Per Serving: Kcal: 475, Protein: 13g, Fat: 47g, Net Carb: 5g

INGREDIENTS:

- 12 mushrooms.
- 8 oz bacon.
- 7 oz cream cheese.
- 3 tbsp fresh chives (finely diced).
- 1 tbsp butter.
- 1 tsp paprika.
- ½ tsp chilli flakes.

INSTRUCTIONS:

1. Preheat the oven at 200 degrees.
2. In a frying pan, cook the bacon until crispy; remove the bacon, leaving the fat in the pan. Allow bacon to cool, then crumble until it resembles large breadcrumbs.
3. Remove stems from the mushrooms and finely chop. Add a little butter to the bacon fat and saute the mushroom cups.
4. In a bowl, mix cream cheese, bacon, chopped mushroom stems, chives, and paprika until well combined.
5. Divide the mixture evenly into each mushroom cup; place on a baking tray and bake for 10-15 minutes or until golden brown.
6. Sprinkle chilli flakes on top.

317. Pumpkin Pie Custard

Made for: Dinner | **Prep Time:** 20 minutes | **Servings:** 04
Per Serving: Kcal: 278, Protein: 5g, Fat: 29g, Net Carb: 3g

INGREDIENTS:

- Four large egg yolks.
- 1 ½ cups (350g) thick whipping cream or double cream.
- 2 tbsp erythritol.
- 2 tsp pumpkin pie spice.
- ¼ tsp vanilla extract.

INSTRUCTIONS:

1. Preheat the oven at 180 degrees.
2. In a saucepan, heat cream, erythritol, pumpkin pie spice, and vanilla extract; bring to the boil.
3. Place the egg yolks into a large bowl and gradually pour in the warm cream mixture, whisking continuously.
4. Pour into an ovenproof dish and place the ovenproof dish into a larger ovenproof dish. Add water to the giant bowl until it is halfway up the side of the first dish.
5. Bake for 25-30 minutes. Allow cooling before serving.

318. Mexican Cabbage Roll

Made for: Dinner | **Prep Time:** 20 minutes | **Servings:** 04
Per Serving: Kcal: 186, Protein: 17g, Fat: 9g, Net Carb: 4g

INGREDIENTS:

- 1 pound (450g) lean ground beef (90% lean)
- 1/2 teaspoon salt
- 3/4 teaspoon garlic powder
- 1/4 teaspoon pepper
- One tablespoon olive oil
- One medium onion, chopped
- 6 cups (540g) chopped cabbage (about one small head)
- Three cans (4 ounces each) chopped green chiles
- 2 cups (500ml) of water
- One can (14-1/2 ounces) reduced-sodium beef broth
- Two tablespoons minced fresh cilantro
- Optional toppings: pico de gallo and reduced-fat sour cream, optional

INSTRUCTIONS:

1. In a large saucepan, cook and crumble beef with seasonings over medium-high heat until no longer pink, 5-7 minutes. Remove from pan.
2. In the same pan, heat oil over medium-high heat; saute onion and cabbage until crisp-tender, 4-6 minutes. Stir in beef, chiles, water, and broth; bring to a boil. Reduce heat; simmer, covered, to allow flavours to blend, about 10 minutes. Stir in cilantro. If desired, top with pico de gallo and sour cream.
3. Freeze option: Freeze cooled soup in freezer containers. To use, partially thaw in refrigerator overnight. Heat through in a saucepan, stirring occasionally.

319. Chicken Provolone

Made for: Dinner | **Prep Time:** 25 minutes | **Servings:** 04
Per Serving: Kcal: 236, Protein: 33g, Fat: 11g, Net Carb: 5g

INGREDIENTS

- Four boneless skinless chicken breast halves (4 ounces each)
- 1/4 teaspoon pepper
- Eight fresh basil leaves
- Butter-flavoured cooking spray
- Four thin slices prosciutto or deli ham
- 4 slices provolone cheese

INSTRUCTIONS:

1. Sprinkle chicken with pepper. In a large skillet coated with cooking spray, cook chicken over medium heat until a thermometer reads 165°, 4-5 minutes on each side.
2. Transfer to an ungreased baking sheet; top with the basil, prosciutto, and cheese. Broil 6-8 in. From the heat until cheese is melted, 1-2 minutes.

320. Lemon-Pepper Tilapia

Made for: Dinner | **Prep Time:** 25 minutes | **Servings:** 02
Per Serving: Kcal: 400, Protein: 34g, Fat: 10g, Net Carb: 4g

INGREDIENTS:

- Two tablespoons butter
- 1/2 pound sliced fresh mushrooms
- 3/4 teaspoon lemon-pepper seasoning, divided
- Three garlic cloves, minced
- Four tilapia fillets (6 ounces each)
- 1/4 teaspoon paprika
- 1/8 teaspoon cayenne pepper
- One medium tomato, chopped
- Three green onions, thinly sliced

INSTRUCTIONS:

1. In a 12-in. Skillet, heat butter over medium heat. Add mushrooms and 1/4 teaspoon lemon pepper; cook and stir 3-5 minutes or until tender. Add garlic; cook 30 seconds longer.
2. Place fillets over mushrooms; sprinkle with paprika, cayenne, and remaining lemon pepper. Cook, covered, 5-7 minutes or until fish just begins to flake easily with a fork. Top with tomato and green onions.

321. Bountiful Bacon, Cheese

Made for: Dinner | **Prep Time:** 30 minutes | **Servings:** 04
Per Serving: Kcal: 273, Protein: 9g, Fat: 29g, Net Carb: 2g

INGREDIENTS:

- 5 oz cheddar cheese (grated).
- 5 oz cream cheese.
- 5 oz bacon.
- 2 oz butter.
- ½ tsp chilli flakes.
- ½ tsp black pepper.
- ½ tsp Italian seasoning.

INSTRUCTIONS:

1. Heat the butter in a large frying pan and

fry the bacon until crispy. Reserve bacon fat and chop the bacon into small pieces.
2. In a bowl, mix cream cheese, cheddar cheese, chilli flakes, pepper, Italian seasoning, and bacon fat until well combined.
3. Place the cream cheese mix in the fridge for 20 minutes.
4. When the mixture is set, roll 24 balls into shape.
5. Roll each ball in the bacon pieces before serving.

322. Sensational Smoked

Made for: Dinner | **Prep Time:** 25 minutes | **Servings:** 04
Per Serving: Kcal: 263, Protein: 10g, Fat: 24g, Net Carb: 3g

INGREDIENTS:
- 8 oz cream cheese
- 7 oz smoked salmon (canned and drained).
- 2 oz iceberg lettuce leaves.
- 5 tbsp mayonnaise.
- 4 tbsp chives (finely chopped).
- ½ lemon zest.

INSTRUCTIONS:
1. In a large bowl, mix everything (except lettuce leaves) together until well combined.
2. Place in the refrigerator for 15-20 minutes.
3. When chilled, scoop onto lettuce leaves and serve.

323. Zucchini Noodles

Made for: Dinner | **Prep Time:** 20 minutes | **Servings:** 04
Per Serving: Kcal: 801, Protein: 21g, Fat: 78g, Net Carb: 7g

INGREDIENTS:
- 32 oz zucchini/courgette.
- 10 oz bacon (diced).
- One ¼ cups (300g) thick cream.
- ¼ cup (60g) mayonnaise.
- 3 oz parmesan (grated).
- 1 tbsp butter.

INSTRUCTIONS:
1. Heat the cream in a large saucepan; bring to a gentle boil and allow to reduce slightly.
2. Heat the butter in a large frying pan and cook the bacon until crispy; set aside and leave grease warming in the pan (low heat).

3. Add the mayonnaise to the cream and turn down the heat.
4. Using a potato peeler, make thin zucchini strips—Cook the zucchini noodles for 30 seconds in a pan of boiling water.
5. Add cream mixture and bacon fat to the zucchini noodles, tossing to ensure all are coated. Mix in the bacon and parmesan

324. Tuna Burgers on a Bed

Made for: Dinner | **Prep Time:** 15 minutes | **Servings:** 04
Per Serving: Kcal: 217, Protein: 21g, Fat: 16g, Net Carb: 2g

INGREDIENTS:
- 16 oz tinned tuna (drained).
- 8 oz baby spinach.
- Two onions (finely diced).
- One large egg.
- ¼ cup (60g) mayonnaise.
- ⅓ cup (35g) almond flour.
- 2 tbsp fresh dill (finely chopped).
- 1 tbsp lemon zest.
- 1 tbsp olive oil.
- 2 tbsp avocado oil.

INSTRUCTIONS:
1. In a large bowl, mix tuna, onions, egg, mayonnaise, almond flour, dill, and lemon zest.
2. From the mixture, form 8 burgers.
3. Heat 1 tbsp avocado oil in a large frying pan, fry four tuna patties for 4-5 minutes, flip and cook for an additional 4 minutes. Repeat with remaining oil and burgers.
4. Place the spinach on a serving plate and drizzle with olive oil, top with burgers.

325. Salmon & Spinach

Made for: Dinner | **Prep Time:** 25 minutes | **Servings:** 04
Per Serving: Kcal: 640, Protein: 37g, Fat: 54g, Net Carb: 5g

INGREDIENTS:
- 10 oz tinned salmon.
- 9 oz spinach (frozen).
- 1 ½ cups (150g) parmesan (grated).
- One cup (240g) of thick cream.
- ½ cup (120g) of almond milk.
- ¼ cup (57.5g) butter.
- Four slices mozzarella.
- One garlic clove (crushed).
- 1 tbsp parsley (dried).

INSTRUCTIONS:
1. Preheat the oven at 180 degrees.
2. In a large saucepan, heat the butter with the garlic. When garlic is browned, add in almond milk and cream.
3. Heat for 5-6 minutes and stir in parmesan, spinach, parsley, and salmon.
4. Continuously stir until the mixture is bubbling...
5. Pour into an ovenproof dish and top with mozzarella cheese.
6. Bake for 25-30 minutes until bubbling and golden.

326. California Burger Wraps

Made for: Dinner | Prep Time: 30 minutes | Servings: 02
Per Serving: Kcal: 400, Protein: 24g, Fat: 15g, Net Carb: 3g

INGREDIENTS:
- 1-pound (450g) lean ground beef (90% lean)
- 1/2 teaspoon salt
- 1/4 teaspoon pepper
- 8 Bibb lettuce leaves
- 1/3 cup (38g) crumbled feta cheese
- Two tablespoons Miracle Whip Light
- 1/2 medium ripe avocado, peeled and cut into eight slices
- 1/4 cup (37.5g) chopped red onion
- Chopped cherry tomatoes, optional

INSTRUCTIONS:
1. In a large bowl, combine beef, salt, and pepper, mixing lightly but thoroughly. Shape into eight 1/2-in.-thick patties.
2. Grill burgers, covered, over medium heat or broil 3-4 in. From heat until a thermometer reads 160°, 3-4 minutes on each side. Place burgers in lettuce leaves. Combine feta and Miracle Whip; spread over burgers. Top with avocado, red onion, and if desired, tomatoes.

327. Chicken Nicoise Salad

Made for: Dinner | Prep Time: 20 minutes | Servings: 02
Per Serving: Kcal: 289, Protein: 24g, Fat: 18g, Net Carb: 5g

INGREDIENTS:
- 1/2-pound fresh green beans, trimmed and halved (about 1 cup)

DRESSING:
- 1/4 cup (60g) olive oil
- Two teaspoons grated lemon zest
- Two tablespoons lemon juice
- Two garlic cloves, minced
- One teaspoon Dijon mustard
- 1/8 teaspoon salt
- Dash pepper

SALAD:
- One can (5 ounces) light tuna in water, drained and flaked
- Two tablespoons sliced ripe olives, drained
- One teaspoon caper, rinsed and drained
- 2 cups (150g) torn mixed salad greens
- One package (6 ounces) ready-to-use Southwest-style grilled chicken breast strips
- One small red onion halved and thinly sliced
- One medium sweet red pepper, julienned
- Two large hard-boiled eggs, cut into wedges

INSTRUCTIONS:
1. In a saucepan, cook green beans in boiling water just until crisp-tender. Remove and immediately drop into ice water to cool. Drain; pat dry.
2. Meanwhile, whisk together dressing ingredients. In a small bowl, lightly toss tuna with olives and capers.
3. Line platter with salad greens; top with tuna mixture, green beans, and remaining ingredients. Serve with dressing.

328. Cauliflower & Ham Bake

Made for: Dinner | Prep Time: 25 minutes | Servings: 04
Per Serving: Kcal: 329, Protein: 19g, Fat: 17g, Net Carb: 7g

INGREDIENTS:
- 2 large eggs.
- Two garlic cloves (crushed).
- ⅔ cup (160g) of almond milk (unsweetened).
- ½ cup (118g) of dry white wine.
- ½ cup (60g) cheddar cheese (grated).
- ½ cup (56g) mozzarella (grated).
- 10 oz spinach (frozen & defrosted).
- 8 oz cooked ham.
- 1 tbsp olive oil.

INSTRUCTIONS:
1. Preheat the oven at 190 degrees.
2. In a large bowl, mix spinach, cauliflower rice, milk, eggs, ⅓ cup mozzarella, and ⅓ cup cheddar.

3. In a large frying pan, heat the olive oil and fry the garlic until lightly browned. Stir in the white wine and cook until wine evaporates; add the ham and cook for 2-3 minutes.
4. Combine the ham mixture to the spinach mixture.
5. Add mixture to an ovenproof dish, sprinkle the remaining cheese on top.
6. Bake for 30-35 minutes until golden brown.

329. Moroccan Cauliflower

Made for: Dinner | **Prep Time:** 20 minutes | **Servings:** 02
Per Serving: Kcal: 226, Protein: 9g, Fat: 19g, Net Carb: 6g

INGREDIENTS
- One large head cauliflower (about 3-1/2 pounds), broken into florets
- 2 cups (480g) vegetable stock
- 3/4 cup (70g) sliced almonds, toasted and divided
- 1/2 cup (30g) minced fresh cilantro, divided
- Two tablespoons olive oil
- 1 to 3 teaspoons harissa chilli paste or hot pepper sauce
- 1/2 teaspoon ground cinnamon
- 1/2 teaspoon ground cumin
- 1/2 teaspoon ground coriander
- 1-1/4 teaspoons salt
- 1/2 teaspoon pepper
- Additional harissa chilli paste, optional

INSTRUCTIONS:
1. In a 5- or 6-qt. Slow cooker, combine cauliflower, vegetable stock, 1/2 cup almonds, 1/2 cup cilantro, and the next seven ingredients. Cook, covered, on low until cauliflower is tender, 6-8 hours.
2. Puree soup using an immersion blender. Or cool slightly and puree the soup in batches in a blender; return to slow cooker and heat through. Serve with remaining almonds and cilantro and, if desired, additional harissa.

330. Coconut Bed of Buttered

Made for: Dinner | **Prep Time:** 25 minutes | **Servings:** 04
Per Serving: Kcal: 768, Protein: 33g, Fat: 69g, Net Carb: 3g

INGREDIENTS:
- 16 oz salmon fillets (frozen & defrosted).
- 16 oz white cabbage.
- 4 oz butter.

- 2 oz shredded coconut (unsweetened).
- 5 tbsp olive oil.
- 1 tsp turmeric.
- ½ tsp onion powder.

INSTRUCTIONS:
1. Cut the salmon into bite-size pieces and drizzle over olive oil.
2. In a small bowl, mix coconut, turmeric, and onion powder. Dip each salmon chunk into the coconut mix until the salmon is well coated.
3. In a frying pan, fry the salmon until golden brown; cover with foil and set aside.
4. Melt the butter in the frying pan and fry the cabbage until it begins to lightly brown.
5. Place the cabbage on a plate and the salmon on top; drizzle with olive oil.

331. Cauliflower Medley

Made for: Dinner | **Prep Time:** 25 minutes | **Servings:** 04
Per Serving: Kcal: 651, Protein: 31g, Fat: 59g, Net Carb: 5g

INGREDIENTS:
- 10 oz beef (minced, frozen & defrosted).
- 8 oz cauliflower (florets).
- 3 oz butter.
- 1 tsp paprika.
- 1 tsp black pepper.
- ½ tsp salt.

INSTRUCTIONS:
1. Melt half of the butter in a large frying pan and fry the beef until almost cooked through.
2. Lower the heat; add the remaining butter, season with paprika, salt, and pepper. Stir in the cauliflower and fry for 5-6 minutes until tender.

332. Butternut Squash

Made for: Dinner | **Prep Time:** 25 minutes | **Servings:** 04
Per Serving: Kcal: 325, Protein: 19g, Fat: 10g, Net Carb: 6g

INGREDIENTS
- One medium butternut squash (about 3 pounds)
- 1 pound Italian turkey sausage links, casings removed
- One medium onion, finely chopped
- Four garlic cloves, minced
- 1/2 cup (45g) shredded Italian cheese blend

- Crushed red pepper flakes, optional

INSTRUCTIONS:
1. Preheat broiler. Cut squash lengthwise in half; discard seeds. Place squash in a large microwave-safe dish, cut side down; add 1/2 in. Of water. Microwave, covered, on high until soft, 20-25 minutes. Cool slightly.
2. Meanwhile, in a large nonstick skillet, cook and crumble sausage with onion over medium-high heat until no longer pink, 5-7 minutes. Add garlic; cook and stir 1 minute.
3. Leaving 1/2-in.-thick shells, scoop pulp from the squash and stir into sausage mixture. Place squash shells on a baking sheet; fill with sausage mixture. Sprinkle with cheese.
4. Broil 4-5 in. From heat until cheese is melted, 1-2 minutes. If desired, sprinkle with pepper flakes. To serve, cut each half into two portions.

333. Keto Cream Cheese

Made for: Dinner | **Prep Time:** 15 minutes | **Servings:** 01
Per Serving: Kcal: 299, Protein: 16g, Fat: 25g, Net Carb: 3g

INGREDIENTS
- 2 eggs
- 2 oz. cream cheese
- 1 tbsp coconut flour
- ½ tsp cinnamon
- 1 packet stevia

INSTRUCTION
1. Beat or blend together the ingredients until the batter is smooth and free of lumps.
2. Two pancakes is equivalent to one serving. On medium-high, heat up a non-stick skillet or pan with coconut oil or salted butter.
3. Ladle the batter on to the pan. Heat until bubbles begin to form on top. Flip over, and cook until the other side is sufficiently browned.
4. Serve.

334. Grilled Peppered Steaks

Made for: Dinner | **Prep Time:** 25 minutes | **Servings:** 04
Per Serving: Kcal: 301, Protein: 48g, Fat: 10g, Net Carb: 1g

INGREDIENTS
- 1-1/2 to 2 teaspoons coarsely ground pepper
- 1 teaspoon onion salt
- 1 teaspoon garlic salt
- 1/4 teaspoon paprika
- 4 boneless beef top loin steaks (8 ounces each)

INSTRUCTION
1. In a small bowl, combine the pepper, onion salt, garlic salt and, if desired, paprika Rub onto both sides of steaks.
2. Grill, covered, over medium heat until meat reaches desired doneness (for medium-rare, a thermometer should read 135°; medium, 140°; medium-well, 145°), 8-10 minutes on each side.

335. Salmon With Garlic Butter

Made for: Dinner | **Prep Time:** 20 minutes | **Servings:** 02
Per Serving: Kcal: 510, Protein: 28g, Fat: 40g, Net Carb: 7g

INGREDIENTS
- 1 small clove garlic, minced
- 1 tbsp fresh chopped parsley
- 3 tbsp freshly squeezed lemon juice (45 ml)
- 2 tbsp melted unsalted butter or ghee (30 ml)
- 3 tbsp extra virgin olive oil (45 ml)
- 3/4 tsp sea salt
- 1/2 tsp cracked black pepper
- 2 salmon fillets (250 g/ 8.8 oz)
- 1 bunch broccolini or broccoli florets (250 g/ 8.8 oz)

INSTRUCTION
1. Preheat oven to 200 °C/ 400 °F (conventional), or 180 °C/ 355 °F (fan assisted). In a small jug, combine lemon juice, melted butter, olive oil, minced garlic, parsley, salt and pepper, and mix to combine.
2. Place the broccolini and salmon on a baking tray and pour over the dressing.
3. Bake on the top oven shelf 10 to 12 minutes until the salmon is just cooked through.
4. For the last 3 minutes, turn the top element (grill/broiler) on high to brown the top. Serve immediately or store for up to a day.

336. Buffalo Pulled Chicken

Made for: Dinner | **Prep Time:** 3 hours | **Servings:** 04
Per Serving: Kcal: 147, Protein: 23g, Fat: 8g, Net Carb: 3g

INGREDIENTS
- 1/2 cup (256g) Buffalo wing sauce
- 2 tablespoons ranch salad dressing mix
- 4 boneless skinless chicken breast halves (6 ounces each)

INSTRUCTION
1. In a 3-qt. slow cooker, mix wing sauce and dressing mix. Add chicken. Cook, covered, on low until meat is tender, 3-4 hours.
2. Shred chicken with 2 forks. If desired, serve on celery, top with additional wing sauce and cheese, and serve with ranch dressing.

337. Cheesy Roasted Broccoli

Made for: Dinner | **Prep Time:** 15 minutes | **Servings:** 02
Per Serving: Kcal: 160, Protein: 8g, Fat: 16g, Net Carb: 4g

INGREDIENTS
- ¼ cup (60g) ranch dressing
- 4 cups (340g) broccoli florets
- ¼ cup (60g) heavy whipping cream or double cream
- ½ cup (56g) cheddar cheese, shredded
- Salt and pepper to taste

INSTRUCTION
1. Preheat your oven to 375 degrees F.
2. Put all the ingredients in a bowl and mix.
3. Arrange the broccoli mix on a baking dish.
4. Bake in the oven for 10 minutes or until tender enough.

338. Garlic-Lime Chicken

Made for: Dinner | **Prep Time:** 50 minutes | **Servings:** 04
Per Serving: Kcal: 191, Protein: 35g, Fat: 9g, Net Carb: 1g

INGREDIENTS
- 1/3 cup (88g) soy sauce
- 1/4 cup (60g) fresh lime juice
- 1 tablespoon Worcestershire sauce
- 1/2 teaspoon ground mustard
- 2 garlic cloves, minced
- 6 boneless skinless chicken breast halves (6 ounces each)
- 1/2 teaspoon pepper

INSTRUCTION
1. In a shallow dish, combine the first 5 ingredients; add chicken and turn to coat. Cover and refrigerate for at least 30 minutes.
2. Drain discard marinade. Sprinkle chicken with pepper. Grill , covered, over medium heat until a thermometer reads, 165°, 7-8 minutes on each side.

339. Keto Fat Bombs

Made for: Dinner | **Prep Time:** 30 minutes | **Bombs:** 10
Per Bomb: Kcal: 176, Protein: 0g, Fat: 15g, Net Carb: 7g

INGREDIENTS
- 8 tablespoons butter
- ¼ cup Swerve
- ½ teaspoon vanilla extract
- Salt to taste
- 2 cups (224g) almond flour
- 2/3 cup (113g) chocolate chips

INSTRUCTION
1. In a bowl, beat the butter until fluffy.
2. Stir in the sugar, salt and vanilla.
3. Mix well.
4. Add the almond flour.
5. Fold in the chocolate chips.
6. Cover the bowl with cling wrap and refrigerate for 20 minutes.
7. Create balls from the dough.

340. Oven-Roasted Salmon

Made for: Dinner | **Prep Time:** 25 minutes | **Servings:** 04
Per Serving: Kcal: 292, Protein: 30g, Fat: 20g, Net Carb: 0g

INGREDIENTS
- 1 center-cut salmon fillet (1-1/2 pounds)
- 1 tablespoon olive oil
- 1/2 teaspoon salt
- 1/4 teaspoon pepper

INSTRUCTION
1. Place a large cast-iron or other ovenproof skillet in a cold oven. Preheat oven to 450°. Meanwhile, brush salmon with oil and sprinkle with salt and pepper.
2. Carefully remove skillet from oven. Place fish, skin side down, in skillet. Return to oven; bake uncovered, until salmon flakes easily and a thermometer reads 125°, 14-18 minutes. Cut salmon into four equal portions.

341. Coconut Crack Bars

Made for: Dinner | **Prep Time:** 30 minutes | **Bars:** 20
Per Bar: Kcal: 147, Protein: 1g, Fat: 16g, Net Carb: 3g

INGREDIENTS

- 3 cups (360g) coconut flakes (unsweetened)
- 1 cup (240g) coconut oil
- ¼ cup (25g) erythritol

INSTRUCTION

1. Line a baking sheet with parchment paper.
2. Put coconut in a bowl.
3. Add the oil and syrup.
4. Mix well.
5. Pour the mixture into the pan.
6. Refrigerate until firm.
7. Slice into bars before serving.

342. Easy Mexican Taco Meatloaf

Made for: Dinner | **Prep Time:** 90 minutes | **Servings:** 04
Per Serving: Kcal: 472, Protein: 30g, Fat: 37g, Net Carb: 4g

INGREDIENTS

- 2 lbs ground beef
- 2 eggs
- 1 jar salsa, divided (16 oz jar)
- 2 tbsp ghee or other cooking oil

FOR THE SEASONING:

- 2 tsp chili powder
- 2 tsp garlic powder
- 1 tsp paprika
- 1 tsp cumin
- 1 tsp onion powder
- 1 tsp oregano
- 1 tsp salt sea salt
- 1/2 tsp pepper
- 1/4 tsp cayenne pepper

INSTRUCTION

1. Preheat oven to 400° Fahrenheit and grease a loaf pan with ghee or oil. Alternatively, you can line the pan with parchment paper for easier cleanup.
2. Make the seasoning by adding all of the seasoning ingredients to a small bowl and mixing well.
3. Place beef in a bowl and add in 1/2 of the salsa, both eggs and the seasoning mix. Using your hands, mix the ingredients until the ingredients are evenly incorporated.
4. Form the beef mixture into the loaf pan. Pour the rest of the salsa over the top of the meatloaf. You may have a little extra salsa left over.
5. Place in the oven to bake for 80-90 minutes, or until the internal temperature reaches 160°.
6. Remove and allow to cool for at least 5 minutes. Carefully pour out any excess liquid from the pan. Cut into thick slices and serve.

343. Keto Pancakes

Made for: Dinner | **Prep Time:** 15 minutes | **Cakes:** 10
Per Cake: Kcal: 84, Protein: 4g, Fat: 8g, Net Carb: 0.5g

INGREDIENTS

- ½ cup (56g) almond flour
- 4 oz. cream cheese
- 4 eggs
- 1 teaspoon lemon zest
- 1 tablespoon butter

INSTRUCTION

1. In a bowl, mix all the ingredients except the butter.
2. Mix until smooth.
3. In a pan over medium heat, put the butter and let it melt.
4. Pour three tablespoons of batter and cook for 2 minutes or until golden.
5. Flip the pancake and cook for another 2 minutes.
6. Repeat the same steps with the rest of the batter.

344. Cream Cheese Muffins

Made for: Dinner | **Prep Time:** 20 minutes | **Muffins:** 06
Per Muffin: Kcal: 247, Protein: 8g, Fat: 32g, Net Carb: 6g

INGREDIENTS

- 4 tablespoons melted butter
- 1 cup (112g) almond flour
- ¾ tablespoon baking powder
- 2 large eggs, lightly beaten
- 2 ounces cream cheese mixed with 2 tablespoons heavy (whipping) cream
- Handfulshredded Mexican blend cheese

INSTRUCTION

1. Preheat the oven to 400°F. Coat six cups of a muffin tin with butter.
2. In a small bowl, mix together the almond flour and baking powder.

3. In a medium bowl, mix together the eggs, cream cheese–heavy cream mixture, shredded cheese, and 4 tablespoons of the melted butter.
4. Pour the flour mixture into the egg mixture, and beat with a hand mixer until thoroughly mixed.
5. Pour the batter into the prepared muffin cups.
6. Bake for 12 minutes, or until golden brown on top, and serve.

345. Palmini Spaghetti Bolognese

Made for: Dinner | **Prep Time:** 35 minutes | **Servings:** 04
Per Serving: Kcal: 474, Protein: 25g, Fat: 27g, Net Carb: 5g

INGREDIENTS
- 2 cans palmini linguine noodles, drained (450 g/1 lb)
- 500 g ground beef (1.1 lb)
- 1 1/4 cups Homemade Marinara Sauce, 1 recipe (300 ml/ 10 fl oz)
- Optional: 4 tbsp grated Parmesan cheese or more, to serve (20 g/ 0.7 oz)
- Optional: fresh basil leaves, to serve

INSTRUCTION
1. Open the Palmini cans and drain the liquid by pouring the content of both cans in a colander. Keto Palmini Spaghetti Bolognese
2. Rinse with water and set aside. The noodles can be eaten as they are or you can place them in a pot with hot water to heat up for 30 to 60 seconds, or heat in a microwave for 30-60 seconds. If you want to warm them up, do that just before serving.
3. Meanwhile, prepare the Marinara Sauce and the beef. Keto Palmini Spaghetti Bolognese
4. Place the ground meat in a cast iron skillet or a non stick pan. (If using cast iron, add a few tablespoons of water.) Cook over a medium-high heat until browned and opaque, for about 10 minutes. Add the Marinara Sauce and cook to heat through. Take off the heat. Keto Palmini Spaghetti Bolognese
5. Place the marinara flavoured meat in a serving bowl and top with the noodles. Keto Palmini Spaghetti Bolognese
6. Optionally serve each with 1 to 2 tablespoons of grated parmesan and a few basil leaves.

7. To store, refrigerate the meat mixture for up to 4 days or freeze for up to 3 months. Palmini are best prepared fresh — it only takes a minute!

346. Carne Asada Recipe

Made for: Dinner | **Prep Time:** 40 minutes | **Servings:** 04
Per Serving: Kcal: 484, Protein: 50g, Fat: 31g, Net Carb: 2g

EQUIPMENT
- Grill

INGREDIENTS
- 2 pounds skirt steak (can use flank, flap or flatiron steak)
  For The Carne Asada Marinade:
- 1/4 cup (55g) avocado oil
- 2 tbsp apple cider vinegar
- 2 limes, juice of
- 1 orange, juice of
- 3 cloves garlic, minced (can sub 1 tsp garlic oil)
- 2 tsp cumin
- 2 tsp chili powder
- 1 teaspoon sea salt
- 1/2 teaspoon black pepper

Instruction
1. Prepare marinade by mixing marinade ingredients in a bowl or jar.
2. Place steak in a shallow dish or zip-top bag. Pour marinade over the steak to coat on both sides. Allow the steak to marinate while your grill heats up, at least 20 minutes. Or, you can marinate it covered in the refrigerator for up to 4 hours. (See recipe notes)
3. Heat a grill to medium-high heat. Once the grill is hot, place the steak on the grill to cook for 4-5 minutes on each side, or until cooked to your liking. While cooking, baste the steak with any remaining marinade using a brush or by simply pouring the marinade over the steak.
4. When the steak is cooked, remove it from the grill and place on a cutting board to rest for 5-10 minutes.
5. Slice the steak into thin strips against the grain. Serve and enjoy.

347. Keto Chicken Wings

Made for: Dinner | **Prep Time:** 60 minutes | **Servings:** 04
Per Serving: Kcal: 419, Protein: 30g, Fat: 32g, Net Carb: 1g

INGREDIENTS

- 3-4 lbs chicken wings separated into the drumette and the flat/tip
- 2 tsp baking powder
- 1/4 tsp salt
- 1/4 tsp pepper
- 1/2 tsp garlic powder
- 1 cup (230g) Frank's Red Hot
- 3 tbsp butter

INSTRUCTION

1. Preheat the oven to 450 degrees.
2. Prepare the chicken wings by separating them into the drumette and the flat/tip portion. Dry them well with a paper towel.
3. Combine the baking powder, salt, pepper, and garlic powder in a bowl. Toss this with the chicken wings.
4. Lightly grease a baking sheet, and place the chicken wings on the baking sheet. (You'll likely need two baking sheets).
5. Place the baking sheets in the oven and cook for 30 minutes. Take the baking sheets out and flip the wings over. Return to the oven and cook for an additional 15-20 minutes.
6. Once the wings are done, melt the butter in a bowl in the microwave. Combine the butter and the hot sauce in a large bowl, and toss the wings in the sauce.
7. Serve as-is, with crumbled blue cheese on top, or with an appropriate blue cheese or ranch dressing for dipping.

348. Mashed Cauliflower with Chives

Made for: Dinner | **Prep Time:** 40 minutes | **Servings:** 04
Per Serving: Kcal: 98, Protein: 9g, Fat: 4g, Net Carb: 6g

INGREDIENTS

- 2 cups (96g) chicken broth
- 2 heads cauliflower, cored and sliced into florets
- ¼ cup (10g) fresh chives, chopped
- ¼ cup (22.5g) Parmesan cheese, grated
- Salt and pepper to taste

INSTRUCTION

1. In a pot over medium heat, pour in the chicken broth.
2. Add the cauliflower.
3. Bring to a boil and then simmer for 20 minutes.
4. Transfer cauliflower to a blender. Pulse until smooth.
5. Stir in the chives and cheese.

6. Season with salt and pepper.

349. Ground beef and green beans

Made for: Dinner | **Prep Time:** 30 minutes | **Servings:** 02
Per Serving: Kcal: 698, Protein: 35g, Fat: 60g, Net Carb: 5g

INGREDIENTS

- 10 oz. ground beef
- 9 oz. fresh green beans
- 3½ oz. butter
- salt and pepper
- 1/3 cup (80g) mayonnaise or crème fraîche (optional)

INSTRUCTION

1. Rinse and trim the green beans.
2. Heat up a generous dollop of butter in a frying pan where you can fit both the ground beef and the green beans.
3. Brown the ground beef on high heat until it's almost done. Add salt and pepper.
4. Lower the heat somewhat. Add more butter and fry the beans for 5 minutes in the same pan. Stir the ground beef every now and then.
5. Season beans with salt and pepper. Serve with remaining butter and add mayonnaise or crème fraiche if you need more fat for satiety.

350. Low-carb baked eggs

Made for: Dinner | **Prep Time:** 20 minutes | **Servings:** 01
Per Serving: Kcal: 499, Protein: 41g, Fat: 35g, Net Carb: 2g

INGREDIENTS

- 3 oz. ground beef
- 2 eggs
- 2 oz. shredded cheese

INSTRUCTION

1. Preheat the oven to 400°F (200°C).
2. Arrange cooked ground-beef mixture in a small baking dish. Then make two holes with a spoon and crack the eggs into them.
3. Sprinkle shredded cheese on top.
4. Bake in the oven until the eggs are done, about 10-15 minutes.
5. Let cool for a while. The eggs and ground meat get very hot!

351. Butter Hardboiled Egg

Made for: Dinner | **Prep Time:** 15 minutes | **Servings:** 01
Per Serving: Kcal: 430, Protein: 14g, Fat: 41g, Net Carb: 1g

INGREDIENTS
- 2 whole Eggs
- 30g (1/8 cup) Butter
- 1 tbsp Mascarpone
- Salt &pepper to taste

INSTRUCTION
1. Hard boil the eggs in a pot. Add a pinch of salt to it so the eggs will peel bet- ter once done.
2. Wash the boiled eggs with cold water. Peel and chop into a large cup.
3. Next, add the mascarpone cheese and butter while the eggs are still hot, mixing well. Season with salt and pepper.

352. Cauliflower Soup

Made for: Dinner | **Prep Time:** 20 minutes | **Servings:** 02
Per Serving: Kcal: 111, Protein: 8g, Fat: 15g, Net Carb: 6g

INGREDIENTS
- Two tablespoons olive oil
- One medium onion, finely chopped
- Three tablespoons yellow curry paste
- Two medium heads cauliflower, broken into florets
- One carton (32 ounces) vegetable broth
- 1 cup (240g) of coconut milk
- Minced fresh cilantro, optional

INSTRUCTION
1. In a large saucepan, heat oil over medium heat. Add onion; cook and stir until softened, 2-3 minutes. Add curry paste; cook until fragrant, 1-2 minutes. Add cauliflower and broth. Increase heat to high; bring to a boil. Reduce heat to medium-low; cook, covered, about 20 minutes.
2. Stir in coconut milk; cook an additional minute. Remove from heat; cool slightly. Puree in batches in a blender or food processor. If desired, top with minced fresh cilantro.

353. The Beastie Bacon Bagel

Made for: Dinner | **Prep Time:** 20 minutes | **Servings:** 02
Per Serving: Kcal: 605, Protein: 30g, Fat: 51g, Net Carb: 5g

INGREDIENTS
- 6 slices bacon (grilled).
- One large egg.
- 1 ½ cups (300g) mozzarella cheese (grated).
- 1 cup (20g) arugula leaves.
- ¾ cup (84g) almond flour.
- 4 tbsp soft cream cheese.
- 2 tbsp pesto.
- 1 tbsp butter (melted).
- 1 tsp xanthan gum.

INSTRUCTION
1. Preheat oven at 390 degrees.
2. Mix the almond flour and xanthan gum. Add the egg and mix until well combined.
3. Over medium heat, melt the mozzarella and 2 tbsp of cream cheese together.
4. Add the cheese mixture to the flour mixture; knead until thoroughly combined and resembles dough.
5. Split the dough into three pieces and roll into long sausage shapes.
6. Put the ends together to make three circles.
7. Brush melted butter over the bagels; place on a baking tray and bake for 15 - 18 minutes or until golden brown. Allow cooling.
8. Spread the bagels with the remaining cream cheese and pesto. Place on the arugula leaves and top with bacon.

354. Easy Coronation chicken

Made for: Dinner | **Prep Time:** 15 minutes | **Servings:** 04
Per Serving: Kcal: 168, Protein: 12g, Fat: 10g, Net Carb: 2g

INGREDIENTS
- 50g (2 oz) mayonnaise
- 40g (2 oz) mango chutney
- 1/2 teaspoon curry powder
- 1/2 dessertspoon lime zest
- 2 tablespoons fresh lime juice
- 1/2 teaspoon salt
- 250g (1/2 lb) skinless, boneless chicken breast fillets - cooked and diced

INSTRUCTION
1. In a large bowl, whisk together the mayonnaise, chutney, curry powder, lime zest, lime juice and salt. Add chicken and toss with the dressing until well coated. Cover and chill until serving.

355. Butter and garlic prawns

Made for: Dinner | **Prep Time:** 30 minutes | **Servings:** 04
Per Serving: Kcal: 430, Protein: 28g, Fat: 40g, Net Carb: 1g

INGREDIENTS

- 250g (9 oz) butter
- 2 tablespoons Dijon mustard
- juice of half a lemon
- 2 cloves garlic, chopped
- half a bunch fresh parsley, chopped
- 1kg (2 lb) medium fresh prawns - shells removed with tails attached, and deveined

INSTRUCTION

1. Preheat oven to 230 C / Gas mark 8.
2. In a small saucepan over medium heat, combine the butter, mustard, lemon juice, garlic and parsley. When the butter melts completely, remove from heat.
3. Arrange prawns in a shallow baking dish. Pour the butter mixture over the prawns.
4. Bake in preheated oven for 12 to 15 minutes or until the prawns are pink and opaque.

356. Keto Milk Chocolate

Made for: Dinner | **Prep Time:** 30 minutes | **Chocolates:** 12
Per Chocolate: Kcal: 170, Protein: 3g, Fat: 17g, Net Carb: 3g

INGREDIENTS

- 5 ounces of cocoa butter
- 5 ounce of baking chocolate, unsweetened, chopped
- 21/2 ounce of powdered erythritol
- 1 ounce of whey protein powder
- 3/4 teaspoon of liquid stevia extract

INSTRUCTION

1. Add together the whey protein and erythritol, blending well to combine to fine powder.
2. Melt the cocoa butter, with continuous stirring, in a double boiler or a small pan over low heat.
3. Add the baking chocolate and keep stirring until smooth.
4. Now add the whey protein and erythritol as well as the stevia, while stirring to mix well.
5. Remove from heat and stir to smoothness.
6. Pour into chocolate molds and place in the refrigerator to cool and hard- ened.
7. Enjoy at room temperature.

357. Garlic Crusted Chicken

Made for: Dinner | **Prep Time:** 55 minutes | **Servings:** 04
Per Serving: Kcal: 307, Protein: 25g, Fat: 19g, Net Carb: 6g

INGREDIENTS

- 4 cloves garlic, crushed
- 4 tablespoons olive oil
- 30g (1 oz) dried breadcrumbs
- 30g (1 oz) grated Parmesan cheese
- 4 skinless, boneless chicken breast fillets

INSTRUCTION

1. Preheat oven to 220 C / Gas mark 7.
2. Warm the garlic and olive oil in a small saucepan to blend the flavours. In a separate dish, combine the breadcrumbs and Parmesan cheese. Dip the chicken breasts in the olive oil and garlic mixture, then into the breadcrumb mixture. Place in a shallow baking dish.
3. Bake in the preheated oven for 30 to 35 minutes, until no longer pink and juices run clear.

358. Bacon and Cheddar stuffed mushrooms

Made for: Dinner | **Prep Time:** 30 minutes | **Servings:** 04
Per Serving: Kcal: 77, Protein: 8g, Fat: 6g, Net Carb: 1g

INGREDIENTS

- 2 slice streaky bacon
- 4 crimini mushrooms
- 1/2 tablespoon butter
- 1/2 tablespoon chopped onion
- 45g (1.5 oz) grated Cheddar cheese

INSTRUCTION

1. place bacon in a large, deep-frying pan. Cook over medium high heat until evenly brown. Remove, dice and set aside.
2. Preheat oven to 200 C / Gas mark 6.
3. Remove mushroom stems. Set aside caps. Chop the stems.
4. In a saucepan over medium heat, melt the butter. Slowly cook and stir the chopped stems and onion until the onion is soft. Remove from heat.
5. In a medium bowl, stir together the mushroom stem mixture, bacon and two thirds of the Cheddar. Mix well and scoop the mixture into the mushroom caps.
6. Bake in the preheated oven 15 minutes, or until the cheese has melted.

7. Remove the mushrooms from the oven, and sprinkle with the remaining cheese.

359. Cream Cheese Crepes

Made for: Dinner | **Prep Time:** 20 minutes | **Servings:** 04
Per Serving: Kcal: 115, Protein: 12g, Fat: 9g, Net Carb: 2g

INGREDIENTS
- 4 egg whites
- 4 eggs
- 4 tablespoons of cream cheese butter
- 2 tablespoons of psyllium husk

INSTRUCTION
1. Blend all the ingredients together in a food processor or regular blender.
2. Melt a little butter in a skillet on medium heat.
3. Add some of the batter and then swirl to distribute evenly, pancake style. Cook over until the top is firm then flip and cook on the other side.
4. Repeat until you run out of batter.

360. Jamaican BBQ chicken

Made for: Dinner | **Prep Time:** 30 minutes | **Servings:** 02
Per Serving: Kcal: 601, Protein: 63g, Fat: 40g, Net Carb: 2g

INGREDIENTS
- 1 spring onion, minced
- 4 tablespoons orange juice
- 1 tablespoon minced fresh ginger root
- 1 tablespoon minced green chilli
- 1 tablespoon lime juice
- 1 tablespoon soy sauce
- 1 clove garlic, minced
- 1 teaspoon ground allspice
- 1/4 teaspoon ground cinnamon
- 1/2 teaspoon ground cloves
- 1 whole chicken, cut into pieces

INSTRUCTION
1. Combine spring onions, orange juice, ginger, chilli, lime juice, soy sauce, garlic, allspice, cinnamon and cloves. Add chicken, and marinate for 8 hours.
2. Preheat barbecue for medium heat. Cook chicken until juices run clear, and drizzle with leftover marinade that has been boiled for 2 to 3 minutes.

361. Courgette Tomato Soup

Made for: Dinner | **Prep Time:** 15 minutes | **Servings:** 02
Per Serving: Kcal: 60, Protein: 3g, Fat: 4g, Net Carb: 2g

INGREDIENTS
- 2 large tomatoes, chopped
- 2 fresh basil leaves, for garnish
- 1 medium zucchini/courgette, julienned
- 1 teaspoon of olive oil
- 1 garlic clove, crushed

INSTRUCTION
1. Add oil to a pan on medium heat.
2. Stir-fry the garlic and zucchini strips for 3-4 minutes.
3. Stir in the tomatoes with its liquid; cook soup for another 3-4 minutes.
4. Ladle soup into bowls and garnish with basil.

362. Easy Keto Ice Cream

Made for: Dinner | **Prep Time:** 40 minutes | **Servings:** 02
Per Serving: Kcal: 238, Protein: 5g, Fat: 22g, Net Carb: 2g

INGREDIENTS
- 4 large eggs
- ¼ tsp cream of tartar
- ½ cup (50g) erythritol
- 1¼ cup (300g) heavy whipping cream/double cream
- 1 tbsp vanilla extract

INSTRUCTION
1. Start by separating your egg yolks from your egg whites, and whisk the egg whites with the cream of tartar. The egg whites will begin to thicken, and as they do you're going to need to add the Erythritol. They should start to form stiff peaks, and you'll need to keep whisking until they do.
2. Take another bowl, and start to whisk your cream. Soft peaks should start to form as the whisk is removed, but you'll need to be careful not to over whisk the cream.
3. In a third bowl, combine your egg yolks with the vanilla.
4. Now you can fold the whisked egg whites into the now whipped cream.
5. Add in your egg yolk mixture, and continue to gently fold with a spatula until thoroughly combined.
6. Place it in a pan, preferably a loaf pan, and let it sit. All hands on time is done,

but it'll need to sit for about two hours.

363. Scrambled Eggs with Bacon

Made for: Dinner | **Prep Time:** 10 minutes | **Servings:** 01
Per Serving: Kcal: 324, Protein: 8g, Fat: 35g, Net Carb: 2g

INGREDIENTS
- 4 slices sugar-free bacon
- 6 large eggs
- 1/2 cup (120g) heavy cream/double cream
- 1/4 teaspoon salt
- 1/4 teaspoon black pepper

INSTRUCTION
1. Cook bacon in a medium skillet over medium heat until crispy, about 10 minutes. Remove bacon from pan and dice.
2. Crack eggs into a medium bowl and whisk together with heavy cream, salt, and pepper. Add egg mixture to bacon grease in pan and stir until scrambled. Add diced bacon to eggs and stir.
3. Remove from heat and serve immediately.

364. Crispy Chicken Wings

Made for: Dinner | **Prep Time:** 60 minutes | **Servings:** 02
Per Serving: Kcal: 592, Protein: 99g, Fat: 16g, Net Carb: 5g

INGREDIENTS
- 2 lbs chicken wings
- 1 ½ tbsp baking powder
- 2 tsp salt

INSTRUCTION
1. Pat chicken wings dry with a paper towel and place in a plastic bag. Sprinkle with baking powder and salt, and shake to coat.
2. Bake at 250°F or 130°C for 30 minutes.
3. Next, increase oven temperature to 425°F or 220°C and continue to bake for another 20 to 30 minutes, until crispy.
4. Toss in a sauce of your choice and enjoy.

365. Barbecued Tandoori Chicken

Made for: Dinner | **Prep Time:** 40 minutes | **Servings:** 02
Per Serving: Kcal: 240, Protein: 40g, Fat: 9g, Net Carb: 0.6g

INGREDIENTS
- 1/2 teaspoon curry powder

- 1/2 teaspoon crushed chillies, such as Schwartz
- 1/2 teaspoon salt
- 1/4 teaspoon ground ginger
- 1/4 teaspoon paprika
- 1/4 teaspoon ground cinnamon
- 1/4 teaspoon ground turmeric
- 2 tablespoons water
- 4 skinless, boneless chicken breast fillets

INSTRUCTION
1. Preheat barbecue for high heat.
2. In a medium bowl, mix curry powder, crushed chillies, salt, ginger, paprika, cinnamon and turmeric with water to form a smooth paste. Rub paste into chicken breasts, and place them on a plate. Cover, and allow to marinate for 20 minutes.
3. Brush cooking grate with oil. Place chicken on the barbecue, and cook 6 to 8 minutes on each side, until juices run clear when pierced with a fork.

366. Keto Pizza Chips

Made for: Dinner | **Prep Time:** 15 minutes | **Chips:** 08
Per Chips: Kcal: 250, Protein: 0g, Fat: 18g, Net Carb: 2g

INGREDIENTS
- 10 oz sliced pepperoni
- 1 (8 oz) bag shredded mozzarella cheese
- 1 (8 oz) bag shredded Parmesan cheese
- 2 tsp Italian seasoning

INSTRUCTION
1. Preheat oven to 400°F or 200°C.
2. Line two cookie sheets with aluminum foil, and place the pepperoni on the sheets.
3. Sprinkle with shredded mozzarella cheese, grated parmesan, and Italian seasoning.
4. Bake for 8-10 minutes.
5. Remove and let cool for about 5 minutes or until crispy.
6. Serve with marinara if you like.

367. Chia Seeds Smoothie

Made for: Dinner | **Prep Time:** 10 minutes | **Servings:** 02
Per Serving: Kcal: 87, Protein: 7g, Fat: 84g, Net Carb: 1g

INGREDIENTS
- 4 Tablespoons of Chia seeds
- 2 Cups of Coconut milk (full fat)
- 1/2 Cup (74g) of blueberries (frozen)

- 4 Tablespoons of Coconut oil (melted)

INSTRUCTION
1. Put the entire ingredients in a blender and blend until combined
2. Serve cold and enjoy

368. Feta Cheese Omelet

Made for: Dinner | **Prep Time:** 15 minutes | **Servings:** 02
Per Serving: Kcal: 243, Protein: 15g, Fat: 20g, Net Carb: 2g

INGREDIENTS
- 4 large eggs
- 1/2 teaspoon of black pepper
- 1 teaspoon heavy cream/double cream
- 3 tablespoons of crumbled feta cheese
- 1 tablespoon vegetable oil

INSTRUCTION
1. Beat eggs with pepper in a small bowl.
2. Combine heavy cream with crumbled cheese in another bowl.
3. Heat oil over medium-high heat in a cast iron skillet. Add beaten eggs and tilt the skillet to cover the bottom evenly.
4. When eggs are set, spoon feta mixture onto the center of the omelet. Use a spatula to fold the eggs on opposite sides to the center, then fold over again.

369. Feta Stuffed Chicken Breasts

Made for: Dinner | **Prep Time:** 60 minutes | **Servings:** 04
Per Serving: Kcal: 570, Protein: 54g, Fat: 38g, Net Carb: 4g

INGREDIENTS
- 4 skinless, boneless chicken breasts
- 125ml mayonnaise
- 75g feta cheese, crumbled
- 2 cloves garlic, chopped
- 285g frozen chopped spinach, thawed and drained
- 4 rashers streaky bacon

INSTRUCTION
1. In a medium bowl, mix mayonnaise, spinach, feta cheese and garlic until well blended. Set aside.
2. Carefully butterfly chicken breasts, making sure not to cut all the way through. Spoon spinach mixture into chicken breasts. Wrap each with a piece of bacon and secure with a cocktail stick. Place in shallow baking dish. Cover.

3. Bake at 190 C / Gas 5 for 1 hour or until chicken is no longer pink.

370. Easy Garlic Chicken

Made for: Dinner | **Prep Time:** 40 minutes | **Servings:** 04
Per Serving: Kcal: 340, Protein: 39g, Fat: 14g, Net Carb: 6g

INGREDIENTS
- 4 skinless, boneless chicken breast fillets
- 3 cloves crushed garlic
- 3 tablespoons ground ginger
- 1 tablespoon olive oil
- 4 limes, juiced

INSTRUCTION
1. Pound the chicken to 1cm (1/2 in) thickness. In a large re-sealable plastic bag, combine the garlic, ginger, oil and lime juice. Seal bag and shake until blended. Open bag and add chicken. Seal bag and marinate in refrigerator for 20 minutes.
2. Remove chicken from bag and barbecue or grill, basting with marinade, until cooked through and juices run clear. Dispose of any remaining marinade.

371. Parmesan Chicken Drumsticks

Made for: Dinner | **Prep Time:** 55 minutes | **Servings:** 04
Per Serving: Kcal: 410, Protein: 42g, Fat: 26g, Net Carb: 1g

INGREDIENTS
- 1 teaspoon salt
- 1 teaspoon freshly ground black pepper
- 200g (7 oz) grated Parmesan cheese
- 1 egg
- 8 chicken drumsticks

INSTRUCTION
1. In a shallow bowl, mix together salt, pepper, and cheese.
2. In a separate bowl, beat egg until lemon colored.
3. Dip chicken in egg, coating well. Dredge in cheese.
4. Bake at 200 C / Gas mark 6 for 45 minutes, or until brown.

372. Chicken with Garlic and Lime

Made for: Dinner | **Prep Time:** 20 minutes | **Servings:** 04
Per Serving: Kcal: 198, Protein: 22g, Fat: 13g, Net Carb: 0.9g

INGREDIENTS

- 3 tablespoons olive oil
- 5 skinless, boneless chicken breast fillets, cut into bite-size pieces
- 2 cloves garlic
- 1/2 lime, juiced
- handful chopped fresh coriander
- salt and pepper to taste

INSTRUCTION

1. Heat the oil in a large frying pan over medium heat. Fry chicken pieces in the hot oil until browned on all sides. Add the garlic, and continue to cook until the chicken is no longer pink in the middle. Stir in the lime juice and coriander, and season with salt and pepper. Cook just until heated through. Remove garlic from pan. Serve chicken with rice and vegetables.

373. Scrambled eggs with tomatoes

Made for: Dinner | Prep Time: 15 minutes | Servings: 02
Per Serving: Kcal: 360, Protein: 18g, Fat: 28g, Net Carb: 1g

INGREDIENTS

- good knob butter
- 1/2 small onion, chopped
- 4 eggs, beaten
- 1 tomato, chopped
- 100g (4 oz) feta cheese, crumbled
- salt and freshly ground black pepper to taste

INSTRUCTION

1. Melt butter in a frying pan over medium heat. Sauté onions until translucent. Pour in eggs. Cook, stirring occasionally to scramble. When eggs appear almost done, stir in chopped tomatoes and feta cheese, and season with salt and pepper. Cook until cheese is melted.

374. Rosemary Chicken and Bacon

Made for: Dinner | Prep Time: 30 minutes | Servings: 04
Per Serving: Kcal: 210, Protein: 29g, Fat: 11g, Net Carb: 2g

INGREDIENTS

- 4 chicken breast halves, skinless, boneless
- 4 slices of bacon
- 4 teaspoons garlic powder
- Salt and pepper to taste
- 4 sprigs of fresh rosemary

INSTRUCTION

1. Preheat your outdoor grill to medium-high heat. Clean the grates and oil them lightly.
2. Place chicken breasts in a bowl and toss with garlic powder, salt and pepper.
3. Place one rosemary sprig on each chicken breast then wrap with a slice of bacon. Hold fast with a toothpick.
4. Transfer to the grill and cook for about 8 minutes per side, or until cooked through.

375. Grilled Turkey Burgers

Made for: Dinner | Prep Time: 20 minutes | Servings: 04
Per Serving: Kcal: 196, Protein: 23g, Fat: 9g, Net Carb: 5g

INGREDIENTS

- 1 pound ground turkey
- 1 packet dry onion soup mix
- 1/2 cup (125ml) water
- 1/2 teaspoon salt
- 1/2 teaspoon ground black pepper

INSTRUCTION

1. Preheat a grill to high heat. Oil the grates lightly.
2. Add ground turkey and the rest of the ingredients to a large bowl. Use your hands to mix until combined then form into 4 patties.
3. Cook the patties until well done, about 5 to 10 minutes per side.

376. Spicy Chicken Wings

Made for: Dinner | Prep Time: 60 minutes | Servings: 04
Per Serving: Kcal: 411, Protein: 21g, Fat: 36g, Net Carb: 5g

INGREDIENTS

- 20 chicken wings, separated at joints, tips removed
- 1/2 cup (231g) red pepper sauce
- 1/2 cup (112g) butter, melted
- 1 1/2 tablespoons chili powder
- 3/4 cup tomato sauce

INSTRUCTION

1. Preheat your oven to 375°F.
2. Combine the red pepper sauce, butter, chili powder and tomato sauce in a large bowl. Add the wings to the sauce and toss to coat.
3. Bake in the oven until cooked through, about 45 minutes.

377. Keto Scrambled eggs

Made for: Dinner | **Prep Time:** 10 minutes | **Servings:** 01
Per Serving: Kcal: 294, Protein: 18g, Fat: 31g, Net Carb: 2g

INGREDIENTS
- 2 large Eggs
- 1 tablespoon Unsalted Butter to cook eggs
- ⅛ teaspoon Salt
- ¼ cup (30g) Grated Cheddar or parmesan - optional if dairy free

   TOPPINGS
- ¼ cup (57g) Avocado
- ¼ diced Tomato

INSTRUCTION
1. In a medium mixing bowl, whisk eggs with salt and pepper.
2. Heat a non-stick skillet over medium-high heat with butter.
3. When the butter has just melted (not brown) pour in the beaten eggs, layer cheese on top, and reduce to medium heat.
4. Let the eggs cook for 30 seconds (no stirring!), then gently move a spatula across the bottom and side of the skillet to break up the eggs and form a soft egg curd.
5. Stop stirring and cook again for 15 seconds to set.
6. Repeat this process of stirring and cooking until the eggs thickened, slightly set but still soft and runny in some places.
7. Serve immediately on a slice of a keto bread loaf or on its own with diced avocado, diced tomatoes, and chives. Feel free to add other toppings like crispy bacon, sour cream, or fried mushrooms.

378. Griddled vegetable

Made for: Dinner | **Prep Time:** 50 minutes | **Servings:** 04
Per Serving: Kcal: 191, Protein: 8g, Fat: 9g, Net Carb: 3g

INGREDIENTS
- 2 tbsp olive oil
- 1 aubergine, sliced
- 2 courgettes, sliced
- 2 red onions, cut into chunky wedges
- 3 large sheets filo pastry
- 10-12 cherry tomatoes, halved
- drizzle of balsamic vinegar
- 85g feta cheese, crumbled
- 1 tsp dried oregano
- large bag mixed salad leaves and low-fat dressing, to serve

INSTRUCTION
1. Heat oven to 220C/200C fan/gas 7. Pop 33 x 23cm baking tray in the oven to heat up. Brush a griddle pan with about 1 tsp of the oil and griddle the aubergines until nicely charred, then remove. Repeat with the courgettes and onions, using a little more oil if you need to.
2. Remove the tray from the oven and brush with a little oil. Brush a large sheet of filo with oil, top with another sheet, add a little more oil and repeat with the final sheet. Transfer the pastry to the hot tray, pushing it into the edges a little.
3. Arrange the griddled veg on top, then season. Add the tomatoes, cut-side up, then drizzle on the vinegar and any remaining oil. Crumble on the feta and sprinkle with oregano. Cook for about 20 mins until crispy and golden. Serve with the dressed mixed salad leaves.

379. Keto oven-baked chicken

Made for: Dinner | **Prep Time:** 60 minutes | **Servings:** 04
Per Serving: Kcal: 1035, Protein: 87g, Fat: 59g, Net Carb: 1g

INGREDIENTS
- 3 lbs chicken, a whole bird
- 2 tsp sea salt
- ½ tsp ground black pepper
- 6 oz. butter
- 2 garlic cloves, minced

INSTRUCTION
1. Preheat the oven to 400°F (200°C). Season the chicken with salt and pepper, both inside and out.
2. Place chicken breast up in a baking dish.
3. Combine the garlic and butter in a small saucepan over medium heat. The butter should not turn brown, just melt.
4. Let the butter cool for a couple of minutes.
5. Pour the garlic butter over and inside the chicken. Bake on lower oven rack for 1-1 ½ hours, or until internal temperature reaches 180°F (82°C). Baste with the juices from the bottom of the pan every 20 minutes.
6. Serve with the juices and a side dish of your choice.

380. Keto fried chicken

Made for: Dinner | **Prep Time:** 20 minutes | **Servings:** 01
Per Serving: Kcal: 774, Protein: 27g, Fat: 66g, Net Carb: 6g

INGREDIENTS
- 6 oz. green cabbage
- 2 oz. butter
- 5 oz. boneless chicken thighs
- salt and pepper

INSTRUCTION
1. Shred the cabbage finely using a sharp knife or a food processor.
2. Heat up a generous dollop of butter in a frying pan large enough to fit both the chicken and the cabbage.
3. Season the chicken. Fry over medium heat for about 4 minutes on each side or until golden brown and fully cooked through.
4. Add more butter and add the cabbage to the same pan. Fry for another 5 minutes.
5. Season the cabbage and serve with the remaining butter.

381. Turkey Arugula Salad

Made for: Dinner | **Prep Time:** 5 minutes | **Servings:** 02
Per Serving: Kcal: 260, Protein: 20g, Fat: 15g, Net Carb: 6g

INGREDIENTS
- 3 oz (100 g) arugula leaves
- 4 oz (115 g) turkey deli meat or turkey breast meat, diced
- 10 raspberries (or blueberries)
- 1 cucumber, peeled and diced
- 2 Tablespoons (30 ml) olive oil
- Juice from 1/2 a lime

INSTRUCTION
1. Toss all the ingredients together in a large bowl and enjoy.

382. Crab-stuffed avocados

Made for: Dinner | **Prep Time:** 10 minutes | **Servings:** 02
Per Serving: Kcal: 389, Protein: 12g, Fat: 38g, Net Carb: 2g

INGREDIENTS
- 100g (1/2 cup) white crabmeat
- 1 tsp Dijon mustard
- 2 tbsp olive oil
- handful basil leaves, shredded with a few of the smaller leaves left whole, to serve
- 1 red chilli, deseeded and chopped
- 2 avocados

INSTRUCTION
1. To make the crab mix, flake the crabmeat into a small bowl and mix in the mustard and oil, then season to taste. Can be made the day ahead. Add the basil and chilli just before serving.
2. To serve, halve and stone the avocados. Fill each cavity with a quarter of the crab mix, scatter with a few of the smaller basil leaves and eat with teaspoons.

383. Cumin Crusted Lamb Chops

Made for: Dinner | **Prep Time:** 30 minutes | **Servings:** 04
Per Serving: Kcal: 702, Protein: 47g, Fat: 60g, Net Carb: 2g

INGREDIENTS
- 2 racks of lamb (3 lb or 1.3 kg)
- ¾ cup (72 g) cumin powder
- 3 Tablespoons (18 g) paprika
- 1 teaspoon (1 g) chili powder (more if preferred)
- 1 Tablespoon (15 g) salt (less if preferred)

INSTRUCTION
1. Cut the racks of lamb into individual lamb chops (approx 20 chops).
2. Combine the spices and salt and dip the lamb chops into it.
3. Grill the lamb until done to the level you enjoy.

384. Masala frittata with avocado salsa

Made for: Dinner | **Prep Time:** 40 minutes | **Servings:** 04
Per Serving: Kcal: 347, Protein: 16g, Fat: 25g, Net Carb: 1g

INGREDIENTS
- 2 tbsp rapeseed oil
- 3 onions, 2½ thinly sliced, ½ finely chopped
- 1 tbsp Madras curry paste
- 500g (3 cup) cherry tomatoes, halved
- 1 red chilli, deseeded and finely chopped
- small pack coriander, roughly chopped
- 8 large eggs, beaten
- 1 avocado, stoned, peeled and cubed
- juice 1 lemon

INSTRUCTION
1. Heat the oil in a medium non-stick, ovenproof frying pan. Tip in the sliced onions and cook over a medium heat for about 10 mins until soft and golden. Add

the Madras paste and fry for 1 min more, then tip in half the tomatoes and half the chilli. Cook until the mixture is thick and the tomatoes have all burst.

2. Heat the grill to high. Add half the coriander to the eggs and season, then pour over the spicy onion mixture. Stir gently once or twice, then cook over a low heat for 8-10 mins until almost set. Transfer to the grill for 3-5 mins until set.

3. To make the salsa, mix the avocado, remaining chilli and tomatoes, chopped onion, remaining coriander and the lemon juice together, then season and serve with the frittata.

385. Beef salad with caper

Made for: Dinner | **Prep Time:** 20 minutes | **Servings:** 04
Per Serving: Kcal: 628, Protein: 40g, Fat: 50g, Net Carb: 2g

INGREDIENTS

- bag green salad leaves, such as rocket and mizuna
- 175g (1 cup) cherry tomatoes, halved
- 4-5 roasted red peppers from a jar, cut into strips
- 8-12 slices cooked roast beef, depending on thickness

For The Dressing
- 2 tbsp lemon juice
- 1 tbsp wholegrain mustard
- 1 tbsp capers, chopped if large
- 3 tbsp chopped parsley
- 5 tbsp olive oil

INSTRUCTION

1. Scatter the salad leaves, tomatoes and red peppers over a serving platter, then arrange the beef slices on top.

2. Put all the dressing ingredients into a small bowl with some salt and pepper, then whisk vigorously with a fork until thickened. Drizzle over the beef and salad and serve.

386. Cheese, Mortadella and Salami

Made for: Dinner | **Prep Time:** 10 minutes | **Servings:** 04
Per Serving: Kcal: 381, Protein: 17g, Fat: 32g, Net Carb: 5g

INGREDIENTS

- 10 slices Provolone cheese
- 4 ounces of mayonnaise
- 10 slices Mortadella
- 10 slices Genoa salami
- 10 pitted olives

INSTRUCTION

1. Add a thin layer of mayonnaise onto each slice of cheese, then add another layer of Mortadella on top of the mayonnaise.

2. Top up with a slice of Genoa salami, roll them up, and place olives on the top.

3. For a party of 10, this is a great way to cut costs.

387. Keto chicken and green beans plate

Made for: Dinner | **Prep Time:** 15 minutes | **Servings:** 02
Per Serving: Kcal: 896, Protein: 75g, Fat: 65g, Net Carb: 2g

INGREDIENTS

- 7 oz. fresh green beans
- 2 tbsp butter for frying
- 1 lb of cooked chicken
- 4 oz. butter for serving
- salt and pepper

INSTRUCTION

1. Fry the green beans in butter over medium heat for a couple of minutes. Season with salt and pepper to taste.

2. Put chicken, green beans and butter on a plate and serve.

388. Chicken and Feta cheese plate

Made for: Dinner | **Prep Time:** 5 minutes | **Servings:** 02
Per Serving: Kcal: 485, Protein: 63g, Fat: 79g, Net Carb: 6g

INGREDIENTS

- 1 lb of rotisserie chicken
- 7 oz. feta cheese
- 2 tomatoes
- 2 cups (400g) leafy greens
- 10 black olives
- 1/3 cup (80g) olive oil
- salt and pepper

INSTRUCTION

1. Slice the tomatoes and put them on a plate together with chicken, feta cheese, lettuce and olives.

2. Season with salt and pepper to taste. Serve with olive oil.

389. Pink Pickled Onion Salad

Made for: Dinner | **Prep Time:** 15 minutes | **Servings:** 04

Per Serving: Kcal: 336, Protein: 18g, Fat: 30g, Net Carb: 4g

INGREDIENTS

- 240g pack peppered smoked mackerel, torn into pieces
- 100g bag watercress
- 250g pack ready-cooked beetroot
- 100g bag honey-roasted mixed nuts

For the dressing
- 1 small red onion, very thinly sliced
- 3 tbsp sherry vinegar
- pinch of sugar
- 4 tbsp extra virgin olive oil

INSTRUCTION

1. Mix together the onion, vinegar, sugar and a pinch of salt. Leave to pickle while you dice the beetroot and roughly chop the nuts.
2. Divide the watercress and smoked mackerel between six plates. Scatter over the beetroot and nuts, then top with a cluster of the pickled onions. Whisk the oil into the pickling vinegar, then drizzle the dressing around the outside of each plate.

390. Mushroom brunch

Made for: Dinner | Prep Time: 20 minutes | Servings: 02
Per Serving: Kcal: 300, Protein: 26g, Fat: 23g, Net Carb: 2g

INGREDIENTS

- 250g (3 cup) mushrooms
- 1 garlic clove
- 1 tbsp olive oil
- 160g (3/2 cup)) bag kale
- 4 eggs

INSTRUCTION

1. Slice the mushrooms and crush the garlic clove. Heat the olive oil in a large non-stick frying pan, then fry the garlic over a low heat for 1 min. Add the mushrooms and cook until soft. Then, add the kale. If the kale won't all fit in the pan, add half and stir until wilted, then add the rest. Once all the kale is wilted, season.
2. Now crack in the eggs and keep them cooking gently for 2-3 mins. Then, cover with the lid to for a further 2-3 mins or until the eggs are cooked to your liking. Serve with bread.

391. Herb omelette with Avocado

Made for: Dinner | Prep Time: 10 minutes | Servings: 01
Per Serving: Kcal: 703, Protein: 28g, Fat: 63g, Net Carb: 3g

INGREDIENTS

- 2 large eggs
- 1/2 cup grated parmesan cheese (30 g/ 1 oz)
- 1 tbsp basil, freshly chopped
- 1/2 tbsp oregano, freshly chopped
- 2 tbsp ghee, butter or coconut oil (30 ml)
- pinch sea salt
- 1/2 small avocado (50 g/ 1.8 oz)
- 1 slice bacon, crisped up (30 g/ 1 oz)

INSTRUCTION

1. Crack the eggs into a bowl and add finely chopped herbs and parmesan cheese. If you don't have basil and oregano, use chives, parsley or the green part of one spring onion.
2. Heat a skillet greased with ghee (or butter, coconut oil) over medium-high heat. Once hot, pour the egg mixture in and lower the heat. Use a spatula to bring in the omelet from the sides towards the centre for the first 30 seconds. This will ensure even cooking.
3. When the top seems firm, flip on the other side for just about 30 seconds. Alternatively, you can fold the omelet in half and cook for another 30-60 seconds. Do not cook for too long or the omelet will be dry.
4. When done, place on a serving plate and top with crisped up bacon and sliced avocado. Serve immediately or refrigerate for up to a day. Reheat before serving.

392. Bacon, Egg & Asparagus

Made for: Dinner | Prep Time: 40 minutes | Servings: 04
Per Serving: Kcal: 609, Protein: 25g, Fat: 53g, Net Carb: 5g

INGREDIENTS

- 4 slices raw bacon (120 g/4.2 oz) - or 64 g/2.2 oz crisped up
- 10-14 asparagus spears, woody ends removed (100 g/ 3.5 oz)
- 1 tbsp butter or ghee (14 g/0.5 oz)
- 2 large eggs
- 1 small head lettuce such as little gem (100 g/3.5 oz)
- 1/2 large avocado, sliced (100 g/3.5 oz)

- 1/3 cup crumbled feta cheese (50 g/1.8 oz)
- 1/3 cup cherry tomatoes, halved (50 g/1.8 oz)
- 2 tsp chopped chives or spring onion
- 1/4 cup flaked almonds, preferably toasted (23 g/0.8 oz)

DRESSING
- 3 tbsp extra virgin olive oil (45 ml/ 1.5 fl oz)
- 1 tsp Dijon mustard
- 2 tsp red wine vinegar
- sea salt and black pepper, to taste

INSTRUCTION
1. Crisp up the bacon in the oven or in a skillet. Oven is better for large batches. If you're only cooking 4 slices it's faster to cook in a lightly greased skillet.
2. Skillet: In a frying pan, fry the bacon rashers for 2 minutes per side until crisp. I dry fried them but you can add a touch of olive oil or ghee if you prefer to prevent sticking. All depends on your pan. Drain on a sheet of kitchen paper.
3. Oven: Preheat the oven to 190 °C/ 375 °F. Line a baking tray with baking paper. Lay the bacon strips out flat on the baking paper, leaving space so they don't overlap. Place the tray in the oven and cook for about 10-15 minutes until golden brown. The time depends on the thickness of the bacon slices.
   When done, remove from the oven and set aside to cool down. Store any leftover bacon in the fridge for up to 4 days.
4. Slice the tomatoes and avocado. Chop the lettuce.
5. Prepare the dressing my mixing the olive oil, mustard, vinegar, salt and pepper together in a small bowl.
6. Place water in the bottom of a steamer pan. Steam the asparagus for 5 – 8 minutes depending on the thickness of the asparagus until el dente. Remove from the pan, coat in 1 tablespoon of butter and chop into chunks.
7. While the asparagus is cooking, boil the eggs to your liking. 3 minutes for soft boiled up to 10 minutes for hard boiled. Run under cold water before peeling off the shell.
8. Toss the lettuce through the tomatoes, crispy bacon and dressing. Top with boiled egg, feta, avocado, asparagus, chives, and almonds.

9. Best eaten fresh but can be stored in the fridge for a day.

393. Soft-boiled eggs with pancetta avocado

Made for: Dinner | **Prep Time:** 15 minutes | **Servings:** 02
Per Serving: Kcal: 517, Protein: 22g, Fat: 46g, Net Carb: 1g

INGREDIENTS
- 4 eggs
- 1 tbsp vegetable oil
- 1 ripe avocado , cut into slices
- 100g (1/2 cup) smoked pancetta rashers

INSTRUCTION
1. Bring a large saucepan of salted water to the boil. Carefully drop the eggs into the water and boil for 5 mins for runny yolks.
2. Meanwhile, heat the oil in a non-stick pan and wrap each avocado slice in pancetta. Fry for 2-3 mins over a high heat until cooked and crisp.
3. Serve the eggs in egg cups with the pancetta avocado soldiers on the side for dipping.

394. Pigeon & hedgerow salad

Made for: Dinner | **Prep Time:** 20 minutes | **Servings:** 02
Per Serving: Kcal: 411, Protein: 18g, Fat: 36g, Net Carb: 2g

INGREDIENTS
- 2 pigeon breasts, skin removed
- 2 tbsp olive oil

For The Dressing
- 3 tbsp olive oil
- 2 tsp Dijon mustard
- 1 tbsp cider vinegar
- 1 bunch chives, half snipped, half finely chopped

For The Salad
- handful shelled hazelnuts, roughly chopped
- 2 large handfuls mixed salad leaves
- small handful parsley leaves
- 100g (1/2 cup) blackberries

INSTRUCTION
1. Toss the pigeon in the olive oil and some cracked black pepper, then set aside until ready to cook. Make the dressing by mixing the oil, mustard and vinegar with

the finely chopped chives, a tiny splash of water and some seasoning. Set aside.

2. Heat a frying pan, dry-fry the hazelnuts, then set aside. Place the pan back on the heat, then pan-fry the pigeon breasts for 2-3 mins on each side until plump. Leave to rest for 5 mins.

3. When the pigeon has rested, remove to a chopping board. Toss the salad ingredients together in a bowl with the snipped chives and a drizzle of dressing, then pile in the centre of 2 plates. Finely slice the pigeon breasts and arrange around the salads. Spoon over the rest of the dressing and serve.

395. Mushroom with poached eggs

Made for: Dinner | Prep Time: 35 minutes | Servings: 04
Per Serving: Kcal: 283, Protein: 15g, Fat: 17g, Net Carb: g

INGREDIENTS

- 1 ½ tbsp rapeseed oil
- 2 large onions, halved and sliced
- 500g closed cup mushrooms, quartered
- 1 tbsp fresh thyme leaves, plus extra for sprinkling
- 500g fresh tomatoes, chopped
- 1 tsp smoked paprika
- 4 tsp omega seed mix (see tip)
- 4 large eggs

INSTRUCTION

1. Heat the oil in a large non-stick frying pan and fry the onions for a few mins. Cover the pan and leave the onions to cook in their own steam for 5 mins more.

2. Tip in the mushrooms with the thyme and cook, stirring frequently, for 5 mins until softened. Add the tomatoes and paprika, cover the pan and cook for 5 mins until pulpy. Stir through the seed mix.

3. If you're making this recipe as part of our two-person Summer Healthy Diet Plan, poach two of the eggs in lightly simmering water to your liking. Serve on top of half the hash with a sprinkling of fresh thyme and some black pepper. Chill the remaining hash to warm in a pan and eat with freshly poached eggs on another day. If you're serving four people, poach all four eggs, divide the hash between four plates, sprinkle with thyme and black pepper and serve with the eggs on top.

396. Chilli avocado

Made for: Dinner | Prep Time: 5 minutes | Servings: 01
Per Serving: Kcal: 102, Protein: 1g, Fat: 10g, Net Carb: 1g

INGREDIENTS

- ½ small avocado
- ¼ tsp chilli flakes
- juice of ¼ lime

INSTRUCTION

1. Sprinkle the avocado with the chilli flakes, lime juice and a little black pepper, and eat with a spoon.

397. Italian keto plate

Made for: Dinner | Prep Time: 5 minutes | Servings: 04
Per Serving: Kcal: 824, Protein: 38g, Fat: 65g, Net Carb: 10g

INGREDIENTS

- 7 oz. fresh mozzarella cheese
- 7 oz. prosciutto, sliced
- 2 tomatoes
- 1/3 cup (80g) olive oil
- 10 green olives
- salt and pepper

INSTRUCTION

1. Put tomatoes, prosciutto, cheese and olives on a plate. Serve with olive oil and season with salt and pepper to taste.

398. Spicy Garlic Lime Chicken

Made for: Dinner | Prep Time: 25 minutes | Servings: 04
Per Serving: Kcal: 220, Protein: 27g, Fat: 11g, Net Carb: 2g

INGREDIENTS

- ¾ teaspoon salt
- ¼ teaspoon black pepper
- ¼ teaspoon cayenne pepper
- ⅛ teaspoon paprika
- ¼ teaspoon garlic powder
- ⅛ teaspoon onion powder
- ¼ teaspoon dried thyme
- ¼ teaspoon dried parsley
- 4 boneless, skinless chicken breast halves
- 2 tablespoons butter
- 1 tablespoon olive oil
- 2 teaspoons garlic powder
- 3 tablespoons lime juice

INSTRUCTION

1. In a small bowl, mix together salt, black pepper, cayenne, paprika,

1/4 teaspoon garlic powder, onion powder, thyme and parsley. Sprinkle spice mixture generously on both sides of chicken breasts.
2. Heat butter and olive oil in a large heavy skillet over medium heat. Saute chicken until golden brown, about 6 minutes on each side. Sprinkle with 2 teaspoons garlic powder and lime juice. Cook 5 minutes more, stirring frequently to coat evenly with sauce.

399. Bacon Cheddar Egg Cups

Made for: Dinner | Prep Time: 35 minutes | Cups: 06
Per Cup: Kcal: 192, Protein: 12g, Fat: 15g, Net Carb: 2g

INGREDIENTS
- 6 medium eggs
- 1 cup (130g) grated turnip or kohlrabi
- 6 slices bacon, cooked (180 g /6.4 oz)
- 1/4 cup (57g) grated cheddar cheese
- pinch of salt and black pepper, to taste

INSTRUCTION
1. Place the bacon in a hot pan and cook for a few minutes. Turn and cook for a few more minutes. The bacon should be cooked but still soft (not too crispy).
2. Preheat oven to 190 °C /375 °F (conventional), or 170 °C /340 °F (fan assisted).
   Divide the grated turnip between 6 silicone muffin molds. Place a strip of bacon into the mold around the edges.
3. Place a tablespoon of cheese into the mold then crack an egg into each mold.
4. Transfer to oven for 20-25 minutes or until set. Eat warm or cold. Store in the fridge for up to 4 days.

400. Avocado, prawn & fennel

Made for: Dinner | Prep Time: 10 minutes | Servings: 04
Per Serving: Kcal: 223, Protein: 13g, Fat: 18g, Net Carb: 1g

INGREDIENTS
For The Dressing
- 4 tbsp extra-virgin olive oil
- 1 segmented orange, plus the juice from the trimmings
- juice 1 lemon

For The Salad
- 1 fennel bulb, trimmed, halved and finely sliced
- 1 avocado, quartered, peeled and sliced

- 200g (1.5 cup) cooked king prawn
- 3 spring onions, sliced
- 55g bag (2 cup) wild rocket

INSTRUCTION
1. Make the dressing by mixing the oil and citrus juices together in a small bowl with some salt and pepper, then set aside.
2. In a bowl, toss all the other ingredients, except the rocket, together with the orange segments and half of the dressing. Scatter the rocket leaves into 4 Martini glasses or small bowls, pile the salad into the centre, then drizzle with the remaining dressing just before serving.

401. Creamy Taco Soup

Made for: Dinner | Prep Time: 35 minutes | Servings: 04
Per Serving: Kcal: 348, Protein: 21g, Fat: 27g, Net Carb: 2g

INGREDIENTS
- 1 lb ground beef or turkey or chicken
- 1 tbsp oil of choice
- 1 small onion diced
- 2-3 cloves garlic minced
- 1 small green bell pepper diced (optional)
- 1 (10 oz) can Rotel tomatoes or 1 large tomato, chopped
- 1 (8 oz) pkg cream cheese or 1 cup heavy cream
- 2 tablespoons teco seasoning homemade or 1 packet
- Salt and pepper to taste
- 1 (14.5) oz can beef broth 1.5 cups

INSTRUCTION
1. Add 1 tablespoon oil to a pot or large pot or dutch oven, brown beef, onion, and garlic over medium-high heat for 7-8 minutes or until the ground beef is browned through.
2. Add the bell pepper, Rotel diced tomatoes, cream cheese, and spices. Stir for 4-5 minutes or until tomatoes are soft and tender and cream cheese is mixed through.
3. Pour in beef broth and reduce heat to low-medium. Simmer 15-20 minutes or until desired thickness is achieved.
4. Serve in small soup bowls. Top with freshly sliced avocado, sour cream, shredded cheese, freshly minced cilantro, jalapeno, and a drizzle of lime.

402. Soft-boiled duck egg with bacon

Made for: Dinner | **Prep Time:** 35 minutes | **Servings:** 04
Per Serving: Kcal: 307, Protein: 21g, Fat: 20g, Net Carb: 8g

INGREDIENTS
- 8 asparagus spears (about 300g), woody ends discarded
- 4 long thin slices rustic bread (preferably sourdough)
- 8 rashers smoked streaky bacon or pancetta
- 4 duck eggs

INSTRUCTION
1. Heat your grill to high. Snap off the woody ends of the asparagus spears and discard. Cut the bread into 12 soldiers, a little shorter than the asparagus.
2. Place a spear onto each soldier and wrap tightly with a rasher of bacon. Place on a baking tray, season and grill for 15 mins or until the bacon is crisp.
3. Bring a pan of salted water to the boil and simmer the duck eggs for about 7 mins, to get a runny yolk and a cooked white. Serve immediately with the warm soldiers for dipping.

403. Tarator-style salmon

Made for: Dinner | **Prep Time:** 25 minutes | **Servings:** 04
Per Serving: Kcal: 398, Protein: 34g, Fat: 27g, Net Carb: 2g

INGREDIENTS
- 50g (1/2 cup) walnuts, finely chopped
- large handful parsley leaves, finely chopped
- 2 tsp sumac
- ½ red onion, finely chopped
- zest and juice 1 lemon
- 4 salmon fillets
- 2 tbsp hummus
- couscous, pitta bread or flatbreads, to serve (optional)
- yogurt, to serve (optional)

INSTRUCTION
1. Heat oven to 200C/180C fan/gas 6. Mix together the chopped walnuts, parsley, sumac, red onion, lemon zest and juice of half the lemon. Season lightly and set aside.
2. Put the salmon on a baking tray and roast for 12 mins, then remove, spread with the hummus and return it to the oven for another 3 mins.

Sprinkle over the walnut mixture and serve with the remaining lemon half to squeeze over along with couscous, pita or flatbreads, and yogurt on the side, if you like.

404. Chicken Broccoli Casserole

Made for: Dinner | **Prep Time:** 25 minutes | **Servings:** 04
Per Serving: Kcal: 842, Protein: 32g, Fat: 104g, Net Carb: 2g

INGREDIENTS
- 2 cups shredded chicken
- 1 medium-sized broccoli (cut into florets)
- 6 oz cream cheese (softened)
- 1/2 cup (50g) chicken stock
- 1/2 cup (56g) cheddar cheese (shredded)
- salt & pepper to taste

INSTRUCTIONS
1. Preheat oven to 390°F (200°C)
2. Place all of your shredded chicken into the casserole and spread it in an even layer
3. In a medium-sized microwave-safe bowl, add in the cream cheese and microwave for 20-30 seconds until it's slightly softened. Add in 1/2 cup chicken stock and whisk them together until you get all the lumps out. Taste the sauce and if needed, add some salt & pepper, I only added a tiny bit since my chicken stock was already quite salty.
4. Spread all of the cream sauce over the shred chicken.
5. Add in broccoli florets in an even layer and push them slightly into the sauce.
6. Sprinkle cheese on top and cook in a preheated oven for 20 minutes, until the cheese is melted and golden.

405. Vegan Keto Green Smoothie

Made for: Dinner | **Prep Time:** 5 minutes | **Servings:** 01
Per Serving: Kcal: 114, Protein: 4g, Fat: 10g, Net Carb: 3g

INGREDIENTS
- 1/2 cup (120g) unsweetened almond milk
- 1/2 lemon juice
- 1 oz Avocado (about 1/8 avocado)
- 1 tbsp hemp seeds
- 1.2 tsp vanilla extract
- One packet keto sweetener
- 1 cup of ice cubes

INSTRUCTIONS
1. Add all your ingredients except ice

cubes to your blender and blend till smooth.
2. Add the ice cubes and blend some more, for about 1 minute.
3. Pour the smoothie into a glass and enjoy!

406. Keto pizza omelette

Made for: Dinner | **Prep Time:** 40 minutes | **Servings:** 04
Per Serving: Kcal: 710, Protein: 45g, Fat: 50g, Net Carb: 6g

INGREDIENTS

Crust
- Eight eggs
- 10 oz. mozzarella cheese, shredded
- 8 tbsp cream cheese
- ½ tsp salt
- 2 tsp garlic powder

Topping
- 6 tbsp tomato sauce
- 12 oz. mozzarella cheese, shredded
- 4 tsp dried oregano

INSTRUCTIONS
1. Preheat the oven to 400°F (200°C).
2. Start by making the crust. Crack eggs into a medium-sized bowl and add the rest of the ingredients. Give it a good stir to combine.
3. Line a pie plate (a normal sized pie plate is big enough for two portions), or any other ovenproof dish, with parchment paper (crumple the sheet before you flatten it out to make it stay down more easily). Pour in the pizza crust batter. Spread it out evenly with a spatula. Bake in the oven for 15 minutes until the pizza crust turns golden.
4. Spread tomato sauce on the crust with the help of the backside of a spoon. Top with cheese.
5. Bake for another 10 minutes or until the pizza has turned a golden brown colour.
6. Sprinkle with oregano and serve.

407. Salmon with Butter and Lemon

Made for: Dinner | **Prep Time:** 15 minutes | **Servings:** 02
Per Serving: Kcal: 580, Protein: 32g, Fat: 50g, Net Carb: 1g

INGREDIENTS
- ½ tbsp olive oil
- 1 lb salmon
- ½ tsp sea salt
- ground black pepper
- 3½ oz. butter
- ½ lemon

INSTRUCTIONS
1. Preheat the oven to 400°F (200°C).
2. Grease a large baking dish with olive oil. Place the salmon, with the skin-side down, in the prepared baking dish. Generously season with salt and pepper.
3. Slice the lemon thinly and place on top of the salmon. Cover with half of the butter in thin slices.
4. Bake on middle rack for about 20-30 minutes, or until the salmon is opaque and flakes easily with a fork.
5. Heat the rest of the butter in a small saucepan until it starts to bubble. Remove from heat and let cool a little. Gently add some lemon juice.
6. Serve with lemon butter and a side dish of your choice. See below for suggestions.

408. Cashew, chilli & crusted fish

Made for: Dinner | **Prep Time:** 25 minutes | **Servings:** 04
Per Serving: Kcal: 356, Protein: 32g, Fat: 22g, Net Carb: 5g

INGREDIENTS
- 1 tbsp vegetable oil
- 1 fat garlic clove, finely grated until it resembles a paste
- 4 skinless sustainable white fish fillets, about 140g each
- 5 tbsp lime juice
- For the crust
- 100g (1/2 cup) cashews
- 4 mild red chillies
- 6 fat garlic cloves, peeled
- thumb-tip-size piece fresh root ginger, roughly chopped
- 1 tbsp cumin powder
- 2 tbsp vegetable oil

INSTRUCTIONS
1. Rub the oil and garlic paste over the fish with 2 tbsp of the lime juice. Season, then marinate for 20-30 mins.
2. Heat oven to 190C/170C fan/gas 5. Whizz together the crust ingredients and the remaining lime juice to make a rough paste. Pat the fish fillets dry with some kitchen paper, then press a quarter of the crust onto each fillet. Lift onto an oiled baking tray, then roast for 12-15 mins until cooked through.

409. Super Packed Cheese Omelette

Made for: Dinner | Prep Time: 15 minutes | Servings: 04
Per Serving: Kcal: 438, Protein: 25g, Fat: 35g, Net Carb: 2g

INGREDIENTS
- Three large mushrooms (sliced).
- Three eggs.
- 1 oz cheddar cheese (grated).
- 1 oz butter.
- ¼ onion (sliced).
- Pinch salt and pepper.

INSTRUCTIONS
1. In a bowl, whisk together the eggs, salt and pepper.
2. In a large frying pan, melt the butter and fry onions and mushrooms until tender.
3. Pour in the egg mixture so that it surrounds the onions and mushrooms.
4. As the sides begin to firm and it is still slightly runny in the middle, sprinkle on the cheese
5. Continue cooking until egg mixture is completely formed and cooked through.

410. Keto Chicken Fajitas

Made for: Dinner | Prep Time: 40 minutes | Servings: 04
Per Serving: Kcal: 208, Protein: 27g, Fat: 9g, Net Carb: 3g

INGREDIENTS
- 1 tablespoon Worcestershire sauce
- 1 tablespoon cider vinegar
- 1 tablespoon soy sauce
- 1 teaspoon chilli powder
- 1 clove garlic, minced
- 1 dash hot pepper sauce, such as Tabasco
- 675g (1 1/2 lb) boneless, skinless chicken thighs, cut into strips
- 1 tablespoon vegetable oil
- 1 onion, thinly sliced
- 1 green pepper, sliced
- 1/2 lemon, juiced

INSTRUCTIONS
1. In a medium bowl, combine Worcestershire sauce, vinegar, soy sauce, chilli powder, garlic and hot pepper sauce. Place chicken in sauce, and turn once to coat. Marinate for 30 minutes at room temperature, or cover and refrigerate for several hours.
2. Heat oil in a large frying pan over high heat. Add chicken strips to the pan, and sauté for 5 minutes.

Add the onion and green pepper, and sauté another 3 minutes. Remove from heat, and sprinkle with lemon juice.

411. Keto crab meat and egg plate

Made for: Dinner | Prep Time: 15 minutes | Servings: 02
Per Serving: Kcal: 620, Protein: 28g, Fat: 62g, Net Carb: 1g

INGREDIENTS
- Four eggs
- 12 oz. canned crab meat
- Two avocados
- ½ cup (80g) cottage cheese
- ½ cup (120g) mayonnaise
- 1½ oz. baby spinach
- 2 tbsp olive oil
- ½ tsp chilli flakes (optional)
- salt and pepper

INSTRUCTIONS
1. Begin by cooking the eggs. Lower them carefully into boiling water and boil for 4-8 minutes depending on whether you like them soft or hard-boiled.
2. Cool the eggs in ice-cold water for 1-2 minutes when they're done; this will make it easier to remove the shell. Peel eggs.
3. Place eggs, crab meat, avocado, cottage cheese, mayonnaise and spinach on a plate.
4. Drizzle olive oil over the spinach. Season with salt and pepper.
Sprinkle optional chilli flakes on the avocado and serve.

412. Keto fried salmon with broccoli

Made for: Dinner | Prep Time: 25 minutes | Servings: 04
Per Serving: Kcal: 926, Protein: 44g, Fat: 80g, Net Carb: 5g

INGREDIENTS
Lemon mayo
- 1 cup (240g) mayonnaise
- 2 tbsp lemon juice

Salmon with broccoli
- 1 lb broccoli
- 1¾ lbs salmon, boneless fillets
- 2 oz. butter, divided
- salt and pepper

INSTRUCTIONS
1. Mix mayonnaise and lemon juice. Set aside for later.

2. Divide the salmon into serving-sized pieces—season with salt and pepper.
3. Rinse and trim the broccoli, including the stem. Chop into bite-sized pieces.
4. Fry the salmon in half the butter over medium heat for a couple of minutes on each side. Lower the heat towards the end. Remove from pan and keep warm.
5. Add the remaining butter to the same skillet and cook the broccoli over medium heat for 3-4 minutes or until it is slightly softened and golden brown—season with salt and pepper to taste.
6. Serve the fried salmon and broccoli together with a hearty dollop of lemon mayo.

413. Keto bacon and eggs plate

Made for: Dinner | **Prep Time:** 15 minutes | **Servings:** 02
Per Serving: Kcal: 974, Protein: 27g, Fat: 90g, Net Carb: 8g

INGREDIENTS
- 5 oz. bacon
- Four eggs
- Two avocados
- 1 oz. walnuts
- One green bell pepper
- salt and Pepper
- 1 tbsp fresh chives, finely chopped (optional)

  ### Serving
- 1 oz. arugula lettuce
- 2 tbsp olive oil

INSTRUCTIONS
1. Fry the bacon over medium heat until crispy.
2. Remove from pan and keep warm. Leave the fat that's accumulated in the pan. Lower the heat to medium-low and fry the eggs in the same frying pan.
3. Place Bacon, eggs, avocado, nuts, bell pepper and arugula on a plate.
4. Drizzle the remaining bacon fat on top of the eggs—season to taste.

414. Keto Lamb chops with butter

Made for: Dinner | **Prep Time:** 20 minutes | **Servings:** 02
Per Serving: Kcal: 725, Protein: 45g, Fat: 62g, Net Carb: 2g

INGREDIENTS
- Four lamb chops
- ½ tbsp butter
- ½ tbsp olive oil

- salt and pepper

  For serving
- 2 oz. herb butter
- ½ lemon, in wedges

INSTRUCTIONS
1. Let the chops reach room temperature before they are fried or grilled. The meat should not be cold when it's cooked, or it won't get a nice brown surface. If you make a few cuts into the fat part, the chop won't curl up.
2. Season with salt and pepper.
3. Fry in butter and some olive oil if you're using a frying pan. If you're grilling, just brush on some olive oil before placing the chops on the grill.
4. Fry for 3-4 minutes, depending on how thick the chops are. Really thick chops will need a longer cooking time. However, it's OK for   lamb to be a little pink inside.
5. Serve with lemon wedges and herb butter.

415. Keto Baked Bacon Omelet

Made for: Dinner | **Prep Time:** 30 minutes | **Servings:** 02
Per Serving: Kcal: 690, Protein: 47g, Fat: 50g, Net Carb: 5g

INGREDIENTS
- 31/2 ounce. Bacon
- 2 ounces. mushrooms, sliced
- 3/4 pounds ground beef
- 1/8 tsp salt & Pepper
- 2 ounces. shredded cheddar cheese
- 1/2 iceberg lettuce, leaves separated and washed

INSTRUCTIONS
1. In a large skillet, cook bacon to desired crispness. Remove from the pan and set aside. Leave the grease in the pan.
2. Add mushrooms to the pan and sauté until browned and tender, about 5 to 7 minutes. Remove from pan and set aside.
3. Add ground beef and season with salt and pepper. Sauté until beef is cooked through, about 10 minutes, breaking up chunks with the back of a wooden spoon.
4. Spoon ground beef into lettuce leaves, sprinkle with cheddar cheese and top with bacon and mushrooms.

416. Keto ground beef and broccoli

Made for: Dinner | **Prep Time:** 20 minutes | **Servings:** 02
Per Serving: Kcal: 740, Protein: 22g, Fat: 70g, Net Carb: 2g

INGREDIENTS
- 2/3 lb (170g) ground beef
- 3 oz. butter
- ½ lb (225g) broccoli
- salt and pepper
- ½ cup (240g) mayonnaise (optional)

INSTRUCTIONS
1. Rinse and trim the broccoli, including the stem. Cut into small florets. Peel the stem and cut into small pieces.
2. Heat up a hearty dollop of butter in a frying pan where you can fit both the ground beef and broccoli.
3. Brown the ground beef on high heat until it is almost done. Season to taste with salt and pepper.
4. Lower the heat, add more butter and fry the broccoli for 3-5 minutes. Stir the ground beef every now and then.
5. Season the broccoli. Top with the remaining butter and serve while still hot. It's also delicious to serve with an extra dollop of crème Fraiche or mayonnaise.

417. Oven-baked chicken in garlic butter

Made for: Dinner | **Prep Time:** 65 minutes | **Servings:** 02
Per Serving: Kcal: 980, Protein: 59g, Fat: 87g, Net Carb: 1g

INGREDIENTS
- 3 lbs chicken, a whole bird
- 2 tsp sea salt
- ½ tsp ground black pepper
- 6 oz. butter
- Two garlic cloves, minced

INSTRUCTIONS
1. Preheat the oven to 400°F (200°C). Season the chicken with salt and pepper, both inside and out.
2. Place chicken breast up in a baking dish.
3. Combine the garlic and butter in a small saucepan over medium heat. The butter should not turn brown, just melt.
4. Let the butter cool for a couple of minutes.
5. Pour the garlic butter over and inside the chicken. Bake on the lower oven rack for 1-1 ½ hours,

or until internal temperature reaches 180°F (82°C). Baste with the juices from the bottom of the pan every 20 minutes.
6. Serve with the juices and a side dish of your choice.

418. Keto Apple Salad

Made for: Dinner | **Prep Time:** 10 minutes | **Servings:** 02
Per Serving: Kcal: 651, Protein: 30g, Fat: 60g, Net Carb: 1g

INGREDIENTS
- 2 cups (170g) broccoli florets, roughly chopped
- 2 ounces pecans, chopped
- One apple, cored and grated
- One green onion stalk, finely chopped
- Salt and black pepper to the taste
- Two teaspoons poppy seeds
- One teaspoon apple cider vinegar
- ¼ cup (60g) mayonnaise
- ½ teaspoon lemon juice ¼ cup sour cream

INSTRUCTIONS
1. In a salad bowl, mix apple with broccoli, green onion and pecans and stir.
2. Add poppy seeds, salt and pepper and toss gently.
3. In a bowl, mix mayo with sour cream, vinegar and lemon juice and whisk well.
4. Pour this over salad, toss to coat well and serve cold for lunch!

419. Baked Eggs and Zoodles with Avocado

Made for: Dinner | **Prep Time:** 25 minutes | **Servings:** 02
Per Serving: Kcal: 633, Protein: 20g, Fat: 53g, Net Carb: 2g

INGREDIENTS
- Nonstick spray
- Three zucchini or courgette, spiralized into noodles
- Two tablespoons extra-virgin olive oil
- Kosher salt and freshly ground black Pepper
- Four large eggs
- Red-pepper flakes, for garnishing
- Fresh basil, for garnishing
- Two avocados, halved and thinly sliced

INSTRUCTIONS
1. Preheat the oven to 350°F. Lightly grease a baking sheet with nonstick spray.

2. In a large bowl, toss the zucchini noodles and olive oil to combine—season with salt and pepper. Divide into four even portions, transfer to the baking sheet and shape each into a nest.
3. Gently crack an egg into the centre of each nest. Bake until the eggs are set, 9 to 11 minutes. Season with salt and pepper; garnish with red pepper flakes and basil. Serve alongside the avocado slices.

420. Grilled Lemon-Garlic Salmon

Made for: Dinner | **Prep Time:** 30 minutes | **Servings:** 04
Per Serving: Kcal: 268, Protein: 29g, Fat: 16g, Net Carb: 1g

INGREDIENTS
- Two garlic cloves, minced
- Two teaspoons grated lemon zest
- 1/2 teaspoon salt
- 1/2 teaspoon minced fresh rosemary
- 1/2 teaspoon pepper
- Four salmon fillets (6 ounces each)

INSTRUCTIONS
1. In a small bowl, mix the first five ingredients; rub over fillets. Let stand 15 minutes. Moisten a paper towel with cooking oil; using long-handled tongs, rub on grill rack to coat lightly.
2. Place salmon on grill rack, skin side up. Grill, covered, over medium heat or broil 4 in. from heat 4 minutes. Turn; grill 3-6 minutes longer
or until fish just begins to flake easily with a fork.

421. Chicken Wings and Tasty Mint Chutney

Made for: Dinner | **Prep Time:** 35 minutes | **Servings:** 04
Per Serving: Kcal: 740, Protein: 22g, Fat: 70g, Net Carb: 2g

INGREDIENTS
- ¼ cup (60g) olive oil
- One red onion, chopped
- Four chicken breasts, skinless and boneless
- Four garlic cloves, minced
- Salt and black pepper to the taste
- ½ cup (90g) Italian olives, pitted and chopped
- Four anchovy fillets, chopped
- One tablespoon capers, chopped

- 1 pound tomatoes, chopped ½ teaspoon red chilli flakes

INSTRUCTIONS
1. Season chicken with salt and pepper and rub with half of the oil.
2. Place into a pan which you've heated over high temperature, cook for 2 minutes, flip and cook for 2 minutes more.
3. Introduce chicken breasts in the oven at 450 degrees F and bake for 8 minutes.
4. Take chicken out of the oven and divide between plates.
5. Heat up the same pan with the rest of the oil over medium heat, add capers, onion, garlic, olives, anchovies, chilli flakes and capers, stir and cook for 1 minute.
6. Add salt, pepper and tomatoes, stir and cook for 2 minutes more.
7. Drizzle this over chicken breasts and serve

422. Delicious Crusted Chicken

Made for: Dinner | **Prep Time:** 50 minutes | **Servings:** 04
Per Serving: Kcal: 402, Protein: 47g, Fat: 23g, Net Carb: 1g

INGREDIENTS
- Four bacon slices, cooked and crumbled
- Four chicken breasts, skinless and boneless
- One tablespoon water
- ½ cup (120ml) avocado oil
- One egg whisked
- Salt and black pepper to the taste
- 1 cup (80g) asiago cheese, shredded
- ¼ teaspoon garlic powder
- 1 cup (90g) parmesan cheese, grated

INSTRUCTIONS
1. In a bowl, mix parmesan cheese with garlic, salt and pepper and stir.
2. Put the whisked egg in another bowl and mix with the water.
3. Season chicken with salt and pepper and dip each piece into egg and then into the cheese mix.
4. Heat up a pan with the oil over medium-high heat, add chicken breasts, cook until they are golden on both sides and transfer to a baking pan.
5. Introduce in the oven at 350 degrees F and bake for 20 minutes.
6. Top chicken with bacon and asiago cheese, introduce in the oven, turn on

the broiler and broil for a couple of minutes.

7. Serve hot.

423. Fried chicken with broccoli

Made for: Dinner | **Prep Time:** 25 minutes | **Servings:** 04
Per Serving: Kcal: 732, Protein: 30g, Fat: 66g, Net Carb: 5g

INGREDIENTS

- 9 oz. broccoli
- 3½ oz. butter
- 10 oz. boneless chicken thighs
- salt and pepper
- ½ cup (232g) mayonnaise, for serving (optional)

INSTRUCTIONS

1. Rinse and trim the broccoli. Cut into smaller pieces, including the stem.
2. Heat up a generous dollop of butter in a frying pan where you can fit both the chicken and the broccoli.
3. Season the chicken and fry over medium heat for about 5 minutes per side, or until golden brown and cooked through.
4. Add more butter and put the broccoli in the same frying pan—Fry for another couple of minutes.
5. Season to taste and serve with the remaining butter.

424. Nut-Free Keto Brownie

Made for: Dinner | **Prep Time:** 30 minutes | **Brownies:** 12
Per Brownie: Kcal: 140, Protein: 14g, Fat: 90g, Net Carb: 2g

INGREDIENTS

- Six medium eggs
- 1 to 2 tbsp. unsweetened cocoa
- 3 to 4 tbsp. melted butter
- One cup softened cream cheese 2 tsp. Vanilla
- ½ tsp. baking powder
- 4 tbsp. granulated sweetener, any of your choice or to taste

INSTRUCTIONS

1. Put the entire ingredients together in a large-sized mixing bowl & blend using a stick blender with the blade attachment until completely smooth.
2. Pour the prepared mixture into a lined square baking dish (preferably 8 ½").
3. Bake until cooked on the middle, for 20 to 25 minutes, at 350F.
4. Slice into your favourite shapes such as rectangle, squares,

bars or triangle wedges.

425. Keto hot chocolate

Made for: Dinner | **Prep Time:** 10 minutes | **Servings:** 01
Per Serving: Kcal: 219, Protein: 2g, Fat: 21g, Net Carb: 1g

INGREDIENTS

- 1 oz. unsalted butter
- 1 tbsp cocoa powder
- 2½ tsp powdered erythritol
- ¼ tsp vanilla extract
- 1 cup (250ml) boiling water

INSTRUCTIONS

1. Put the ingredients in a tall beaker to use with an immersion blender.
2. Mix for 15–20 seconds or until there's a fine foam on top.
3. Pour the hot cocoa carefully into cups and enjoy.

426. Keto Ground Beef Enchiladas

Made for: Dinner | **Prep Time:** 25 minutes | **Servings:** 04
Per Serving: Kcal: 485, Protein: 29g, Fat: 38g, Net Carb: 6g

INGREDIENTS

- 1 pound (450g) ground beef
- homemade keto taco seasoning
- 2 cups Mexican blend cheese, shredded
- 1/2 cup (130g) red enchilada sauce, warmed in the microwave
- Eight teaspoons sour cream
- Two green onions, sliced

INSTRUCTIONS

1. Cook ground beef in a skillet on the stove with homemade keto seasoning. Set aside.
2. Preheat oven to 350 degrees. Prepare a baking sheet pan with parchment paper or a silicone mat.
3. Arrange shredded cheese into eight separate flat circles on the sheet pan, using about 1/4 cup cheese for each one. You may have to use two sheet pans to make eight enchilada shells.
4. Bake for about 6 minutes until cheese is bubbling and the outside of the cheese circles starts to brown.
5. While still warm and bendable, flip each cheese circle over. Roll each one with 1/2 cup ground beef, and pour warm enchilada sauce over the top.
6. Add one teaspoon of sour cream to each enchilada,

and a few sliced onions to the tops.

427. Avocado Chips

Made for: Dinner | **Prep Time:** 45 minutes | **Chips:** 15
Per Chip: Kcal: 120, Protein: 7g, Fat: 10g, Net Carb: 3g

INGREDIENTS
- One large ripe avocado
- 3/4 cup (67.5g) freshly grated Parmesan
- 1 tsp. lemon juice
- 1/2 tsp. garlic powder
- 1/2 tsp. Italian seasoning
- Kosher salt
- Freshly ground black pepper

INSTRUCTIONS
1. Preheat oven to 325° and line two baking sheets with parchment paper. In a medium bowl, mash avocado with a fork until smooth. Stir in Parmesan, lemon juice, garlic powder, and Italian seasoning. Season with salt and pepper.
2. Place heaping teaspoon-sized scoops of mixture on the baking sheet, leaving about 3" apart between each scoop. Flatten each scoop to 3" wide across with the back of a spoon or measuring cup. Bake until crisp and golden, about 30 minutes, then let cool completely. Serve at room temperature.

Keto Vegitarian Recipes

428. Broccoli Cheese Bites

Made for: Dinner | **Prep Time:** 55 minutes | **Chips:** 24
Per Chip: Kcal: 120, Protein: 7g, Fat: 10g, Net Carb: 3g

INGREDIENTS
- 2 heads Broccoli
- 1/2 cup (78g) frozen spinach defrosted and drained well
- 1/4 cup (25g) Scallions sliced
- 1 Lemon Zest only
- 1 cup (120g) Cheddar Cheese grated
- 1/4 cup (22.5g) Parmesan cheese grated
- 2 eggs
- 1/3 cup (80g) Sour Cream
- 1/2 teaspoon Pepper
- 1/4 teaspoon Salt

INSTRUCTIONS:
1. Preheat oven to 180C/355F.

2. Cut broccoli into evenly sized florets and place in a microwave safe container with ¼ cup of water. Microwave on high for 3 minutes or until the broccoli is tender. Drain well and allow to cool.
3. Chop the broccoli into very small pieces, You should end up with approximately 2-2 ½ cups.
4. Place the chopped broccoli in a bowl with all the remaining ingredients and mix well.
5. Pour the mixture into a 11 x 7in rectangle brownie pan, lined with parchment paper, and smooth into an even layer.
6. Bake for 25 minutes, until the bites are puffed and browning.
7. Allow to cool for 10 minutes, before cutting into 24 squares.

429. Cauliflower Keto Casserole

Made for: Dinner | **Prep Time:** 45 minutes | **Servings:** 02
Per Serving: Kcal: 469, Protein: 18g, Fat: 40g, Net Carb: 9g

INGREDIENTS:
- ½ head cauliflower florets
- 1 cup (90g) shredded Cheddar cheese
- ½ cup (120g) heavy cream/double cream
- 1 pinch salt and freshly ground black pepper to taste

INSTRUCTIONS:
1. Preheat the oven to 400 degrees F (200 degrees C).
2. Bring a large pot of slightly salted water to a boil and cook cauliflower until tender but firm to the bite, about 10 minutes. Drain.
3. Combine Cheddar cheese, cream, salt, and pepper in a large bowl. Arrange cauliflower in a casserole dish and cover with cheese mixture.
4. Bake in the preheated oven until cheese is bubbly and golden brown, about 25 minutes.

430. Keto Strawberry Muffins

Made for: Dinner | **Prep Time:** 25 minutes | **Muffins:** 12
Per Muffin: Kcal: 181, Protein: 5g, Fat: 17g, Net Carb: 5g

Equipment
- Non-stick Muffin Pan (12 holes)
- Cupcake Paper Cups

INGREDIENTS:
- 3 tbsp flaxseeds grinded

- 6 tbsp water
- 2 cups almond flour
- 2 tsp baking powder
- 1/2 cup (120g) plant-based milk
- 1/3 cup (80g) coconut oil melted
- 1 tbsp vanilla extract
- 1/4 cup (23g) liquid sweetener stevia, erythritol or monk fruit
- 1 1/4 cup (175g) fresh strawberries diced

INSTRUCTIONS:
1. Preheat oven to 180°C/356°F.
2. In a small cup or bowl combine flaxseeds and water and let it sit for a few minutes.
3. In another, large bowl, combine almond flour and baking powder. Add coconut oil, milk, vanilla extract, and liquid sweetener. Stir well.
4. Add prepared flaxseed "egg". Combine with a wooden spatula.
5. Gently fold into diced strawberries.
6. Place the muffin paper cups in your non-stick muffin pan. Spoon the muffin batter into each paper cup. Place in the oven and bake for 12 minutes or until a wooden stick comes out clean.

431. Low-Carb Spinach

Made for: Dinner | **Prep Time:** 35 minutes | **Servings:** 04
Per Serving: Kcal: 110, Protein: 20g, Fat: 23g, Net Carb: 4g

INGREDIENTS:
- 8.8 oz spinach (8.8 oz = 250g) (if frozen, let defrost)
- 5 eggs
- 1.5 cup cheddar cheese (1 cup = 125g)
- 2 tomatoes
- ½ tsp garlic powder (or garlic salt)
- 1 tsp nutmeg
- 1 tsp onion powder
- 1 tbsp basil (dried is also fine)
- 1 tbsp oregano (dried is also fine)
- Salt and pepper to taste
- 1 tbsp olive oil (for greasing the tray)

INSTRUCTIONS:
1. Preheat the oven to 200°C/390°F.
2. Beat the eggs in a large bowl.
3. Add the garlic, nutmeg, onion powder, salt and pepper.
4. Grate the cheese.
5. Give it all a stir then mix in the spinach and cheese.
6. Make sure everything is thoroughly coated in egg and spice mix.

7. Pour into a 9 inch pie tin (grease with a little oil first), spread it evenly and get it in the oven!
8. Slice the tomatoes.
9. After about 20 minutes of cooking, take out the pie and layer the tomatoes on top.
10. Cook for another 15-20 mins.
11. When ready, sprinkle on the basil, oregano and a little more salt and pepper.
12. Done! Serve, and enjoy.

432. Keto Vegetable Soup

Made for: Dinner | **Prep Time:** 30 minutes | **Servings:** 04
Per Serving: Kcal: 108, Protein: 2g, Fat: 8g, Net Carb: 2g

INGREDIENTS:
- 2 tablespoons olive oil
- ½ small onion (diced)
- 1 clove garlic (minced)
- 2 stalks celery (diced)
- 1 tablespoon tomato paste
- 2 teaspoons Italian seasoning
- 1 cup (150g) green beans (chopped)
- 1 cup (156g) broccoli (chopped)
- 3 cups (700g) vegetable stock
- 2 cups (60g) baby spinach

INSTRUCTIONS:
1. In a large pot, heat the olive oil over medium heat.
2. Once the oil is hot, add the onion, garlic, and celery, then cook, stirring frequently, until the onion starts to soften, about 2-3 minutes.
3. Stir in the tomato paste and Italian seasoning, then cook an additional 1-2 minutes.
4. Add the green beans, broccoli, and vegetable stock.
5. Bring everything to a light boil, then allow to simmer for 10-15 minutes or until the beans are soft.
6. Stir in the spinach.
7. Remove from heat and serve warm.

433. Roasted Veggies

Made for: Dinner | **Prep Time:** 35 minutes | **Servings:** 04
Per Serving: Kcal: 86, Protein: 3g, Fat: 4g, Net Carb: 3g

INGREDIENTS:
- 1 ½ cups (174g) radishes
- 1 ½ cups (132g) Brussels sprouts
- 1 yellow squash

- 1 zucchini/courgette
- 1 Red pepper
- 1 Yellow Pepper
- Salt and pepper to taste
- 1 tsp. Oregano
- 1 tsp basil
- 1 tsp parsley
- 1 Tbsp Coconut oil, melted

INSTRUCTIONS:

1. Preheat the oven to 425°F.
2. Wash all veggies well first, peel the zucchini and squash first if you like.
3. Rough chop everything into bite size pieces, in general I cut brussel sprouts and radishes in half unless they were very large. These take longer to cook and will cook more evenly in smaller pieces.
4. In a large bowl toss together the chopped veggies, coconut oil, and herbs until all vegetables are well coated in oil and seasoning.
5. Spread vegetables out as much as you can over a large baking sheet, drizzle a little more oil on them if they are not wet enough, healthy oils are our friend.
6. Salt and pepper to taste, I like to use a fresh ground black pepper and coarse ground sea salt when roasting veggies to really bring out the flavors.
7. Let your vegetables roast for 20-30 minutes, depending on how softened and browned you like them. I like to leave mine in longer and get that delicious caramelized flavor and char on the tips.
8. Remove from oven and serve with your favorite protein and healthy fats for a tasty and pretty meal!

434. Vegetable Bake with Creamy Pesto

Made for: Dinner | **Prep Time:** 35 minutes | **Servings:** 04
Per Serving: Kcal: 265, Protein: 8g, Fat: 19g, Net Carb: 4g

INGREDIENTS:

- 1 zucchini/courgette
- 1 red capsicum
- 1/2 red onion
- 1 head of broccoli
- Sauce
- 1/2 cup (125g) pesto
- 1/4 cup (60g) cream
- 4 tablespoons parmesan cheese
- 1/4 teaspoon salt
- Fresh basil or celery leaves to serve

INSTRUCTIONS:

1. Preheat the oven to 180C / 356F and grease a small baking dish
2. Chop the vegetables into rough chunks and the onion into small wedges, separating the layers.
3. Combine the sauce ingredients and toss through the chopped vegetables and pour into the baking dish.
4. Bake for 30 minutes, stirring halfway through and serve warm with fresh basil

435. Loaded Cauliflower

Made for: Dinner | **Prep Time:** 25 minutes | **Servings:** 04
Per Serving: Kcal: 165, Protein: 6g, Fat: 11g, Net Carb: 3g

INGREDIENTS:

- 1 head cauliflower (steamed) or 6 cups Steamed Cauliflower Rice
- 1 cup shredded cheddar cheese, divided
- 1/2 cup (120g) sour cream
- 2 teaspoons dry ranch seasoning
- 1 teaspoon onion powder
- 1 teaspoon garlic powder
- 4 tablespoons real bacon bits, divided

INSTRUCTIONS:

1. preheat oven to 350
2. You need to first steam your fresh cauliflower head. Break apart the head of the cauliflower and discard the green leaves. Steam cauliflower until a fork can easily be stuck into the vegetable. Mash cauliflower in a large mixing bowl. Season with salt and pepper.
3. If you prefer to use cauliflower rice, you need approximately 6 cups of steamed cauliflower rice.
4. Set aside 1 tablespoon shredded cheddar cheese and then add remaining cheddar cheese, sour cream, ranch seasoning, onion powder, garlic powder and 3 tablespoons of bacon bits to the cauliflower and mix well. If you are adding whole whipping cream as the optional ingredient, add at this stage.
5. Transfer cauliflower into a small baking dish and heat for 35 minutes until hot.
6. Remove from oven and immediately sprinkle with remaining cheddar cheese and 1 tablespoon bacon bits.
7. Serve white hot and melty.

436. Keto Sausage Veggie Sheet Pan

Made for: Dinner | **Prep Time:** 30 minutes | **Servings:** 04
Per Serving: Kcal: 405, Protein: 16g, Fat: 33g, Net Carb: 6g

INGREDIENTS:

- 1 (16 ounce) package keto-friendly Smoked Sausage
- 3 cups (255g) broccoli florets
- 1 cup (150g) red bell pepper, cut into chunks (about 1 large bell pepper)
- 1 tablespoon olive oil
- 2 teaspoons cajun seasoning
- Instructions

INSTRUCTIONS:

1. Preheat the oven to 400 degrees F.
2. Lightly spray the pan with cooking spray. Place the sliced sausage evenly in one layer.
3. In a mixing bowl combine the broccoli and bell pepper. Toss with the olive oil and seasonings. Place the vegetables in the pan with the sausage. Try to evenly distribute the ingredients, it is okay if things overlap a little bit because everything shrinks as it cooks.
4. Bake at 400 degrees for 15 minutes, toss and bake an additional 10-15 minutes until the vegetables have reached your desired texture.

437. Greek Cucumber Salad

Made for: Dinner | **Prep Time:** 10 minutes | **Servings:** 04
Per Serving: Kcal: 54, Protein: 2g, Fat: 3g, Net Carb: 2g

INGREDIENTS:

- 2 cucumbers, chopped
- 1 cup (200g) tomatoes, chopped
- 1/2 cup (75g) red onion, chopped
- 1/4 cup (80g) jarred pepperoncini peppers
- 1/4 cup (20g) olives (green, black or kalamata)
- 1/4 cup (60g) olive oil
- 1 tablespoon lemon juice
- 1/2 cup (75g) crumbled feta cheese
- salt and pepper to taste

INSTRUCTIONS:

1. Combine all chopped vegetables, peppers and olives.
2. Drizzle with olive oil, lemon juice and salt and pepper to taste. Stir well
3. Fold in crumbled feta cheese when ready to serve.

438. Keto Tzatziki

Made for: Dinner | **Prep Time:** 30 minutes | **Servings:** 04
Per Serving: Kcal: 125, Protein: 3g, Fat: 10g, Net Carb: 0.4g

INGREDIENTS:

- 1 english cucumber, seeded and finely diced
- 1 ⅕ cups (272g) greek yogurt
- 4 tbsp olive oil
- 1 tbsp lemon juice
- 2 tbsp fresh dill, chopped
- 2 tbsp minced garlic
- 1 tsp sea salt
- 1 tsp pepper

INSTRUCTIONS:

1. Slice and seed the cucumber, finely chop.
2. Combine all ingredients and mix well.
3. Allow the dip to chill overnight for best flavor.

439. Protein Pancakes

Made for: Dinner | **Prep Time:** 20 minutes | **Servings:** 04
Per Serving: Kcal: 323, Protein: 16g, Fat: 27g, Net Carb: 3g

INGREDIENTS:

- 2 scoops organic soy protein (chocolate flavor)
- 1 cup (112g) almond flour
- 1 tsp. glucomannan powder
- 2 tbsp. ground flaxseed
- 1½ cup (375ml) water
- 1 tbsp. flaxseed oil
- 2 tbsp. olive oil
- 1 tsp. vanilla extract
- 1 tsp. baking powder

INSTRUCTIONS:

1. Put the glucomannan powder and ground flaxseed into a medium-sized
2. bowl with ½ cup of water and set aside for a couple of minutes.
3. In another medium-sized bowl, combine the soy protein, baking powder,
4. and almond flour and set it aside, as well.
5. Mix the vanilla extract and flaxseed oil into the bowl with the soaked
6. glucomannan powder and ground flaxseed.
7. Slowly stir the remaining water into the first mixture and combine
8. thoroughly.

9. Add the glucomannan mixture to the bowl with the flour mixture and stir
10. well, making sure no lumps remain in the batter.
11. Put a medium-sized non-stick frying pan on the stove over medium heat
12. and add the olive oil.
13. When the oil is warm, add a tablespoon of batter to the frying pan and
14. spread it into a ¼-inch thick pancake.
15. Cook the pancake for 3 minutes on each side. Repeat this process for the
16. remaining 3 pancakes, or until all the batter is used.
17. Enjoy the pancakes right away. Alternatively, store the pancakes in an
18. airtight container in the fridge, and consume within 3 days.

440. Spicy keto roasted nuts

Made for: Dinner | Prep Time: 30 minutes | Servings: 04
Per Serving: Kcal: 285, Protein: 4g, Fat: 30g, Net Carb: 2g

INGREDIENTS
- 8 oz. pecans or almonds or walnuts
- 1 tsp salt
- 1 tbsp olive oil or coconut oil
- 1 tsp ground cumin
- 1 tsp paprika powder or chilli powder

INSTRUCTIONS
1. Mix all ingredients in a medium frying pan, and cook on medium heat until the almonds are warmed through.
2. Let cool and serve as a snack with a drink. Store in a container with a lid at room temperature.

441. Roasted cabbage

Made for: Dinner | Prep Time: 40 minutes | Servings: 04
Per Serving: Kcal: 367, Protein: 3g, Fat: 62g, Net Carb: 7g

INGREDIENTS
- 2 lbs (900g) green cabbage
- 6 oz. butter
- 1 tsp salt
- ¼ tsp ground black pepper

INSTRUCTIONS
1. Preheat the oven to 400°F (200°C).
2. Melt the butter in a saucepan over medium-low heat.
3. Split the green cabbage into wedges and remove the thick stem in the middle.

Cut slices — less than an inch thick — and place on a baking sheet lined with parchment paper or in a large baking dish.
4. Season with salt and pepper and pour the melted butter on top.
5. Bake for 20 minutes or until the cabbage is roasted.

442. Keto cinnamon coffee

Made for: Dinner | Prep Time: 10 minutes | Servings: 04
Per Serving: Kcal: 142, Protein: 4g, Fat: 17g, Net Carb: 2g

INGREDIENTS
- 4 tbsp ground coffee
- 2 tsp ground cinnamon
- 4 cups (960ml) of water
- 2/3 cup (160g) heavy whipping cream/double cream

INSTRUCTIONS
1. Mix ground coffee and cinnamon. Add piping hot water and brew as usual.
2. Whip the cream using a whisk or a mixer until medium stiff peaks form.
3. Serve the coffee in a tall mug (a glass mug is fun if you have it) and add the whipped cream on top. Finish with a small sprinkle of ground cinnamon.

443. Dairy-Free Vanilla Custard

Made for: Dinner | Prep Time: 10 minutes | Servings: 02
Per Serving: Kcal: 214, Protein: 5g, Fat: 20g, Net Carb: 1g

INGREDIENTS
- Three egg yolks
- ¼ cup (60ml) unsweetened almond milk
- ½ tsp vanilla extract
- ½ tsp erythritol (optional)
- 2 tbsp melted coconut oil or unsalted butter

INSTRUCTIONS
1. Whisk together egg yolks, almond milk, vanilla and optional sweetener in the medium metal bowl.
2. Slowly mix in the melted coconut oil or butter. Be sure the oil isn't too hot, or the eggs may cook unevenly.
3. Place the bowl over a saucepan of simmering water. Whisk the mixture constantly and vigorously until thickened. Your instant-read thermometer should register 140°F for

three full minutes. Usually, this means about 5 minutes of total cooking time. (When ready, it should coat the back of a spoon.)

4. Remove the custard from the water bath. Serve either warm or chilled. (If serving chilled, it can be prepared 1-3 days ahead and refrigerated. Re-whisk before serving.)

444. Roasted Vegetable Scramble

Made for: Dinner | **Prep Time:** 50 minutes | **Servings:** 02
Per Serving: Kcal: 256, Protein: 5g, Fat: 11g, Net Carb: 1g

INGREDIENTS

- One tablespoon avocado oil or olive oil
- One medium zucchini squash halved lengthwise and chopped
- One medium yellow squash halved lengthwise and chopped
- Two carrots peeled and chopped
- 4 cups (120g) baby spinach loosely packed
- Six large eggs well are beaten.
- sea salt to taste
- 1/2 ripe avocado sliced

INSTRUCTIONS

1. Preheat the oven to 420 degrees F. Place chopped zucchini squash, yellow squash, and carrots on a large baking sheet and drizzle with avocado oil and sprinkle with sea salt. Use your hands to toss everything together until the vegetables are well coated. Spread vegetables into a single layer on the baking sheet. Roast 20 to 25 minutes in the preheated oven, until golden brown. Remove from oven.
2. Heat a medium-sized skillet over medium heat with enough oil to lightly coat the surface, about two teaspoons. Add the baby spinach and cover. Cook, occasionally stirring, until wilted, about 2 minutes. Transfer the roasted vegetables to the skillet. Evenly pour the beaten eggs over the vegetables and sprinkle liberally with sea salt. Allow eggs to sit untouched for 1 to 2 minutes. Use a spatula to flip the eggs and cook another 1 to 2 minutes. Continue cooking and flipping until eggs are cooked through.
3. Serve scramble with fresh fruit and sliced avocado

445. Warm keto kale salad

Made for: Dinner | **Prep Time:** 40 minutes | **Servings:** 02
Per Serving: Kcal: 488, Protein: 10g, Fat: 48g, Net Carb: 5g

INGREDIENTS

- ¾ cup (180g) heavy whipping cream/double cream
- 2 tbsp mayonnaise
- 1 tsp Dijon mustard
- 2 tbsp olive oil
- One garlic clove, minced or finely chopped
- salt and Pepper
- 2 oz. butter
- 8 oz. kale
- 4 oz. blue cheese or feta cheese

INSTRUCTIONS

1. Mix together heavy cream, mayonnaise, mustard, olive oil and garlic in a small beaker—salt and pepper to taste.
2. Rinse the kale and cut into small, bite-size pieces. Remove and discard the thick stem.
3. Heat a large frying pan and add the butter. Sauté the kale quickly, so it turns a nice colour, but no more than that—salt and pepper to taste.
4. Place in a bowl and pour the dressing on top. Stir thoroughly and serve with crumbled blue cheese or another flavorful cheese of your choice.

446. Broccoli Mash

Made for: Dinner | **Prep Time:** 10 minutes | **Servings:** 04
Per Serving: Kcal: 134, Protein: 4g, Fat: 10g, Net Carb: 9g

INGREDIENTS

- 1 pound Broccoli 2 medium heads
- 1/2 teaspoon salt
- 1/2 teaspoon Pepper
- 1 ounce Butter
- 3 ounces Sour Cream
- Two tablespoons chives finely chopped

INSTRUCTIONS

1. Bring a large pot of water to the boil.
2. Cut the broccoli into evenly sized florets.
3. Gently add the broccoli to the boiling water and cook for 3-5 minutes, until the broccoli is tender.
4. Drain the broccoli and return it to the warm pot, add the butter, sour cream, salt and pepper.

5. Blend the broccoli with a stick blender until there are no lumps.
6. Stir through the chives and adjust the seasoning.

447. Keto Vegetable Soup

Made for: Dinner | Prep Time: 45 minutes | Servings: 4
Per Serving: Kcal: 75, Protein: 4g, Fat: 3g, Net Carb: 5g

INGREDIENTS
- One tablespoon butter
- One tablespoon olive oil
- One medium onion, chopped
- Three stalks celery, chopped
- Two carrots, peeled and chopped
- Four cloves garlic, minced
- 2 cups (225g) chopped cauliflower florets
- 1 ½ cups fresh green beans, trimmed and cut into 1-inch pieces
- 30 ounces canned diced tomatoes
- 4 cups (960g) beef broth
- One tablespoon Worcestershire sauce
- One tablespoon Italian seasoning
- One teaspoon salt
- One teaspoon cracked Pepper
- 2 cups fresh spinach

INSTRUCTIONS
1. Add the butter and olive to a large stockpot over medium heat until the butter has melted.
2. Add the onions, celery, carrots, and garlic and cook for 5 minutes, stirring often.
3. Add the cauliflower, green beans, tomatoes, beef broth, Worcestershire sauce, and Italian seasoning. Stir to combine.
4. Bring to a boil, reduce to a simmer, and cook for 25 minutes or until vegetable are tender.
5. Season with the salt and pepper and add the spinach to the pot. Stir well and continue cooking for 1-2 minutes until the spinach has wilted.
6. Taste and add additional salt and pepper, if needed. Serve immediately.

448. Easy Seed & Nut Granola

Made for: Dinner | Prep Time: 5 minutes | Servings: 4
Per Serving: Kcal: 400, Protein: 9g, Fat: 30g, Net Carb: 9g

INGREDIENTS
- A small handful of nuts (10 almonds, 3 Brazil nuts, five cashews)
- 2 Tablespoons (17 g) pumpkin seeds
- 1 Tablespoon (12 g) cacao nibs
- 1 Tablespoon (5 g) coconut flakes
- 1/4 cup (60 ml) unsweetened coconut or almond milk

INSTRUCTIONS
1. Mix together all the dry ingredients. If you're making a large batch, then store leftovers in an airtight container. Serve with coconut or almond milk.

449. Delicious Broccoli Soup

Made for: Dinner | Prep Time: 45 minutes | Servings: 4
Per Serving: Kcal: 352, Protein: 10g, Fat: 30g, Net Carb: 6g

INGREDIENTS
- One white onion, chopped
- One tablespoon ghee
- 2 cups (480g) veggie stock
- Salt and black pepper to the taste
- 2 cups (500ml) of water
- Two garlic cloves, minced
- 1 cup (240g) heavy cream/double cream
- 8 ounces cheddar cheese, grated
- 12 ounces broccoli florets ½ teaspoon paprika

INSTRUCTIONS
1. Heat up a pot with the ghee over medium heat, add onion and garlic, stir and cook for 5 minutes.
2. Add stock, cream, water, salt, pepper and paprika, stir and bring to a boil.
3. Add broccoli, stir and simmer the soup for 25 minutes.
4. Transfer to your food processor and blend well.
5. Add cheese and blend again.
6. Divide into soup bowls and serve hot.

450. Keto fried halloumi cheese

Made for: Dinner | Prep Time: 15 minutes | Servings: 2
Per Serving: Kcal: 830, Protein: 36g, Fat: 74g, Net Carb: 7g

INGREDIENTS
- 10 oz. mushrooms
- 10 oz. halloumi cheese
- 3 oz. butter
- Ten green olives
- salt and pepper

INSTRUCTIONS
1. Rinse and trim the mushrooms, and cut or slice.

2. Heat up a hearty dollop of butter in a frying pan where you can fit both halloumi cheese and mushrooms.
3. Fry the mushrooms on medium heat for 3-5 minutes until they are golden brown—season with salt and pepper.
4. If necessary, add more butter and fry the halloumi for a couple of minutes on each side. Stir the mushrooms every now and then. Lower the heat towards the end. Serve with olives.

451.   Keto tuna and avocado salad

Made for: Dinner | Prep Time: 20 minutes | Servings: 4
Per Serving: Kcal: 642, Protein: 41g, Fat: 45g, Net Carb: 5g

INGREDIENTS
- 24 oz. can of tuna in water
- Three avocados, cut into eights
- 3 oz. red bell peppers, sliced
- 2 oz. red onions, sliced
- 5 oz. cucumber quartered
- 2 oz. celery stalks, diced
- 2 tbsp lime juice
- 1/3 cup (80ml) olive oil
- salt and pepper to taste

INSTRUCTIONS
1. Drain the tuna. Use a fork to flake the tuna onto a plate.
2. Slice red bell pepper and red onion into thin slices.
3. Quarter the cucumber, lengthways, remove seeds and slice.
4. Halve the celery, lengthways, and then cut into small pieces. Then peel and de-stone the avocado and cut into eighths.
5. Arrange all ingredients in layers on a large serving platter, or onto individual plates.
6. Place the lime juice and olive oil in a small jar and shake well to combine. Drizzle dressing over salad and finish off with salt and pepper to taste.

452.   Overnight Blueberry

Made for: Dinner | Prep Time: 20 minutes | Servings: 4
Per Serving: Kcal: 233, Protein: 9g, Fat: 10g, Net Carb: 2g

INGREDIENTS
- 1 cup (120g) raw almonds (unsalted)
- ½ cup (80g) flaxseeds
- ¼ cup (37g) frozen blueberries
- 3 cups (750ml) water
- 2 tbsp. lemon juice

- 2 tsp. glucomannan powder
- Optional: ¼ tsp. vanilla extract
- Optional: ¼ tsp. cinnamon

DIRECTIONS
1. Put the almonds and flaxseeds in a medium-sized heat-safe bowl.
2. Bring the 3 cups of water to a boil, then pour it onto the almonds and
3. flaxseeds.
4. Stir in the glucomannan powder and lemon juice, as well as the optional
5. ingredients, if desired.
6. Put the hot almond mixture in a heat-safe blender and process until all
7. ingredients are combined into a smooth mixture.
8. Stir in the blueberries and pour the mixture into a canning jar or an airtight
9. container. Set aside for about 15 minutes to let it cool down.
10. Seal the jar or container once the mixture is cool and refrigerate for a few
11. hours or until the next morning before serving.
12. Serve the pudding for breakfast or as a guilt-free snack and enjoy!
13. Consume within 4 days, or store in the freezer for a maximum of 30 days
14. and thaw in the fridge before serving.

Snack and Desserts Recipes

453.   Keto Cups

Prep Time: 20 minutes | Cups: 18
Per Cup: Kcal: 120, Protein: 2g, Fat: 10g, Net Carb: 4g

INGREDIENTS:
- 2 cups (340g) keto chocolate chips
- 1/4 tsp (60ml) coconut oil
- 1/2 cup (115g) coconut butter softened

INSTRUCTIONS:
1. Line a 18-count mini muffin tin with mini muffin liners and set aside.
2. In a microwave safe bowl or stove top, melt your coconut oil with chocolate chips.
3. Moving quickly, coat the bottom and sides of the muffin liners with melted chocolate. Ensure a little is leftover to top with later. Place the chocolate coated muffin tins in the freezer to firm up.

4. Once firm, drizzle the coconut butter amongst the cups. Top with the remaining chocolate and freeze until firm.

454. Chocolate Chip Cookies

Prep Time: 20 minutes | **Cookies:** 18
Per Cookie: Kcal: 137, Protein: 2g, Fat: 11g, Net Carb: 0.5g

INGREDIENTS:
- 1/2 cup (115g) butter softened
- 1/3 cup (53g) Swerve confectioners sugar (Erythritol sweetener)
- 1 teaspoon pure vanilla extract
- 1/2 teaspoon kosher salt
- 2 cup (224g) almond flour
- 9 ounces dark chocolate chips (I used Lily's)
- 8 ounces sugar-free chocolate chips (I used Hershey's)

INSTRUCTIONS:
1. In a large bowl beat butter until light and fluffy, using a hand mixer. Mix in sugar, salt, and vanilla and mix until combined.
2. Add in almond flour a little at a time and mix until dough consistency forms. Pour in dark chocolate chips and mix. Cover with plastic wrap and place in the refrigerator for 10-15 minutes.
3. Remove dough from fridge and use a cookie scoop or measuring spoon to form 1-inch balls (about 1 heaping tablespoon). Place on a rimmed baking sheet lined with parchment paper.
4. In a microwave-safe dish melt, sugar-free chocolate chips in 30-second increments, stirring between each round of heating until smooth.
5. Dip each chilled fat bomb in melted chocolate and then put back onto the lined baking sheet. Place in freezer for 5 minutes, or until chocolate has hardened.

455. Keto Brownie Cookies

Prep Time: 20 minutes | **Cookies:** 18
Per Cookie: Kcal: 57, Protein: 12g, Fat: 19g, Net Carb: 1g

INGREDIENTS:
- oz cream cheese, room temperature
- 1/3 cup Swerve confectioners sweetener
- 1 egg, beaten
- 1 teaspoon baking powder

- 6 tablespoons cocoa powder* (I recommend Guittards or Divine)
- 1/3 cup ChocZero or Lilys low carb chocolate chips*
- ¼ teaspoon SweetLeaf vanilla liquid stevia

INSTRUCTIONS:
1. Preheat oven to 350 degrees F. Line a cookie sheet with parchment paper and set aside.
2. Using a hand mixer, cream the Swerve sweetener and cream cheese. When nice and creamy add in the baking powder, stevia, cocoa powder and egg.
3. Mix well until a dough forms. Add the chocolate chips and mix with a spoon to incorporate.
4. Spoon out the cookies on the cookie sheet. The dough is very sticky. Flatten the cookie dough with your fingers. Or take a piece of wax paper and spray it generously with cooking spray. Then place it on the cookies and flatten them with your hand. That way you won't get your hands messy.
5. Bake for 8-10 minutes. You want the cookies to be firm to the touch but not too firm.
6. Take out of the oven and let cool completely before eating. Eat immediately or store in the refrigerator or freezer.
7. For the chocolate chips I used low carb ChocZero or Lily's dark chocolate stevia sweetened mini chips.

456. Butter Fat Bombs

Prep Time: 20 minutes | **Bombs:** 12
Per Bomb: Kcal: 167, Protein: 1g, Fat: 19g, Net Carb: 1g

INGREDIENTS:
- 2 cups (480g) heavy whipping cream or double cream (very cold)
- 1 teaspoon vanilla
- 2 to 3 tablespoons sweetener {to taste}
- 3 tablespoons peanut butter

INSTRUCTIONS:
1. Place the cold whipping cream in a medium mixing bowl mixing at medium speed.
2. Add the vanilla. At the soft peak stage add the sugar substitute followed by the peanut butter.
3. Whip until combined.

4. Place 12 cupcake liners in a muffin tin. Set aside.
5. Using a plastic baggie or icing bag, pipe peanut butter mixture into liners.
6. Place into freezer for 2 hours or until frozen. Then place in a sealed container in the freezer for storage.

457. Chewy Keto Eggless Cookies

Prep Time: 50 minutes | **Cookies:** 14
Per Cookie: Kcal: 147, Protein: 3g, Fat: 42g, Net Carb: 2g

INGREDIENTS:
- 3/4 stick unsalted butter, room temperature (85 g/3 oz)
- 1/2 cup Allulose (100 g/ 3.5 oz)
- 1 tsp sugar-free vanilla extract
- 1 1/2 cups (150g) almond flour
- 1/2 tsp xanthan gum
- pinch of sea salt
- 1/2 cup (90g) 90% dark chocolate chips or sugar-free chocolate chips

INSTRUCTIONS:
1. Prepare all the ingredients. Cut the butter into pieces and let it come to room temperature. In a bowl mix the almond flour with xanthan gum and salt.
2. Place the butter in a bowl and add the Allulose and vanilla extract. Using an electric mixer (or a stand mixer), process until well combined. Slowly add the almond flour while beating and process until thick and sticky cookie dough is formed.
3. Note: You can substitute the Allulose with another erythritol-based sweetener, just remember that the cookies won't be chewy.
4. Add the chocolate chips and combine well.
5. Using your hands, form into a big ball. Transfer onto a piece of cling film and form into a log, about 25 cm (10 inch) long, wrapping it all around. Transfer into a freezer for 20 to 30 minutes, or place in the fridge for up to a day.
6. Preheat the oven to 165 °C/ 330 °F (fan assisted), or 185 °C/ 365 °F (conventional). Remove the dough from the freezer and cut into 14 pieces, each about 1 1/2 – 2 cm (1/2 – 3/4 inch) thick.
7. Transfer the cookie slices onto a tray lined with parchment paper. Make sure to leave at least 2 cm (1 inch) between the cookies. Bake for 10 to 15 minutes, turning the tray (not the cookies as they are fragile) once to ensure even baking. We are baking these on low and slow so the cookies should only be lightly browned.
8. Remove from the oven and let the cookies cool down completely before removing them from the tray. Store them at room temperature in a sealed container for up to 2 weeks. For longer storage freeze for up to 3 months.

458. Cheesecake Bites

Prep Time: 30 minutes | **Bites:** 20
Per Bite: Kcal: 36, Protein: 1g, Fat: 2g, Net Carb: 0.2g

INGREDIENTS:
- 3.4 ounces package low-carb/sugar-free instant chocolate pudding
- 8 ounces cream cheese (room temperature)
- 1 teaspoon vanilla extract
- 1/4 teaspoon salt
- 1/3 cup (34g) Powdered Erythritol Sweetener (or Powdered Swerve Sweetener)
- 1/3 cup (34g) unsweetened cocoa powder

INSTRUCTIONS:
1. In a medium bowl, mix the chocolate pudding, cream cheese, vanilla, salt, powdered sugar.
2. Chill the mixture for 30 minutes.
3. Add cocoa powder to a small bowl.
4. Use a 1 tablespoon cookie scoop to form the dough into balls then dip in a small bowl of cocoa powder until coated.
5. Chill for 30 minutes and enjoy!

459. Chocolate Fat Bombs

Prep Time: 20 minutes | **Bombs:** 10
Per Bomb: Kcal: 46, Protein: 1g, Fat: 1g, Net Carb: 0.4g

INGREDIENTS:
- 1/2 cup (120g) coconut oil
- 1/2 cup (220g) swerve sweetener (granular and brown sugar work)
- 1/2 cup (120g) low carb peanut butter
- 3/4 cup (112.5g) Lilly's Dark Chocolate Chips

INSTRUCTIONS:
1. Heat a medium size sauce pan to medium low heat.

2. Add the coconut oil first and wait until it has completely melted.
3. Then add the sugar substitute, peanut butter and chocolate chips.
4. Stir the mixture continuously until it has completely melted.
5. Remove from heat and allow mixture to cool 5-10 minutes.
6. Carefully spoon into a silicone mini muffin tin until 3/4 full. (This makes 34 for me)
7. Sprinkle with sea salt if desired.
8. Freeze until firm.

460. S'mores Recipe

Prep Time: 20 minutes | **Smores:** 6
Per Smores: Kcal: 115, Protein: 3g, Fat: 10g, Net Carb: 06g

INGREDIENTS:
- 12 Keto Graham Crackers
- 6 squares Lindt 90% Dark Chocolate
- 6 Keto Marshmallows

INSTRUCTIONS:
1. Place 6 crackers onto a cookie sheet lined with parchment paper, top each with the square of chocolate.
2. Grill/Broil for 3-5 minutes until the chocolate has melted slightly.
3. Top each with a marshmallow, followed by another graham cracker.
4. Enjoy immediately.

461. Strawberry Cheesecake

Prep Time: 20 minutes | **Cake:** 6
Per Cake: Kcal: 121, Protein: 3g, Fat: 15g, Net Carb: 0.3g

INGREDIENTS:
- 8 oz. cream cheese, room temperature
- ⅓ cup (48g) fresh or frozen strawberries
- 4 tbsp unsalted butter
- 1 scoop Vanilla MCT Powder
- 1 tbsp monk fruit (or another low carb sweetener)
- Splash of vanilla extract or the paste of 1/2

INSTRUCTIONS:
1. Puree the strawberries in a small blender or using a hand mixer.
2. Add a small splash of vanilla and mix to incorporate.
3. Prepare a muffin tray with muffin liners.
4. Melt the cream cheese and butter together.

5. In a medium-sized mixing bowl, combine the dairy mixture and the strawberry mixture, and mix well.
6. Pour evenly in muffin tins or silicone mold and place in the freezer to chill for no less than 40 minutes.

462. Chocolate Chip

Prep Time: 20 minutes | **Chips:** 10
Per Chip: Kcal: 286, Protein: 1g, Fat: 1g, Net Carb: 04g

INGREDIENTS:
Crust
- 8 tablespoons butter (1 stick)
- 1 ¼ cup (90g) almond flour
- 2 tablespoons swerve

Cheesecake Filling
- 2 8oz packages cream cheese
- 1 egg
- 1 tablespoon vanilla
- ½ cup (80g) powdered swerve (confectioners sugar)
- 1 cups (150g) chocolate chips (lily's sugar-free)

INSTRUCTIONS:
1. Preheat oven to 350°
2. Line a 9x9 baking pan with parchment paper or aluminum foil, lightly spray with cooking spray and set aside.
3. Melt butter
4. Combine butter, almond flour and swerve. Mix well.
5. Pat crust into pan and bake for 6 minutes
6. Cheesecake Filling
7. Combine cream cheese, egg, vanilla, and powdered swerve in a bowl and beat with an electric mixer until well combined
8. Fold in chocolate chips
9. Evenly press the cheesecake filling into the pan and bake 30 minutes until a toothpick placed in the center comes out clean.

463. Keto Chocolate Heaven

Prep Time: 35 minutes | **Slices:** 15
Per Slice: Kcal: 250, Protein: 4g, Fat: 21g, Net Carb: 8g

INGREDIENTS:
- 300 g (10.5 oz) 70% chocolate
- 175 g (6 oz) butter
- 2 teaspoon vanilla extract

- 6 eggs - medium
- 6 tablespoon heavy whipping cream
- 4 teaspoon granulated sweetener of choice or more, to your taste

INSTRUCTIONS:
1. Melt the chocolate and butter together over a low heat in a saucepan. Remove from the heat and allow to cool slightly before adding the vanilla extract.
2. In another bowl beat the eggs, cream and sweetener together for 3-4 minutes (use a stick blender or hand whisk). It will go frothy and remain runny.
3. Slowly add the egg mixture to the chocolate mixture in the saucepan, stirring all the time. As you add more egg mixture, the chocolate and butter will thicken to the consistency of custard.
4. Pour into a prepared tin (see below). Grease a loose bottom cake tin with butter then line the loose bottom with baking paper and push through the outer ring so the baking paper adds a seal and stops the cake mixture from leaking.
5. Bake at 180C/ 350F for 20 ~ 30 minutes, or more depending on your oven. Bake until it is just set in the centre, do not overcook the cake.

464. Keto No Bake Cookies

Prep Time: 30 minutes | Cookies: 48
Per Cookie: Kcal: 70, Protein: 1g, Fat: 7g, Net Carb: 0.7g

INGREDIENTS:
- 3/4 cup (180ml) coconut oil
- 3/4 cup (187.5g) creamy low carb peanut butter or almond butter
- 1/4 cup (25g) cocoa powder
- 1 cup swerve sweetener (brown sugar or granular)
- 1 teaspoon vanilla extract (optional)
- 1 1/2 cup (180g) UNSWEETENED coconut flakes
- 2 tablespoons hulled hemp seeds, also called hemp hearts (you can use an extra 2 tablespoons of coconut flakes if you don't have this. I like the mixed texture and it adds a bit of fiber)
- sea salt for topping (optional)

INSTRUCTIONS:
1. In a medium size sauce pan combine the coconut oil and the peanut butter over medium low heat.

2. As the mixture begins to melt stir until well combined.
3. Stir in the cocoa powder, vanilla (if using) and the .
4. Increase heat to medium or just over medium and slowly bring the mixture to a simmer.
5. When the mixture is simmering and the sweetener has completely melted (your fudge mixture should be smooth with no visible granulars) remove from heat and stir in the coconut flakes and the hemp seeds.
6. Set aside and allow mixture to cool slightly.
7. Carefully spoon into silicone mini muffin tins until 3/4 full.
8. Sprinkle with sea salt if desired.
9. Freeze for 15 minutes until set. Remove from tins and store in an air tight container in the freezer.

465. Keto Cheesecake Bites

Prep Time: 60 minutes | Bites: 8
Per Bite: Kcal: 370, Protein: 9g, Fat: 16g, Net Carb: 1g

INGREDIENTS:
- 2/3 cup (75g) Almond Flour
- 1 tbsp Powdered Erythritol
- 2 tbsp Unsalted Butter melted
- Pinch of Salt
- 8 oz Cream Cheese in room temperature
- 1/4 cup (25g) Erythritol
- 1 Egg in room temperature
- 1/4 tsp Vanilla Extract
- 1/2 tsp Lemon Zest
- 1/4 cup (37.5g) Fresh Strawberries smashed

INSTRUCTIONS:
1. Preheat oven to 350°F. Grease a muffin tin or line it with six muffin liners.
2. In a small bowl, stir together almond flour, powdered erythritol, and salt. Add melted butter and mix until combined. Divide the almond crust batter into six equal parts. Then, add batter to each muffin liner. Press the almond mixture to the bottom of muffin tins to make the crust for the cheesecake bites.
3. Bake in the preheated oven for 10 minutes or until lightly golden. Remove from the oven and let them cool at room temperature while preparing the cheesecake filling.
4. Using a hand mixer, beat together cream cheese and sweetener. Add one egg,

vanilla extract, and lemon zest. Beat until combined. Using a spatula, stir in smashed strawberries.

5. When the crusts for the cheesecake bites have cooled, top each muffin liner with the cream cheese filling. Bake for 15-25 minutes. Keto Cheesecake bites are ready when the center is almost set. Let them cool completely at room temperature before removing the cheesecake bites from the muffin tin.

466. Keto Chocolate Lava Cake

Prep Time: 20 minutes | Servings: 1
Per Serving: Kcal: 257, Protein: 8g, Fat: 22g, Net Carb: 03g

INGREDIENTS:
- 2 Tablespoons Almond Flour
- 4 teaspoons Unproccesed Cocoa Powder
- 2 Tablespoons Sugarless Sugar or other natural sweetner
- pinch of salt
- 1/2 teaspoon vanilla
- 1 Tablespoon Kerrigold Irish Grassfed Butter {Softnened}
- 1 Egg

INSTRUCTIONS:
1. Preheat oven to 350 degrees
2. Prepare Ramekin by spraying with cooking spray - set aside
3. Mix ingredients in mixing bowl until well combined and smooth
4. Use spatula to spoon into prepared ramekin
5. Bake in oven for 12-15 minutes until set.

467. Strawberry Cheesecake

Prep Time: 25 minutes | Servings: 1
Per Serving: Kcal: 117, Protein: 1g, Fat: 22g, Net Carb: 07g

INGREDIENTS:
- 8 ounces cream cheese softened
- ⅔ cup (100g) fresh strawberries chopped
- ½ cup (120g) heavy cream/double cream
- ¼ cup (60g) butter softened
- ¼ cup (40g) Allulose powdered
- 1 teaspoon vanilla extract

INSTRUCTIONS:
1. Add all the ingredients to the bowl of a food processor and blend. Scrape down the sides of the bowl and continue mixing until everything is well combined.

2. Using a cookie scooper, add the batter into 24 silicone mini muffin molds or other small fat bomb molds that you have on hand.
3. Freeze for 1-2 hours or until they are completely set.
4. Store leftovers in the fridge for several days or freeze.

Keto Chicken Recipes

468. Garlic Parmesan chicken wings

Prep Time: 55 minutes | Servings: 6
Per Serving: Kcal: 259, Protein: 17g, Fat: 20g, Net Carb: 2g

INGREDIENTS:
- 14-16 chicken wings, cut at joints (~ 1.4 kg/ 3 lbs) - freeze the wingtips for later to make chicken stock or bone broth.
- 1/4 cup butter, melted (57 g/ 2 oz)
- 4 garlic cloves, minced
- 2 tbsp minced parsley
- 1 cup grated Parmesan cheese (90 g/3.2 oz)
- Optional: paleo Caesar dressing or Homemade Ranch Dressing, for serving

INSTRUCTIONS:
1. Preheat oven to 230 °C/ 450 °F (conventional), or 210 °C/ 410 °F (fan assisted). Dry the chicken wings by patting them with a paper towel.
2. Heat a large cast iron skillet over medium high heat and sear the wings 2-3 minutes per side.
3. Transfer to the oven and bake another 20-30 minutes until golden and crisp. (Tip: For extra crispy chicken wings, follow this oven-baked method using baking powder.)
4. Add the garlic and butter to the skillet with the wings, stirring so that every wing gets coated in the sauce. Sprinkle in the parmesan and continue to cook just until melted.
5. Toss with the cooked wings and serve with Caesar dressing.
6. Serve immediately with the Caesar dressing.

469. Garlic Chicken with Broccoli

Prep Time: 20 minutes | Servings: 1
Per Serving: Kcal: 309, Protein: 27g, Fat: 22g, Net Carb: 09g

INGREDIENTS:

- 1 pound (450g) chicken breasts cut into 1" pieces
- 2 tablespoons olive oil
- 1 teaspoon Italian seasoning
- 1/4 teaspoon crushed pepper optional
- salt and pepper to taste
- 3-4 cloves garlic minced
- 1/2 cup (100g) tomatoes chopped
- 2 cups (170g) broccoli florets
- 2 cups (60g) baby spinach
- 1/2 cup (112g) shredded cheese mozzarella, cheddar, parmesan, or favorite melting cheese
- 4 oz cream cheese

INSTRUCTIONS:

1. Heat 2 tablespoons olive oil in a large saucepan over medium-high heat. Add the chopped chicken breasts, season with Italian seasoning, crushed red pepper, and salt & pepper. Sautee for 4-5 minutes or until chicken is golden and cooked through.
2. Add the garlic and saute for another minute or until fragrant. Add the tomato, broccoli, spinach, shredded cheese, and cream cheese. Cook for another 3-4 minutes or until the broccoli is cooked through.
3. Serve with cooked pasta, rice, zucchini noodles.

470. Cheesy Jalapeño Chicken

Prep Time: 20 minutes | Servings: 4
Per Serving: Kcal: 425, Protein: 40g, Fat: 5g, Net Carb: 03g

INGREDIENTS:

- 4 small chicken breast (this was about 1.5 pounds for me)
- 1 teaspoon cumin
- 1/2 teaspoon chili powder
- 1/2 teaspoon garlic powder
- 1/2 teaspoon salt
- 1/2 teaspoon pepper
- 1 tablespoon butter
- 1/2 cup (75g) chopped onion (half of one small onion)
- 2 jalapenos, seeded and diced
- 1 teaspoon minced garlic
- 1/4 cup (60) heavy cream or double cream
- 1/3 cup (32g) chicken broth
- 2 ounces cream cheese
- 1 cup (112g) shredded cheddar cheese (divided)

INSTRUCTIONS:

1. Combine the cumin, chili powder, garlic powder, salt and pepper, set aside.
2. Heat a 12-inch skillet over medium heat, spray with nonstick spray or add up to 1 tablespoon olive oil.
3. Sprinkle the chicken breast with the spice mixture on each size.
4. Sear the chicken in the skillet 2-3 minutes on each side until nicely browned, remove from skillet and set aside.
5. Add 1 tablespoon butter in the skillet and add the onion, jalapenos and garlic and sauté for 3-4 minutes, stirring occasionally.
6. Add the cream, broth, cream cheese and reduce heat to low.
7. Stir mixture until cream cheese melts completely and add 1/2 cup of the shredded cheese to the sauce, stir well.
8. Add the chicken to the skillet and cover with the remaining cheese.
9. Place a lid on the skillet and let simmer over low for 6-8 minutes.

471. Chicken Cheese Bake

Prep Time: 60 minutes | Servings: 10
Per Serving: Kcal: 541, Protein: 29g, Fat: 47g, Net Carb: 07g

INGREDIENTS:

- 1 pound bacon
- 8 ounce package cream cheese
- ½ cup (45g) grated Parmesan cheese
- 1 ½ cups (168g) sharp cheddar cheese, shredded
- 1/3 cup (60g) avocado mayonnaise
- 1 cup (240g) heavy cream or double cream
- ½ teaspoon hot sauce, we used Cholula
- 1 teaspoon dry mustard
- ½ teaspoon white pepper
- ½ teaspoon garlic powder
- ½ teaspoon onion powder
- ½ teaspoon paprika
- 1 store bought cooked rotisserie chicken, meat removed and chopped into bite sized pieces
- 1 ½ cups (225g) red onion, diced
- 8 ounces baby bella mushrooms, sliced
- 1 tablespoon fresh garlic, minced
- 8 ounces baby spinach
- 2 cups (225g) mozzarella cheese, shredded

INSTRUCTIONS:

1. Preheat oven to 375 degrees F.
2. In a large skillet, cook bacon to crisp, remove to paper towels and reserve three tablespoons of bacon fat.
3. While the bacon is cooking, in a medium sauce pan, place cream cheese, Parmesan cheese, cheddar cheese, avocado mayonnaise, heavy cream, hot sauce, mustard, pepper, garlic powder, onion powder and paprika.
4. Cook over medium heat and stir with a wooden spoon until creamy.
5. Crumble bacon and add to the cream mixture.
6. Clean skillet and add two tablespoons of the bacon fat and saute onions over medium high heat for three minutes.
7. Add the remaining tablespoon of bacon fat and add the mushrooms and saute for five minutes.
8. Add the garlic and spinach and toss to coat the spinach and cook until wilted, about two minutes.
9. Add the cream mixture and cooked chicken and heat then pour into an 8X12 inch casserole dish.
10. Sprinkle on the two cups of mozzarella cheese and bake for 20 minutes.
11. Place under the broiler and brown, 1-2 minutes.

472. Crispy Parmesan Crusted Chicken

Prep Time: 15 minutes | Servings: 4
Per Serving: Kcal: 364, Protein: 36g, Fat: 22g, Net Carb: 1g

INGREDIENTS:

- 1 pound (500g) chicken breasts 2-3 chicken breasts
- 1 teaspoon Italian seasoning or seasoning of choice
- 1/2 teaspoon garlic powder
- Pinch of salt and pepper
- 1 cup (100g) grated or zested parmesan cheese
- 1/2 cup (112g) almond flour
- 2 eggs
- 3 tablespoons olive oil or butter or oil of choice

INSTRUCTIONS:

1. Preheat the oven to 400°F (200°C).
2. Mix cream and cream cheese with pesto and lemon juice. Salt and pepper to taste.

3. In a large pan over medium-high heat, melt the butter. Add the chicken, season with salt and pepper, and fry until they turn a nice golden brown.
4. Place the chicken in a greased 9 x 13" (23 x 33 cm) baking dish, and pour in the cream mixture.
5. Top chicken with leek, tomatoes, and cauliflower.
6. Sprinkle cheese on top and bake in the middle of the oven for at least 30 minutes or until the chicken is fully cooked. If the casserole is at risk of burning before it's done, cover it with a piece of aluminium foil, lower the heat and let cook for a little longer.

473. Low-carb garlic chicken

Prep Time: 50 minutes | Servings: 4
Per Serving: Kcal: 540, Protein: 42g, Fat: 39g, Net Carb: 03g

INGREDIENTS:

- 2 oz. butter
- 2 lbs (900g) chicken drumsticks
- salt and pepper
- 1 lemon, the juice
- 2 tbsp olive oil
- 7 garlic cloves, sliced
- ½ cup (1 oz.) fresh parsley, finely chopped

INSTRUCTIONS:

1. Preheat the oven to 450°F (225°C).
2. Place the chicken pieces in a butter-greased baking pan. Salt and pepper generously.
3. Drizzle the lemon juice and olive oil over the chicken pieces. Sprinkle the garlic and parsley on top.
4. Bake the chicken until golden and the garlic slices have turned brown and roasted, about 30–40 minutes. The baking time may be longer, if your drumsticks are on the larger size. Lower the temperature a little towards the end.

474. Cheesy Chicken Fritters

Prep Time: 40 minutes | Servings: 4
Per Serving: Kcal: 396, Protein: 47g, Fat: 21g, Net Carb: 02g

INGREDIENTS:

- 1.5 lb (700g) skinless boneless chicken breast
- 2 medium eggs
- 1/3 cup (40g) almond flour

- 1 cup (110g) shredded mozzarella cheese
- 2 Tbsp fresh basil - finely chopped
- 2 Tbsp chives - chopped
- 2 Tbsp parsley - chopped
- 1/2 tsp garlic powder
- a pinch of sea salt and fresh ground black pepper - or to taste
- 1 Tbsp olive oil - or more to fry

INSTRUCTIONS:

1. Place the chicken breast on a chopping board and using a sharp knife, chop it into tiny pieces, then place them in a large mixing bowl.
2. Into the large bowl, stir in almond flour, eggs, mozzarella, basil, chives, parsley, garlic powder, salt, and pepper. Mix well to combine.
3. Heat oil in a large non-stick pan, over medium-low heat. With an ice cream scoop or a large spoon, scoop into the chicken mixture and transfer it to the pan, then slightly flatten to create a fritter. Don't overcrowd the pan, cook the fritters in batches, about 4 per batch.
4. Fry until golden brown on both sides, about 6-8 minutes. Keep in mind that you need to cook them at medium-low temp, otherwise they will burn on the outside but won't get well cooked on the inside.
5. Serve with your favorite dip

475. Sticky chicken wings

Prep Time: 50 minutes | Servings: 4
Per Serving: Kcal: 489, Protein: 33g, Fat: 31g, Net Carb: 03g

INGREDIENTS:

- 2 lbs chicken wings
- ¼ cup (60g) coconut aminos
- 2 tbsp tamari soy sauce
- 1 tbsp coconut oil
- ¼ tsp ground ginger
- ¼ tsp onion powder
- ¼ tsp garlic powder
- ¼ tsp chili flakes

INSTRUCTIONS:

1. Preheat oven to 450°F (225°C).
2. Place the wings with the thicker skin-side up on a rimmed baking sheet with wire racks. (The wire rack helps promote even cooking).
3. Bake the wings for 40 minutes.
4. When the wings have about 12 minutes left to bake, start making the sauce.

5. Heat a medium to a large skillet over medium heat, and add the coconut aminos, soy sauce, coconut oil, and seasoning.
6. Once the sauce comes to a simmer, begin stirring. Continue to stir periodically, adjusting the heat as needed to maintain a gentle simmer.
7. Once the sauce has thickened slightly—as you stir it, it should take a few seconds for the sauce to fill back behind your spoon or spatula—you can reduce the heat to low while the wings finish cooking.
8. Place the wings in a large heatproof bowl and pour the sauce over them. Stir to evenly coat with the sauce, and serve.

476. Paprika Chicken with Rutabaga

Prep Time: 50 minutes | Servings: 4
Per Serving: Kcal: 1090, Protein: 41g, Fat: 90g, Net Carb: 9g

INGREDIENTS:

- 2 lbs chicken thighs (bone-in with skin) or chicken drumsticks
- 2 lbs rutabaga or celery root, peeled and cut into 2" (5 cm) pieces
- 1 tbsp paprika powder
- salt and pepper
- ¼ cup (60g) olive oil
- Garlic and paprika mayo
- 1 cup (230g) mayonnaise
- 1 tsp garlic powder
- 1 tsp paprika powder
- salt and pepper, to taste

INSTRUCTIONS:

1. Preheat the oven to 400°F (200°C).
2. Place the chicken and the rutabaga in a baking dish. Season with salt, pepper, and paprika powder. Drizzle with olive oil and mix well.
3. Bake in the oven until the chicken is well done, about 40 minutes. Lower the heat towards the end of the chicken or rutabaga is getting too golden brown.
4. Mix the mayonnaise with seasoning and serve together with the roasted chicken and rutabaga.

477. Keto Chicken Korma

Prep Time: 40 minutes | Servings: 4
Per Serving: Kcal: 440, Protein: 34g, Fat: 31g, Net Carb: 03g

INGREDIENTS:

- ¼ cup (60g) ghee
- ½ (2 oz.) red onion, thinly sliced
- 4 oz. Greek yogurt
- 3 whole cloves
- 1 bay leaf
- 1 cinnamon stick
- 1 star anise
- 3 green cardamom pods
- 8 whole black peppercorns
- 1½ lbs chicken drumsticks
- 1 tsp ginger garlic paste
- ½ tsp turmeric
- 1 tsp kashmiri red chili powder
- 1 tsp ground coriander seed
- ½ tsp garam masala seasoning
- 1 tsp ground cumin
- salt, to taste
- fresh cilantro, for garnish

INSTRUCTIONS:

1. Heat the ghee in a wok or non-stick saucepan and deep-fry the onions on low-medium heat until they get a nice golden brown color.
2. Remove the fried onions from the pan. Mix yogurt with the onions in a blender to get a creamy paste.
3. Reheat the ghee in the saucepan. Once it gets hot add cloves, bay leaf, cinnamon stick, star anise, green cardamom pods, and black peppercorns. Fry for 30 seconds or until they start to sizzle.
4. Add the chicken drumsticks. Season thoroughly with salt. Add the ginger-garlic paste, combine well and fry for about 2 minutes.
5. Add turmeric, red chili powder, coriander powder, garam masala, and cumin powder. Combine well and fry for 2 more minutes.
6. Add the fried onion yogurt paste, combine well. Add some water. You can use the water to rinse out the blender so don't waste any of the paste. Mix well.
7. Cover and cook for 10-15 minutes or until the chicken is thoroughly cooked and tender.
8. Garnish with fresh cilantro.

478. Keto chicken wings

Prep Time: 45 minutes | Servings: 4
Per Serving: Kcal: 1260, Protein: 65g, Fat: 99g, Net Carb: 9g

INGREDIENTS:

Baked chicken wings
- ½ orange, juice and zest
- ¼ cup (60g) olive oil
- 2 tsp ground ginger
- 1 tsp salt
- ¼ tsp cayenne pepper
- 3 lbs chicken wings

Creamy broccoli
- 1½ lbs broccoli
- 1 cup (230g) mayonnaise
- ¼ cup (1/10 oz.) chopped fresh dill
- salt and pepper, to taste

INSTRUCTIONS:

1. Preheat the oven to 400°F (200°C).
2. Mix juice and zest from the orange with oil and spices in a small bowl. Place the chicken wings in a plastic bag and pour in the marinade.
3. Give the bag a good shake to cover the wings thoroughly. Put aside to marinate for at least 5 minutes but preferably more.
4. Place the wings in one layer in a greased baking dish or on a broiler rack, for extra crispiness.
5. Bake on middle rack in the oven for about 45 minutes or until the wings are golden brown and thoroughly cooked.
6. In the meantime, divide the broccoli into small florets and parboil in salted water for a couple of minutes. They're only supposed to soften a bit but not lose their shape or color.
7. Strain the broccoli and let some of the steam evaporate before adding the remaining ingredients. Serve the broccoli with the baked wings.

479. Keto chicken curry pie

Prep Time: 50 minutes | Servings: 4
Per Serving: Kcal: 1003, Protein: 48g, Fat: 96g, Net Carb: 5g

INGREDIENTS:

Pie crust
- ¾ cup (3 oz.) almond flour
- 4 tbsp sesame seeds
- 4 tbsp coconut flour
- 1 tbsp ground psyllium husk powder
- 1 tsp baking powder
- 1 pinch salt
- 3 tbsp olive oil or coconut oil
- 1 egg
- 4 tbsp water

Filling

- 11 oz. cooked chicken
- 1 cup mayonnaise
- 3 eggs
- ½ (2½ oz.) green bell pepper, finely chopped
- 1 tbsp curry powder
- 1 tsp paprika powder
- 1 tsp onion powder
- ¼ tsp ground black pepper
- 4 oz. cream cheese
- 1¼ cups (5 oz.) cheddar cheese, shredded

INSTRUCTIONS:

1. Preheat the oven to 350°F (175°C). Put all the ingredients for the pie crust into a food processor for a few minutes until the dough firms up into a ball. If you don't have a food processor, you can also mix the dough with a fork or by hand.
2. Attach a piece of parchment paper to a springform pan, no larger than 10" (23 cm) in diameter (the springform pan makes it easier to remove the pie when it's done). Grease the bottom and sides of the pan.
3. Spread the dough into the pan. Use an oiled spatula or your fingers. Pre-bake the crust for 10–15 minutes.
4. Mix all other filling ingredients together, and fill the pie crust. Bake for 35–40 minutes or until the pie has turned a nice, golden brown.
5. Let it cool before serving.

480. Kristie's chicken Philly

Prep Time: 50 minutes | Servings: 8
Per Serving: Kcal: 750, Protein: 41g, Fat: 61g, Net Carb: 07g

INGREDIENTS:

- 1 tbsp butter
- 2 lbs boneless chicken thighs, cubed
- 4 oz. (2/3 cup) yellow onions, sliced
- 6 oz. green bell peppers, sliced
- 8 oz. mushrooms, sliced
- 2 garlic cloves, minced
- ½ tsp salt
- ½ tsp pepper
- 2 tsp Italian seasoning, divided
- 8 oz. cream cheese, softened
- ½ cup mayonnaise
- 2 tbsp Worcestershire sauce
- 2 cups (8 oz.) cheddar cheese, shredded
- 12 oz. (2½ cups) provolone cheese, sliced

INSTRUCTIONS:

1. Preheat the oven to 375°F (190°C).
2. In a large skillet on medium-high heat, brown the chicken in butter.
3. When the meat is cooked, add onions, pepper, mushrooms, half of the garlic, salt, pepper, and half of the Italian seasoning. Continue cooking until vegetables are just tender, but not soft. Remove from heat and set aside.
4. In a large bowl, mix cream cheese, mayonnaise, the rest of the garlic, the rest of the Italian seasoning, Worcestershire, and cheddar cheese. Add the meat mixture and combine.
5. Spoon into a 9" by 13" (23x33) glass baking dish and top with the slices of provolone cheese.
6. Bake in the oven for 25 to 30 minutes or until the casserole is bubbly and slightly browned.

481. Keto chicken casserole

Prep Time: 55 minutes | Servings: 4
Per Serving: Kcal: 768, Protein: 31g, Fat: 61g, Net Carb: 05g

INGREDIENTS:

- ¾ cup (180g) heavy whipping cream or double cream
- ½ cup (112g) cream cheese
- 3 tbsp green pesto
- 1 tbsp lemon juice
- salt and pepper
- 1½ oz. butter
- 2 lbs skinless boneless chicken thighs, cut into bite-sized pieces
- 6 oz. leeks, finely chopped
- 4 oz. cherry tomatoes, halved
- ¾ lb cauliflower, cut into small florets
- 2 cups (8 oz.) cheddar cheese, shredded

INSTRUCTIONS:

1. Preheat the oven to 400°F (200°C).
2. Mix cream and cream cheese with pesto and lemon juice. Salt and pepper to taste.
3. In a large pan over medium-high heat, melt the butter. Add the chicken, season with salt and pepper, and fry until they turn a nice golden brown.
4. Place the chicken in a greased 9 x 13" (23 x 33 cm) baking dish, and pour in the cream mixture.
5. Top chicken with leek, tomatoes, and cauliflower.
6. Sprinkle cheese on top and bake in the

middle of the oven for at least 30 minutes or until the chicken is fully cooked. If the casserole is at risk of burning before it's done, cover it with a piece of aluminium foil, lower the heat and let cook for a little longer.

482. Keto chicken pesto

Prep Time: 50 minutes | Servings: 4
Per Serving: Kcal: 618, Protein: 25g, Fat: 41g, Net Carb: 05g

INGREDIENTS:
- 11/3 lbs boneless chicken thighs
- 1/3 cup (2¾ oz.) sugar-free green pesto
- 5 oz. cherry tomatoes, halved
- 4 oz. feta cheese, crumbled or cubed
- 12 oz. zucchini or zucchini noodles
- 3 tbsp olive oil

INSTRUCTIONS:
1. Place the chicken thighs in a medium pot and add cold water until the chicken is just covered.
2. Bring to a boil. Then reduce the heat to medium-low and simmer for 15 minutes or until the chicken is thoroughly cooked.
3. Remove the chicken from the water and shred it using two forks. Set aside.
4. Spiralize the zucchini and place the zoodles in a large mixing bowl.
5. Pour the pesto over the zoodles, and toss with tongs to completely coat the zoodles.
6. Add shredded chicken, tomatoes, and feta to the zoodles and gently toss with tongs until evenly combined. Drizzle with olive oil.

483. Keto chicken fajita bowl

Prep Time: 30 minutes | Servings: 4
Per Serving: Kcal: 845, Protein: 31g, Fat: 51g, Net Carb: 05g

INGREDIENTS:
- 10 oz. Romaine lettuce
- 5 oz. cherry tomatoes
- 2 (14 oz.) avocados
- 4 tbsp fresh cilantro
- 1 (4 oz.) yellow onion
- 1 (5 oz.) green bell pepper
- Bell pepper, green
- Green bell pepper
  Also, known as pepper and capsicum
- 1½ lbs boneless chicken thighs
- 3 oz. butter

- salt and pepper
- 2 tbsp Tex-Mex seasoning
- 1 cup (4 oz.) Mexican cheese or cheddar cheese, shredded
- 1 cup sour cream (optional)

INSTRUCTIONS:
1. Prepare the toppings. Tear the lettuce, chop tomatoes, dice avocados, and clean and chop the cilantro. Set aside.
2. Slice onion and pepper fairly thin.
3. On a separate cutting board, cut the chicken into thin strips.
4. Fry the chicken in butter in a large skillet over medium high heat. Salt and pepper to taste. When the chicken is almost cooked through, add onion, pepper and Tex-Mex seasoning.
5. Lower the heat and continue to fry while stirring for a couple of minutes until the chicken is thoroughly cooked and the vegetables have softened just a bit.
6. Place lettuce in a bowl and add the chicken mixture. Add shredded cheese, diced avocado, chopped tomatoes, fresh cilantro and perhaps a dollop of sour cream.

484. Keto turkey burgers

Prep Time: 30 minutes | Servings: 4
Per Serving: Kcal: 885, Protein: 33g, Fat: 75g, Net Carb: 06g

INGREDIENTS:
Chicken patties
- 1½ lbs ground turkey or ground chicken
- 1 egg
- ½ (2 oz.) yellow onion, grated or finely chopped
- 1 tsp kosher or ground sea salt
- ½ tsp ground black pepper
- 1 tsp dried thyme or crushed coriander seed
- 2 oz. butter, for frying

Fried cabbage
- 1½ lbs green cabbage
- 3 oz. butter
- 1 tsp salt
- ½ tsp ground black pepper

Whipped tomato butter
- 4 oz. butter
- 1 tbsp tomato paste
- 1 tsp red wine vinegar (optional)
- sea salt and pepper to taste

INSTRUCTIONS:

1. Preheat the oven to 220°F (100°C). Mix all ingredients for the patties in a bowl.
2. Shape the ground turkey into patties using wet hands. Fry in butter on medium-high heat until golden brown and fully cooked through. Place in the oven to keep warm.
3. Shred the cabbage using a sharp knife, mandolin slicer, or food processor.
4. Fry the cabbage in a generous amount of butter on medium-high heat until browned on the edges, but still has somebody. Stir occasionally to make sure it cooks evenly. Season with salt and pepper. Lower the heat towards the end.
5. Place all ingredients for the tomato butter in a small bowl and whip them together using an electric hand mixer. Plate the turkey patties and fried cabbage and place a dollop of tomato butter on top.

485. Keto chicken and Feta cheese

Prep Time: 20 minutes | Servings: 2
Per Serving: Kcal: 1203, Protein: 63g, Fat: 99g, Net Carb: 9g

INGREDIENTS:
- 1 lb of rotisserie chicken
- 7 oz. feta cheese
- 2 (8 oz.) tomatoes
- 2 cups (4 oz.) leafy greens
- 10 black olives
- 1/3 cup olive oil
- salt and pepper

INSTRUCTIONS:
1. Slice the tomatoes and put them on a plate together with chicken, feta cheese, lettuce and olives.
2. Season with salt and pepper to taste. Serve with olive oil.

486. Keto chicken pesto

Prep Time: 10 minutes | Servings: 2
Per Serving: Kcal: 716, Protein: 33g, Fat: 61g, Net Carb: 07g

INGREDIENTS:
- 2 tbsp butter
- 1½ lbs boneless, skinless boneless chicken thighs, cut into 1" (3 cm) pieces
- 1½ tsp garlic powder
- 1 cup heavy whipping cream
- 3 tbsp green pesto

- 1 lb zucchini, spiralized
- 8 oz. (1¼ cups) tomatoes, diced, or cherry tomatoes cut in half
- salt and ground black pepper, to taste

INSTRUCTIONS:
1. Melt the butter in a large frying pan, over medium-high heat.
2. When the butter starts to bubble, add the garlic powder and chicken to the pan. Sauté for about 10 minutes, or until lightly browned.
3. Reduce the heat to medium-low, and add the cream and pesto. Simmer for a couple of minutes, stirring together until the mixture is creamy and well-combined.
4. Add the zucchini noodles and tomatoes. Toss to combine, and let simmer for about 2 minutes, just until the zucchini noodles become slightly tender, but still have some crispness. Season with salt and pepper to taste. Serve immediately.

487. Keto chicken stir-fry

Prep Time: 10 minutes | Servings: 2
Per Serving: Kcal: 737, Protein: 33g, Fat: 67g, Net Carb: 06g

INGREDIENTS:
- ½ lb shirataki noodles
- ¾ lb boneless chicken thighs
- 3 tbsp coconut oil or light olive oil
- 3 oz. (¾ cup) celery stalks
- 5 oz. oyster mushrooms
- ½ yellow beet
- salt and ground black pepper

Hot sauce
- 2 tbsp sesame oil or light olive oil
- 2 tbsp water
- 1 tbsp rice vinegar or cider vinegar
- 1 tbsp tamari soy sauce
- 1 tbsp sriracha sauce
- 1 garlic clove, minced

INSTRUCTIONS:
1. Place the noodles in a colander and rinse well under running water for 1-2 minutes. Squeeze out all the water. The less water, the better the texture will be.
2. Cut the chicken into thin strips. Heat up oil in a frying pan or wok and fry the chicken for a few minutes. Season with salt and pepper.
3. Add vegetables and noodles and keep frying for a few more minutes.

4. Mix all ingredients for the sauce in a small bowl. Combine well.
5. Add half the sauce to the wok and toss to combine. Save the rest for serving so you can adjust the flavor to suit your taste.

488. Crispy baked chicken with BBQ

Prep Time: 50 minutes | **Servings:** 4
Per Serving: Kcal: 992, Protein: 82g, Fat: 87g, Net Carb: 07g

INGREDIENTS:
- 1/3 cup (1¼ oz.) coconut flour
- 1 tsp garlic powder
- 1 tsp chili powder
- 1 tsp salt
- ½ tsp ground black pepper
- 2 lbs (900g) chicken thighs (bone-in with skin)

  BBQ-mayo
- 1 cup (230g) mayonnaise or vegan mayonnaise
- 2 tbsp tomato paste
- 1 tbsp Dijon mustard
- ½ tsp smoked paprika powder
- salt and pepper

  Salad
- 4 oz. (32/3 cups) baby spinach
- 2 (10 oz.) green bell peppers, sliced
- ½ (2 oz.) red onion, sliced
- 2 tbsp olive oil
- salt and pepper to taste

INSTRUCTIONS:
1. Preheat the oven to 450°F (200°C). Combine coconut flour and spices in a plastic bag.
2. Place the chicken in the bag and shake gently to properly cover with the flour and spices.
3. Place the chicken skin side up in a greased baking dish. Bake in the oven for 30 minutes. Use a meat thermometer if you're unsure; the internal temperature in the thighs should be 165°F (74°C).
4. While the chicken is baking, chop the ingredients for the salad and prepare the sauce by mixing all the ingredients in a bowl.
5. Serve the chicken on top of the salad with a dollop of the BBQ-mayo.

489. Spicy keto chicken

Prep Time: 60 minutes | **Servings:** 4
Per Serving: Kcal: 1126, Protein: 76g, Fat: 75g, Net Carb: 07g

INGREDIENTS:
- 1½ lbs chicken breasts (without skin), cut into bite-sized pieces
- 10 oz. bacon, coarsely chopped
- 2 garlic cloves, pressed
- 5 oz. broccoli, cut into small florets
- 7 oz. cauliflower, cut into small florets
- 2 tsp sambal oelek
- 2 tbsp tomato paste
- 2 cups heavy whipping cream
- Heavy whipping cream
  Also, known as thickened cream or double cream
- 1 cup (4 oz.) shredded cheese
- salt and pepper
- butter, to grease casserole dish
- For serving
- 4 oz. (2 cups) leafy greens
- 1 (4 oz.) small red onion, divided and thinly sliced
- 7 oz. cherry tomatoes, cut into quarts

INSTRUCTIONS:
1. Preheat the oven to 400°F (200°C). Lightly grease a 9 x 12 casserole dish with butter.
2. Heat a large frying pan over medium heat. Add the bacon and fry until crispy. Remove from pan and distribute it in a casserole dish.
3. Using the bacon fat, fry the chicken together with garlic and salt and pepper for about 15 minutes, until chicken is no longer pink. Add chicken to the casserole dish.
4. Distribute cauliflower and broccoli evenly among the chicken in the baking dish.
5. In a saucepan over medium heat, whisk together heavy whipping cream, tomato paste, and sambal oelek.
   Season with salt and pepper and bring to a boil.
6. Pour the sauce into the baking dish, distributing well among chicken, vegetables, and bacon.
7. Cover with foil to prevent from burning. Bake in the oven for 30 minutes.
8. Remove the aluminum foil and add shredded cheese on the top of the casserole. Put the baking dish back into

the oven, uncovered, and bake for about 15 minutes or until the cheese is bubbly and light gold.
9. Serve with a fresh salad.

490. Keto chicken club

Prep Time: 50 minutes | Servings: 4
Per Serving: Kcal: 1214, Protein: 63g, Fat: 105g, Net Carb: 5g

INGREDIENTS:
- 2 lbs rotisserie chicken
- 2 (8 oz.) tomatoes
- 5 oz. cooked bacon
- 1 dill pickle
- ½ cup (115g) mayonnaise
- 1½ cups (6 oz.) shredded cheddar cheese
- salt and pepper

Serving
- 6 oz. (3 cups) leafy greens
  4 tbsp olive oil

INSTRUCTIONS:
1. Preheat the oven to 400°F (200°C).
2. Shred the rotisserie chicken into bite-sized pieces and place in a medium-sized bowl.
3. Dice (cooked) bacon and chop up the tomatoes and pickles. Mix all three together with the chicken. Add mayonnaise and ⅔ of the cheese and stir. Season with salt and pepper to taste.
4. Pour the mixture into a greased baking dish. Sprinkle the remaining cheese on top and bake for about 20 minutes or until golden brown.
5. Serve with leafy greens and olive oil.

491. Chicken with roasted vegetables

Prep Time: 60 minutes | Servings: 4
Per Serving: Kcal: 847, Protein: 60g, Fat: 62g, Net Carb: 08g

INGREDIENTS:
Roasted vegetables tricolore
- 16 oz. fresh Brussels sprouts, whole
- 8 oz. cherry tomatoes, whole
- 8 oz. mushrooms, sliced or whole
- 1 tsp sea salt
- ½ tsp ground black pepper
- 1 tsp dried rosemary
- ½ cup olive oil

Fried chicken
- 4 (1½ lbs) chicken breasts (without skin)

- 2 tbsp unsalted butter or olive oil, for frying
- salt and pepper, to taste
- 4 oz. herb butter, for serving

INSTRUCTIONS:
1. Preheat the oven to 400°F (200°C).
2. Place the vegetables in a roasting pan. Sprinkle the salt, pepper and rosemary over the vegetables. Pour the olive oil on top and stir to evenly coat.
3. Bake for 20 minutes or until the vegetables are gently caramelized.
4. Meanwhile, heat the olive oil or butter in a large frying pan over medium heat. Season the chicken with salt and pepper and sauté for about 20 minutes, or until the internal temperature reaches 165°F (74°C).
5. For serving, plate the chicken and roasted vegetables, and then spread the herb butter onto the chicken for added flavor!

492. Keto cauliflower chicken

Prep Time: 40 minutes | Servings: 4
Per Serving: Kcal: 1051, Protein: 40g, Fat: 62g, Net Carb: 7g

INGREDIENTS:
- 5 oz. bacon, diced
- 1½ lbs boneless chicken thighs
- 2 oz. butter
- 4 garlic cloves, minced
- 7 oz. (6½ cups) baby spinach
- 1½ cups heavy whipping cream
- 1 cup (2¾ oz.) shredded Parmesan cheese
- salt and pepper
- 1¼ lbs cauliflower

INSTRUCTIONS:
1. Fry the bacon until crispy and cooked through. Drain, and set aside in a bowl or on a plate.
2. Cut the chicken into strips. Add butter in the same frying pan with the remaining bacon fat and sauté the chicken and garlic. Set aside when the chicken is thoroughly cooked.
3. Sauté the spinach until it shrinks, but no more. Set aside.
4. Add cream to the pan and let boil for a few minutes. Add parmesan cheese, bacon, chicken, and spinach. Salt and pepper to taste.
5. Lower the heat and let simmer while parboiling the cauliflower.

6. Divide the cauliflower into small florets, no bigger than walnuts. You can use either fresh or frozen.
7. Parboil the cauliflower in lightly salted water for a few minutes. Let drain thoroughly. Add the chicken and sauce. Stir and serve.

493. Coconut Chicken flour

Prep Time: 40 minutes | Servings: 4
Per Serving: Kcal: 370, Protein: 15g, Fat: 31g, Net Carb: 06g

INGREDIENTS:
- 1 cup coconut oil or avocado oil, for frying
- 1 (4 oz.) small yellow onion, diced
- 3 (4¼ oz.) celery stalks
- 1 tsp salt
- 1 tsp dried oregano
- 1 tsp ground cumin
- 13 oz. boneless chicken thighs, skinless
- 2 large eggs
- ¾ cup (2½ oz.) fine coconut flour

INSTRUCTIONS:
1. Heat a large, 9-inch (23 cm) cast iron skillet over medium heat. Add in the oil and let it come to temperature while you prepare the fritters.
2. Add the onion, celery and seasonings to the bowl of your food processor. Process until minced. Add the chicken thighs and the eggs to the food processor and process until a thick paste forms.
3. Put the coconut flour on a large plate. Scoop two tablespoons of chicken paste, shape into a ball and put it on the coconut flour mound, then turn it over to bread it all over with coconut flour.
4. Gently toss between your hands to shake off excess flour and place it on the rim of the plate. Repeat until the whole chicken paste is used and all the balls are breaded.
5. Insert a wooden spoon into the oil to make sure it is hot enough, the oil should sizzle. Add fritters to the hot oil in batches, make sure they are not touching. Fry for 3 minutes each side.
6. When removing the fritters from the oil use a slotted spoon and place them on a plate lined with paper towel. Repeat until all of the chicken paste is gone. When they are all ready, serve with dipping sauces and enjoy warm.

494. Keto coconut curry chicken

Prep Time: 50 minutes | Servings: 4
Per Serving: Kcal: 790, Protein: 33g, Fat: 70g, Net Carb: 08g

INGREDIENTS:
- 2 stalks of lemon grass
- 2 tbsp coconut oil
- 1 tbsp curry powder
- 1½ lbs boneless chicken thighs
- 1 (3 oz.) leek
- 1 thumb-sized piece of fresh ginger
- 2 garlic cloves
- 1 (5 oz.) red bell pepper, sliced
- ½ red chili pepper, finely chopped
- 14 oz. coconut cream
- 1 lime, the finely grated zest

INSTRUCTIONS:
1. Crush the rough part of the lemongrass with the broad side of a knife or a pestle.
2. Cut the chicken into coarse pieces.
3. Gently heat the coconut oil in a wok or a large frying pan.
4. Grate the ginger and fry together with the lemongrass and curry.
5. Add half of the chicken and sauté over medium heat until the strips are golden. Salt and pepper to taste.
6. Set aside and fry the rest of the chicken in the same way, perhaps add a little more curry for the second batch. The lemon grass can remain in the pan.
7. Slice leaks into pieces and sauté them in the same pan together with the other vegetables and finely chopped garlic. The vegetables should turn golden, but retain their crispiness.
8. Add the coconut cream and chicken and let simmer for 5–10 minutes until everything is warm.
9. Remove the lemon grass and sprinkle over the lime zest.

495. Keto Butter Chicken

Prep Time: 30 minutes | Servings: 4
Per Serving: Kcal: 385, Protein: 26g, Fat: 26g, Net Carb: 06g

INGREDIENTS:
- 1 lb (500g) chicken breast
- 1 cup (240g) Heavy Whipping Cream or double cream
- 2 tbsp Butter
- 1.5 tbsp tomato paste
- 2 cloves garlic
- 1/4 medium Onion

- 1.5 tsp turmeric powder
- 1 tsp ground ginger
- 1 tsp Pink Himalayan Salt
- 3/4 tsp chili powder
- 1/2 tsp ground cinnamon

INSTRUCTIONS:

1. Cut the chicken up into bite sized chunks and generously coat them in the turmeric, ginger, salt, chili powder and cinnamon. Set aside in a bowl.
2. Heat a skillet to medium heat and add the butter. As the butter melts dice the onion and garlic and add it to the pan. Cook for 2-3 minutes until the onions are translucent and fragrant.
3. Increase the pan heat to medium-high and add the chicken. Cook it almost entirely through – the outside should be white and this will take about 3-5 minutes.
4. Once the chicken looks almost fully cooked add in the heavy whipping cream and tomato paste. Using a spatula mix in the tomato paste so it runs smooth through the heavy whipping cream. It should be an orange color at this point. Turn the heat to medium-low and cover with a lid for 5-7 minutes.
5. Remove lid and combine. The chicken is fully cooked and you should be able to eat it. However, if you like a thicker curry sauce allow it to reduce with the lid off until it reaches the consistency you like.
6. Serve with low carb naan or over cauliflower rice. Enjoy!

496. Keto Chicken Cheese

Prep Time: 30 minutes | Servings: 4
Per Serving: Kcal: 416, Protein: 31g, Fat: 60g, Net Carb: 07g

INGREDIENTS:

- 1 pound broccoli cut into florets
- 1 rotisserie chicken meat shredded
- 8 ounces cream cheese
- 3/4 cup (180g) heavy cream or double cream
- 1/2 cup (120g) unsweetened almond milk
- 1 tablespoon dijon mustard
- 1 teaspoon garlic powder
- 1/2 teaspoon salt
- 1/4 teaspoon pepper ground
- 1/4 cup (15g) fresh basil chopped
- 1 cup (112g) cheddar cheese shredded

INSTRUCTIONS:

1. Preheat your oven to 200C/390F.
2. Place a saucepan of water over high heat and boil the broccoli florets until al dente. Drain well and add to a large mixing bowl along with the shredded chicken.
3. In a small saucepan, add the cream cheese, cream, almond milk, mustard, garlic, salt and pepper and place over low heat. Whisk until the sauce is smooth.
4. Pour the warm sauce into the broccoli and chicken mixture, add the basil, and mix well.
5. Pour the mixture into a casserole dish and top with the shredded cheese.
6. Bake in the oven for 20-30 minutes, until warmed through and the cheese has browned.
7. Serve immediately.

497. Keto Chicken Salad

Prep Time: 40 minutes | Servings: 4
Per Serving: Kcal: 289, Protein: 24g, Fat: 29g, Net Carb: 01g

INGREDIENTS:

- 1.5 lb (700g) chicken breast
- 3 ribs celery, diced
- 1/2 cup (115g) mayo
- 2 tsp brown mustard
- 1/2 tsp pink Himalayan salt
- 2 tbsp fresh dill, chopped
- 1/4 cup (30g) chopped pecans

INSTRUCTIONS:

1. Preheat oven to 450°F and line baking sheet with parchment paper.
2. Bake chicken breast until cooked throughout, about 15 minutes.
3. Remove chicken from oven and allow to cool. After completely cooled, cut chicken into bite-sized pieces.
4. In a large bowl, add chicken, celery, mayo, brown mustard, and salt. Toss until chicken is fully coated and ingredients are well-combined.
5. Cover bowl with lid or plastic wrap and refrigerate until chilled, about 1-2 hours.
6. When ready to serve, add fresh dill and chopped pecans and lightly toss. Serve chilled and enjoy.

498. Skillet Creamy Garlic Chicken

Prep Time: 30 minutes | **Servings:** 4
Per Serving: Kcal: 447, Protein: 31g, Fat: 29g, Net Carb: 04g

INGREDIENTS:

- 2 pounds (907 g) boneless chicken breasts (or chicken thighs)
- salt , to taste
- fresh cracked black pepper , to taste
- 1/2 teaspoon (2.5 ml) paprika
- 4 tablespoons (60 ml) butter , divided
- 4 cloves (4 cloves) garlic , minced
- 10.5 ounces (300 g) (1 can) Condensed Cream of Chicken Soup , or more if needed
- 1 cup (240 ml) water
- 2 cups (240 ml) chopped broccoli (or spinach, kale, cauliflower, green beans, carrots, etc.)

INSTRUCTIONS:

1. Preheat oven to 450°F and line baking sheet with parchment paper.
2. Bake chicken breast until cooked throughout, about 15 minutes.
3. Remove chicken from oven and allow to cool. After completely cooled, cut chicken into bite-sized pieces.
4. In a large bowl, add chicken, celery, mayo, brown mustard, and salt. Toss until chicken is fully coated and ingredients are well-combined.
5. Cover bowl with lid or plastic wrap and refrigerate until chilled, about 1-2 hours.
6. When ready to serve, add fresh dill and chopped pecans and lightly toss. Serve chilled and enjoy.

499. Keto Breaded Chicken

Prep Time: 30 minutes | **Servings:** 4
Per Serving: Kcal: 587, Protein: 18g, Fat: 36g, Net Carb: 01g

INGREDIENTS:

- 1 1/2 pounds thinly sliced chicken breast
- Kosher salt
- 2 cups (225g) almond flour
- 3 large eggs
- 1/2 cup (45g) grated Parmesan
- 1 1/2 teaspoons paprika
- 1/2 teaspoon garlic powder
- Ghee or avocado oil, for frying
- Lemon wedges, for serving

INSTRUCTIONS:

1. If any of the chicken slices are thicker than 1/4 inch, pound them out one at a time between 2 sheets of plastic wrap with a meat mallet to a thickness of 1/4 inch.
1. Lay out the chicken on a baking sheet or plate and sprinkle all over with salt and just enough of the almond flour to lightly coat both sides.
2. Beat the eggs in a wide shallow bowl. In another wide, shallow bowl, mix the remaining almond flour with the Parmesan, paprika and garlic powder.
3. Dip 1 to 2 slices of chicken in the eggs to coat. Let the excess drip off, then coat thoroughly in the almond flour-Parmesan mixture. Return to the baking sheet or plate and repeat with the remaining chicken.
4. Heat 1/4 inch of ghee or avocado oil in a large skillet over medium-high heat until hot but not smoking. Add half the chicken and cook until golden on one side, about 3 minutes. Flip and cook until golden on the other side, another 3 minutes. Transfer to a paper towel-lined plate and repeat with the remaining chicken, adding more ghee or oil if needed. Serve with lemon wedges.

500. Keto Chicken Soup

Prep Time: 30 minutes | **Servings:** 4
Per Serving: Kcal: 687, Protein: 65g, Fat: 31g, Net Carb: 01g

INGREDIENTS:

- 1 tbsp butter or extra virgin olive oil
- 1 1/4 small yellow onion finely diced (87g)
- 2 medium carrots peeled and chopped (122g)
- 1 small leek chopped (67g)
- 3 medium stalks celery chopped (120g)
- 1 tbsp thyme leaves chopped
- 8 g fresh parsley
- 1 garlic clove minced
- 1.5 litres chicken stock
- 2 bay leaves
- 1/2 tsp salt or to taste (dependant on how salty your stock is)
- 1/4 tsp black pepper or to taste
- 300 g cooked chicken 300g
- 1 cup chopped cavolo nero or kale 50g

  To serve
- Squeeze of lemon juice
- 1 tbsp olive oil
- 1 tsp fresh parsley

INSTRUCTIONS:

1. Heat 1 tbsp of butter or olive oil in a non stick soup pot and sauté on a medium heat the onion, carrots, leek and celery with chopped thyme and about 2/3rds of the parsley for about 5 minutes until beginning to soften. Add the garlic and sauté for another 2 - 3 minutes.
2. Add the stock, bay leaves, season and bring to boil. Reduce to a simmer and cook with lid on for 15 minutes.
3. Add the cooked chicken. Remove half mixture and bay leaves and pulse with stick blender. This thickens the soup and adds flavour.
4. Add the rest of soup back into the pan along with the greens and simmer until they soften (about 1 minute.)
5. Mix the lemon juice with olive oil and swirl into the soup and top with fresh parsley. Adjust seasoning to taste and enjoy. To make it even more delicious I like to swirl through a little butter at the end before serving too!

501. Crispy Chicken Thighs

Prep Time: 50 minutes | **Servings:** 4
Per Serving: Kcal: 145, Protein: 23g, Fat: 31g, Net Carb: 0.91g

INGREDIENTS:
- 1kg/2.2lbs Chicken Thighs
- 2-4 Tablespoons Extra Virgin Olive Oil
- Salt & Pepper, to taste
- Paprika

INSTRUCTIONS:

1. Preheat the oven to 200C/400F and get out a large oven proof dish.
2. Place the chicken into the oven proof dish, drizzle over the oil and toss the chicken well to cover in the oil.
3. Shake over salt and paprika and toss the chicken once again, moving them all to be skin side down.
4. You can shake over more salt and paprika, plus your seasoning of choice then move to the preheated oven for 20 minutes.
5. Remove from the oven, turn the chicken over so that all of the pieces are skin side up and return to the oven for a final 25 minutes or until the chicken is cooked through and skin is crisp to your liking.

502. Parmesan Crusted Chicken

Prep Time: 15 minutes | **Servings:** 4
Per Serving: Kcal: 261, Protein: 22g, Fat: 18g, Net Carb: 0.8g

INGREDIENTS:
- 1 lb (450g) chicken breasts (2 large pieces)
- 1/2 tsp garlic powder
- 1 tsp Italian herb seasoning
- 1/2 tsp salt
- 1/4 tsp pepper
- 1 egg
- 1/2 cup (50g) shredded Parmesan cheese
- 2-3 tbsp vegetable oil

INSTRUCTIONS:

1. Place the chicken breasts out on a cutting board, and cut in half horizontally into two thin pieces. Season both sides with garlic powder, herbs, salt, and pepper; Set aside.
2. In a shallow plate, whisk the egg. In another shallow plate, place the Parmesan.
3. Dip each chicken cutlet in the egg, and let the excess drip off. Press the cutlet into the Parmesan cheese to coat. Turn and coat the other side. Repeat with the remaining chicken pieces.
4. Heat the oil in a large NON-STICK skillet over medium-high heat. Place the chicken cutlets in the pan in a single layer, and DO NOT move them around. Cook for 5-6 minutes on each side, flipping just once, until golden and crispy.

RECIPE INDEX

Recipe Index (Recipe No.)

CONCLUSION

One of the primary keys to any successful diet or lifestyle change has always been the recipes that fit in with the principles of the diet. I am sure there are many ways to achieve ketosis and to attain that weight loss goal. However, you do not want to get there by just having the same old dishes over and over again.

Variety is the name of the game here, which is crucial in ensuring the sustainability of the ketogenic diet. With the flavorful and delicious recipes found in this step by step keto cookbook, they will be useful additions for any keto dieter at any stage of their ketogenic journey. I have yet to see anyone complain about having too many easy yet delicious recipes!

ONE LAST THING...

If you enjoyed this book or found it useful, I'd be very grateful if you'd post a short review on Amazon. Your support really does make a difference, and I read all the reviews personally so I can get your feedback and make this book even better.

Thanks, again for your support!

Printed in Great Britain
by Amazon